JAVABEANS

Developer's Resource

Prentice Hall PTR
Developer's Resource Series

JavaBeans

Developer's Resource

Prashant Sridharan

Prentice Hall PTR
Upper Saddle River, NJ   07458
http://www.prenhall.com/mail_lists/

Editorial/production Supervision: Patti Guerrieri
Acquisitions Editor: Mark L. Taub
Editorial Assistant: Tara Ruggiero
Development Editor: Jim Markham
Manufacturing Manager: Alexis R. Heydt
Marketing Manager: Dan Rush
Cover Design: Design Source
Cover Design Director: Jerry Votta
Art Director: Gail Cocker-Bogusz
Series Design: Meg VanArsdale
CD-ROM Design: Cynthia L. Mason

© 1997 Prentice Hall PTR
Prentice-Hall, Inc.
A Simon & Schuster Company
Upper Saddle River, NJ 07458

Prentice Hall books are widely used by corporations and government agencies
for training, marketing, and resale.

The publisher offers discounts on this book when ordered in bulk quantities.
For more information, contact: Corporate Sales Department, Phone: 800-382-3419;
Fax: 201-236-7141; E-mail: corpsales@prenhall.com; or write: Prentice Hall PTR,
Corp. Sales Dept., One Lake Street, Upper Saddle River, NJ 07458.

All products or services mentioned in this book are the trademarks or service marks of their
respective companies or organizations.

Printed in the United States of America
10 9 8 7 6 5 4 3 2 1

ISBN   0-13-887308-9

Prentice-Hall International (UK) Limited, *London*
Prentice-Hall of Australia Pty. Limited, *Sydney*
Prentice-Hall Canada Inc., *Toronto*
Prentice-Hall Hispanoamericana, S.A., *Mexico*
Prentice-Hall of India Private Limited, *New Delhi*
Prentice-Hall of Japan, Inc., *Tokyo*
Simon & Schuster Asia Pte. Ltd., *Singapore*
Editora Prentice-Hall do Brasil, Ltda., *Rio de Janeiro*

For Jim Haber, who got me started.

For Fred Kuhl, who kept me going.

"How bold the teacher's doctrine, sanctified
By truth, shall spread, throughout the world dispersed."

William Wordsworth, 1770–1850

Trademarks

Java, JavaBeans, Java Development Kit (JDK), Write Once, Run Anywhere, and JDBC are trademarks of Sun Microsystems, Inc.

Marimba, Castanet, and Bongo are trademarks of Marimba, Inc.

ActiveWeb is a trademark of Active Software, Inc.

Microsoft, Microsoft Visual J++, DCOM, COM, OLE, Microsoft Access, Microsoft Windows 95, and ActiveX Technologies are trademarks of Microsoft Corporation.

Visual Café is a trademark of Symantec Corporation.

SuperMojo is a trademark of Penumbra Software, Inc.

LiveConnect and JavaScript are registered trademarks of Netscape Communications Corporation.

BMW and BMW Z3 Roadster are trademarks of BMW NA, Inc.

Porsche is a registered trademark of Porsche of America, Inc.

Volvo is a registered trademark of Volvo America, Inc.

Baltimore Orioles is a registered trademark of the Baltimore Orioles Baseball Club.

Seattle Mariners is a registered trademark of the Seattle Mariners.

National Football League, NFL, Washington Redskins, San Francisco 49ers, and Dallas Cowboys are trademarks of NFL Properties, Inc.

Sears is a trademark of Sears Roebuck, Inc.

Starbucks is a trademark of Starbucks Coffee, Inc.

Contents

Part One: Introduction to Java and Components 1

JavaBeans Developer's Resource

CHAPTER 4   **Bean Properties   111**

Part Three: Advanced Beans   218

CHAPTER 9   **Bean Integration   253**

CHAPTER 10   **Bean Networking   279**

Acknowledgments

This entire book could have been written in the first person plural as a nod to the various people that helped here and there. I want to take a brief moment to just point out who all those people are.

Jennifer Schlegelmilch is the love of my life, and did her best not to nag for a diamond ring too much. Of course, a ton of credit goes to my mom, my sister, and my little old puppy. I'm very lucky to have such a wonderful family.

Doug Jelen and Helen Schryver, my new neighbors, are truly great friends. I managed to attend Dave Krause's wedding in the process, and wouldn't have missed it for the world. Dave calls me dutifully every week to cheer me up about the Redskins lack of faith in the mighty Heath Shuler. Jon Hogue was still out there. (Admiral) Daniel Orchard-Hays launched a missile that missed my ear by two inches.

A bunch of people from Sun Microsystems supported me every step of the way during this entire process. My manager, Jeff Zank, rescued me while I was floundering elsewhere in the company and brought me to Market Development Engineering. Jeff's the best manager I've ever had, and I really couldn't have found time to finish this book without him. The folks at MDE are truly terrific and, unlike much of my experience thus far, are very customer-focused. They know what Java is and why it's important. Matt Thompson, Paul Comey, and Mark Chisam provided invaluable encouragement and criticism to the work as a whole.

Gina Centoni helped by encouraging this book. Leeba Aminoff was instrumental in getting the licensing done so that we could give you the Java Developer's Kit and Beans Developer's Kit on the CD-ROM. Mark Taub signed me up to write this book. Cindy Mason helped put the CD together. Jim Markham made sure the text made sense, while Beth Dickens edited my engineer English. Patti Guerrieri made the book printable.

Near the end of the writing phase of the book, I bolted for Microsoft. Here's the best place for me to explain why I made such a decision. After all, I was a Software Architect and Java Evangelist with Sun, the founder and progenitor of the Java Revolution. The answer is quite simple, really. Microsoft is an extremely customer-focused company. They recognize what the customer wants and they provide it. I don't get involved in Holy Wars, and don't really pay attention to zealots on either side of the fence. I saw what Microsoft was doing with Java and wanted to be a part of it. We're not out to steal Java, but we are out to make it work for real applications.

A whole slew of people helped out in many places. Bill Rieken provided advice on security and was his usual jolly mad scientist self. Ron Kleinmann made me laugh and filled me with Java enthusiasm. Sydney Springer and Maurice Balick brought me to Silicon Valley in the first place, and I hope I've made them proud. Edith Crowe, Ken Oestreich, Manish Punjabi, James McIlree, Laraine Peterson, Hellene Garcia, Janet Koenig, and Karin Stok-Harrisson were my support group in many ways.

Lastly, thanks to every single man, woman, and child that makes Silly Valley such a wonderful place. Without your enthusiasm, passion, drive, and determination, I would not be as fortunate as I am today.

Prashant Sridharan

Introduction

This book was designed from the ground up for people who have a strong desire to learn all about Java and JavaBeans, in particular. It is *not* a marketing brochure and it is *not* a gee-whiz propeller-head technical tome. It is an honest account and appraisal of JavaBeans technology, both the good and the bad. JavaBeans is a wonderful component architecture embraced by, of course, Sun Microsystems and its loyal legion of followers, as well as Microsoft and the other 85 percent of the computing world. For that reason alone, JavaBeans is the single most important API for Java.

This book takes a very hands-on approach to teaching JavaBeans technology. There are several code examples, and all of them build on one another from chapter to chapter. The book is designed to be very accessible; you won't see language intended to be understood only by PhDs from Berkeley. Rather, the book attempts to teach you the basics and advanced concepts of JavaBeans with easy to understand examples and code fragments. It is neither insulting nor impossible. All that's required is a firm grasp of the fundamentals of object-oriented programming and Java in particular.

What You'll Need

The CD included with this book supports both the Windows 95/Windows NT platform as well as the Solaris platform. While Java's write once-run everywhere mantra dictates that the code examples included with the book should run on any Java Virtual Machine that supports Java 1.1.1, any seasoned Java programmer will quickly note that *write once-run everywhere* is a myth along the lines of Paul Bunyan. Nevertheless, the code has been tested on only Win32 and Solaris platforms. In addition, included is the Java Developer's Kit 1.1.1 for Win32 and Solaris only. Time considerations hampered the ability to include a Macintosh VM.

How to Read This Book

This book is divided into four parts, and further divided by chapter from there. Because it is highly unusual for a technical book to be read cover-to-cover, the text contains several things that make life easier for those that like to jump around. You will find, interspersed throughout the text, several icons that are designed to grab your attention and point out important features. The API Tip (an example of which can be found later in this introduction), will allow you to search for specific methods contained within a JavaBeans API. The Design Pattern Tip lets you in on some suggested naming conventions for JavaBeans objects. Ideally, of course, the book should be read in order of chapter, but sometimes that is simply not realistic. The icons are there to help you.

Parts Is Parts

Part One deals with Java and Component Models and provides the foundation for much of your work in JavaBeans throughout this book. In Chapter 1, you will get an understanding of the basic language constructs, including Objects, Serialization, Reflection, and more. In addition, Chapter 2 discusses what components are all about, and how people have been using them in the past and where Java will take them in the future.

Part Two addresses the nuts and bolts of JavaBeans. Here, you'll see how to take three different Beans, add events, properties, introspection, and persistence to them, and connect them together. Chapter 3 covers the JavaBeans Event Model, while Chapter 4 talks about JavaBeans and Properties. In Chapter 5 you'll get the low down on JavaBeans and Introspection, and Chapter 6 closes out with Persistence and Packaging.

Part Three moves you beyond the daily rigors of coding and covers several Advanced Beans Concepts. The GUI Builder is the single most important aspect of Bean development, and Chapter 7 shows you how to use a GUI Builder to assemble disparate Beans and build an application or applet. Chapter 8 talks about several Bean-related GUI issues that can make your applications prettier and more component-ized. Chapter 9 delves into Bean integration with Microsoft's ActiveX component model and Netscape's JavaScript programming language. Chapter 10 introduces Bean networking by talking about Java Remote Method Invocation

(RMI) and Java Interface Definition Language (IDL), the Java binding to industry-standard CORBA objects.

Part Four is a lovingly fluffy marketing brochure that was slipped into an otherwise highly technical book. Chapter 11 discusses in marketing-level detail what Beans can accomplish in the real world and what other companies, like Corel and Lotus, are doing with Beans. This had to be thrown in to make Product Marketing Managers happy. Besides, you do want to know why you should do Beans, right?

Note: Throughout this book JavaBeans may be referred to as *Beans* or *Beans components*. The technical, trademarked name is JavaBeans. But, for the general flow and beauty of the text, from time to time the official name may be shortened.

Appendixes

There are also three Appendixes that will show you how to do some of the more mundane things with Bean development. Appendix A is a Quick Start Guide that maps out where advanced Java and Beans developers should go for information. Appendix B is a quick guide to the features and bugs of the Bean Development Kit's Bean Box. Finally, Appendix C will show you how to install and run the applications on the CD-ROM included with this book.

CD-ROM

The CD provided with this book contains some very useful items. The first of these items is the latest and greatest version (1.1.1) of the Java Developer's Kit (JDK). The JDK contains all of the Beans classes and objects that you need to build JavaBeans applications. However, a second component, the Beans Developer's Kit (BDK), is also included. The BDK contains a sample container (discussed in Appendix B) and several example Beans.

In addition, the major source code from every chapter is also included. The `RainbowButton` Bean that is used as an example throughout the book is here in all its glory and excitement. In addition, you can play with examples of reflection, serialization, and more.

Conventions

Throughout this book, you will see the use of various typographic conventions, which are outlined here.

Icons

Icons represent called-out material that is of significance and that you, the reader, should be alerted to. These include:

 A *Warning* icon is used to point out a bug, mistake, or common error made by Beans developers.

 A *Note* is a brief discussion about something that might be useful to you along the way.

 A *Tip* is a helpful bit of advice for developers. It may range from something as mundane as how to compile an object, or to something as complex as how to properly multiplex an event.

 An *API Tip* is a special kind of Tip that points out a specific use of a method in one of the various Beans APIs that are discussed throughout this book. It will describe the method itself, the parameters to the method, any return types for the method, as well as any exceptions that may be thrown by the method.

 A *Design Pattern Tip* is a suggested way of naming a function. This kind of tip describes that design pattern in detail and shows you how to properly construct a function using it.

(Because of the large number of times the *API Tip* and *Design Pattern Tip* are used in succession in the book, their discussions will appear in normal text with a ■ at the end to denote their conclusion.)

Code

Code samples, code extracts within text, and other specific items (like methods, arrays, objects, or classes) are denoted by using the Courier font, like this:

```
public class Jenny
{
}
```

Any later additions to the code will be represented in bold face type, like this:

```
public class Jenny
{
    String loves = "Prashant";
}
```

Note: I never quite understood what a *program listing* was, and as you will see, I keep showing fragments of code, followed by additions to the fragments as I go along. You will also notice that whenever I add a pile of code to an existing pile of code, the new code is bolded. I have always appreciated it when authors don't skimp on listings and show as much as possible, in as coherent a manner as possible.

Sidebars

At the end of Chapters 1-4, 7, 8, and 11, a sidebar is used for some light-hearted relief. Each one will supply you with some background information on various Beans. Not computer Beans, but coffee Beans. After all, for the truly geeky among us, a good cup of Java is as important as a good line of Java.

Closing Thoughts

Finally, I would like to thank you for buying this book. I wrote this book because I believe in Java. I do not apologize for my enthusiasm, rather I celebrate it. If work isn't fun, it just isn't worth doing. Java makes Computer Science fun, and JavaBeans makes Java extremely useful. Writing on JavaBeans was easy because of folks like Graham Hamilton and Larry Cable whose genius produced such a wonderfully practical toy to play with.

I know there might be some errors here and there throughout this book. For that I apologize. Such is the nature of the technical writing business. I will maintain a published list of errors on the Web site for this book (www.prenhall.com/developers_resource_series) and welcome your feedback. Writing a book is a labor of love, and there's no doubt I had fun through the whole thing. It's made possible by folks like you who take the time to praise and criticize when necessary.

Thanks!

PART ONE

Introduction to Java and Components

The book opens with a simple object-oriented programming and Java tutorial. It emphasizes those aspects of the object-oriented paradigm and Java language that are of importance to readers of this book and Beans programmers in general. It is not a comprehensive study of the language; that's saved for the many Java books on the shelf today. Instead, the intention is to provide a common base of terminology from which to discuss the finer points of Beans later in this book. This part also introduces the notion of components as an extension to the tried and true object-oriented programming to which everyone is accustomed. It discusses components in a general sense before briefly skimming the Beans Component Model.

CHAPTER 1
Advanced Java

- Objects, objects everywhere!
- Serialization
- Java Events
- Reflection

This discussion of JavaBeans begins with a brief tutorial on object-oriented programming, in order to set the base terminology that is used throughout this book. It is not intended to provide a complete education of the knowledge that comes from some of the other books mentioned in Appendix A, *Quick Start Guide*.

Basic Java

When beginners first take to C++, their primal screams can be heard for miles. Often, emergency crews are dispatched immediately to prevent the serious injuries that are typically endured when beginners are first confronted with the dreaded *pointer-> and associated memory management problems.

Enough to make a grown man cry, C++ is a powerful yet incredibly difficult language.

Enter Java. Java is object-oriented, modular, elegant, and—in the hands of a master—quite poetic! Java code can be beautiful and powerful, fun and exciting, and most importantly, incredibly useful!

This chapter focuses on some of the advanced concepts you need to grasp in order to support further endeavors using Java. Throughout the discussion, you will see sample code that highlights some of Java's inherently object-oriented features: *encapsulation* and *information hiding*, *modularity, inheritance*, and *elegance*. This chapter is intended to provide a base of terminology, not a comprehensive Java language tutorial.

Beginners should be forewarned: This book assumes you know the language. Much of what is discussed in this chapter are fundamental design aspects of an object-oriented language. For seasoned programmers, the urge to skip this chapter will be strong. However, many of the advanced features of Java, as well as the architectural decisions that must be made for a JavaBeans application, are based on the fundamental concepts described in this chapter and are of great importance to the veteran and rookie Beans developer alike.

Object-Oriented Design Using Java

In Java, classes are defined as a collection of operations performed on a set of data. Because data cannot be passed by reference (Java is a pointer-free language—let the cheering begin!), Java classes are needed to contain data so that it can be modified within other classes.

CLASSES VERSUS INTERFACES

The prevailing assumption about Java is that you are unable to separate implementations from interfaces. However, this assumption is false. Java provides an interface component that is similar to its class counterpart except that it is not permitted to have member functions. Indeed, this interface must be reused by other objects that will implement its method and variable definitions, as the following code snippet illustrates:

```
public interface MyAdvancedJavaInterface
{
    public abstract void methodOne();
```

```
        void methodTwo();
}
publicclassMyAdvancedJavaClassimplementsMyAdvancedJavaInterface
{
    MyAdvancedJavaClass()
    {
    }

    public void methodOne()
    {
        ...
    }

    public void methodTwo()
    {
        ...
    }
}
```

All member functions declared within interfaces are, by default, *public* and *abstract*. This means they are available for public consumption and must be implemented in a class before they can be used. Furthermore, interfaces do not have constructors and must be extended before they can be used.

DATA MEMBERS

Good object-oriented style dictates that all data members of a class should be declared private, hidden from any operations other than those included in the class itself. But, any experienced OO programmer will tell you in no uncertain terms that this is often stupid and inane for small classes. Because structures (as they are known in C and C++) are not available in Java, you can group data into one container by using a *class*. Whether you subscribe to the artificially enforced private-data-member scheme of C++ or the language-enforced scheme of Smalltalk is entirely up to you. Java, however, assumes data members are public unless otherwise instructed, as the following snippet suggests:

```
public class MyAdvancedJavaClass
{
    public int numItems;
    private int itemArray[];
};
```

METHODS

Another important component of the Java class is the operation, or method. Methods allow outside classes to perform operations on the data contained in your class. By forcing other classes to utilize data through the classes, you enforce implementation hiding. It doesn't matter to other classes that your collection of data is an array, for as far as those classes are concerned, it could be a *Vector*. Somewhere down the line, you could change the implementation to a *HashTable* if efficiency becomes a concern. The bottom line is that the classes that use your methods don't care, and don't need to know how the data is collected, as long as the *method signature* (the method name and its accompanying parameters) remains the same. The following code shows how a method can be introduced within a class:

```
public class MyAdvancedJavaClass
{
    public int numItems;
    private int itemArray[];

    public void addItem(
        int item
    )
    {
        itemArray[numItems] = item;

        numItems++;
    };
};
```

CONSTRUCTORS

There is one small problem in this example; the data is never initialized! This is where the notion of constructors comes in. Constructors set up a class for use. Classes don't need to specify a constructor, indeed a constructor is, by default, simply a function call to nothing. In this case, however, our class must call a constructor because our data needs to be initialized before it can be used.

In Java, everything is inherited from the superclass *Object*. All `Objects` must be initialized, or allocated, before they are used. For example, the declaration

```
public int numItems;
```

specifies an integer value. The `int` is a primitive type, but it is just like an Object, and therefore `int` needs to be initialized. You can do so either in the declaration itself:

```
public int numItems = 0;
```

or you can use the constructor and initialize the array as well, like this:

```java
public class MyAdvancedJavaClass
{
    public int numItems;
    private int itemArray[];

    MyAdvancedJavaClass()
    {
        numItems = 0;
        itemArray = new int[10];
    }

    public void addItem(
        int item
    )
    {
        itemArray[numItems] = item;

        numItems++;
    };
};
```

Keep in mind that initializing a variable at its declaration affords little flexibility for any classes or methods that subsequently will use the object. A constructor can be modified easily to accept incoming data as well, enabling you to modify the object depending on the context of its use:

```java
public class MyAdvancedJavaClass
{
    public int numItems;
    private int itemArray[];

    MyAdvancedJavaClass(
        int initialValue,
        int arrayLength
    )
    {
        numItems = initialValue;
        itemArray = new int[arrayLength];
    }

    public void addItem(
        int item
    )
    {
        itemArray[numItems] = item;

        numItems++;
    };
};
```

An object is allowed to have several constructors, as long as no two constructors have the same method signature (parameter list):

```java
public class MyAdvancedJavaClass
{
    public int numItems;
    private int itemArray[];

    MyAdvancedJavaClass()
    {
        numItems = 0;
        itemArray = new int[10];
    }

    MyAdvancedJavaClass(
        int initialValue,
        int arrayLength
    )
    {
        numItems = initialValue;
        itemArray = new int[arrayLength];
    }

    public void addItem(
        int item
    )
    {
        itemArray[numItems] = item;

        numItems++;
    };
};
```

Sometimes, confusion may arise when there are several constructors that all do the same thing, but with different sets of data. In Java, constructors are allowed to call themselves, eliminate duplicate code, and enable you to consolidate all constructor code in one place:

```java
MyAdvancedJavaClass()
{
/*  Instead of...
    numItems = 0;
    itemArray = new int[10];
*/
    // call the more specific constructor
    this(0, 10);
}

MyAdvancedJavaClass(
    int initialValue,
```

```
         int arrayLength
    )
    {
         numItems = initialValue;
         itemArray = new int[arrayLength];
    }
```

Constructors are powerful tools. They enable you to create classes and use them dynamically without any significant hard-coding. As you will see, good constructor design is essential to an object-oriented architecture that works.

CREATING AND INITIALIZING AN OBJECT

It was mentioned earlier that all Java classes inherit from the `Object` superclass. The constructor for an `Object` is invoked using the `new` operation. This initialization operation is used at object creation, and is not used again during the object's lifecycle. One example of an object being initialized is the array initialization in our sample class. The `new` operation first allocates memory for the object and then invokes the object's constructor.

Because two kinds of constructors were created, the sample class can be invoked in one of two ways:

```
myAdvancedJavaInstance1 =
  new MyAdvancedJavaClass();


myAdvancedJavaInstance2 =
  new MyAdvancedJavaClass(10, 100);
```

The first instance of the class is initialized to the default values 0 and 10. When you invoked the new operation in this instance, the new operation set the values appropriately, and created a new instance of Array within the class instance. The second instance of our class set `numItems` to 10 and created a 100 item `Array`.

As you can see, this kind of dynamic class creation is very flexible. You could just as easily create another instance of our class with entirely different (or the same) initial values. This is one of the basic principles of object-oriented design espoused by languages such as Java.

Each instance of the object maintains a similar-looking, but *entirely different* set of variables. Changing the values in one instance does not result in a change in the values of the variables of the other instances. Remember, an instance of a class is like a BMW 328i Convertible.

As the analogy in Figure 1.1 illustrates, it looks as cool as every other BMW 328i, but just because you modify yours to remove the annoying electronic inhibition of speed, doesn't mean every other Beemer also will be changed!

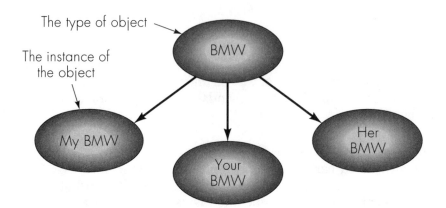

The type of object

The instance of the object

My BMW

BMW

Your BMW

Her BMW

Figure 1.1: *Just as customizing a BMW makes it different from other BMWs, modifying variables in one instance doesn't change them in all instances.*

Applying Good Object-Oriented Design Skills

Maybe you're tired of driving a mini-van. What you really want is a BMW Z3 Roadster. So, you drive your behemoth Toyota van down to the nearest BMW dealer and trade it in for the Z3. Now, because you have a different car, does that mean you have to learn how to drive all over again? Obviously not (unless you have just traded in a Volvo, in which case you have to learn how to drive to begin with). That's because the world, yes the same world that brought you Elvis and Bob Dole, is inherently object-oriented.

INHERITANCE

A BMW Z3, and every other car on the road, is a car, pure and simple. All cars have accelerators, brakes, steering wheels, and, even though you don't use them in a Beemer, turn signals. If you take this analogy further, you can say that every car inherits from the same *base class*, as illustrated in Figure 1.2.

A base class is a special kind of object that forms the foundation for other classes. In Java, a base class is usually inherited later on. Think of derived classes as *kinds of* base classes. In other words, a BMW Z3 is a kind of car. With that in mind, you can create the following class structure:

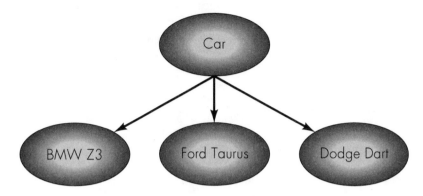

Figure 1.2: *In any object-oriented environment, classes inherit the characteristics of their base classes.*

```
public class Car
{
}

public class BMWZ3 extends Car
{
}
```

The extends keyword tells the BMWZ3 class to utilize the properties, values, and behavior of the Car base class. But there is one small problem. Can you ever drive a generic car? No, because there is no such thing. There are always kinds of cars, but never a specific thing that is known simply as a car. Java gives us the notion of an *abstract base class*.

An abstract base class is, quite simply, a class that must be inherited. It can never be used as a stand-alone class. In Java, the abstract keyword gives a class this unique property:

```
public abstract class Car
{
    int topSpeed;
}

public class BMWZ3 extends Car
{
}
```

In this situation, the Car class can never be instantiated or used as is. It must be inherited. When the BMWZ3 class inherits from Car, it also obtains all of the variables and methods within the Car class. So, the BMWZ3 class gets to use topSpeed as if it were its own member variable.

Somewhere in your code you might want to check what type of variable you are using. Java provides the `instanceof` keyword to enable you to inquire as to what the abstract base class of an object is. For example, the following two code snippets would return the value True:

```
BMWZ3 bmwVariable;
FordTaurus fordVariable;

if(bmwVariable instanceof Car) …

if (fordVariable instanceof Object) …
```

Whereas the following code snippet would return the value false:

```
if(bmwVariable instanceof PandaBear)
```

 Notice that Java's inheritance model is quite simple. In C++, objects are allowed to inherit from one or more abstract base class and can be made to inherit the *implementation* of those interfaces as well. Java, as a matter of simplicity, does not allow this, nor does it plan to at any time in the future.

There are ways to get around multiple implementation inheritance, but they do not really involve inheritance at all. The bottom line is that if you need to use multiple implementation inheritance, you probably won't want to use Java.

CODE REUSE

Let's say you are putting together your son's bicycle on Christmas morning. The instructions call for you to use a Phillips-head screwdriver. You take the screwdriver out of the toolbox, use it, and put it back. A few minutes later, you need the screwdriver again. Surely you would use the same screwdriver, not go to the hardware store and buy a new one!

Likewise, code reuse is of vital importance to the programmer on a tight schedule. You will need to streamline your code so that you can distribute commonly used tasks to specific modules. For example, many of the online demonstrations provided with this book include animation examples. Rather than recreate the animation routines, the same set of animation tools that were developed beforehand, were reused. Because the animators were coded with reuse in mind, we were able to take advantage of a strong interface design and an effective inheritance scheme.

OOP Strong, Efficient, and Effective

Whew! Whether this is your first foray using the Java language or your 101st, all design begins in this one place. There are three keys to creating an object that you can use time and again:

- Strong interface design

- Efficient class implementation

- Effective inheritance

With the fundamentals of object-oriented programming under your belt, you are ready to explore the simplicity with which you can create programs in Java that handle input and output (I/O). The Java I/O routines are not only easy, but extremely powerful. Bringing your C++ I/O to Java will result in as little functional loss as migrating object-oriented design techniques to Java from C++.

Introduction to Threading in Java

Multithreaded (MT) programs are the current rage in computer science. Books upon books have been written that describe the benefits of threading, the threading features inherent in various operating systems, and the various forms of threaded architectures.

So, what on earth are threads? How can you use them in your programs? Will threading continue to work in those applications that run native on operating systems that do not support threading? What does it mean to be MT-safe, and how do you design an MT-safe program?

The entire realm of multithreaded and multitasked programming transcends the scope of this book. We will confer only that knowledge of the topic that is directly related to the ideas of Beans programming, and in cases where more research may be warranted, direct you to the appropriate resources.

What are Threads?

Let's say you're sitting in your living room watching another Washington Redskins victory.

You get bored watching the massacre of the Dallas Cowboys, and you decide that you would like to see the San Francisco 49ers game in progress. In the good old days, you would have to actually switch channels and choose between one or the other. But, these days, televisions have Picture-in-Picture (PIP) capability. By pressing the PIP button on your trusty remote control, you can watch the Redskins demolish the Cowboys on a little box in the corner of the TV while watching the 49ers on the rest of the screen.

This is a prime example of multithreaded programming. The little screen and the big screen share resources (in this case, the area of the full television screen), but are not able to affect one another. In the areas in which the two games collide, one screen gives way to another.

THREADS IN YOUR COMPUTER

In the computer world, multithreaded applications exist similarly to the television world. They share the same area, in our case the television screen, which in reality is the physical process in which the application resides and is permitted to execute. MT applications, as they are known, are simultaneously able to execute multiple series of executable steps. Each of these series of steps is known as a *thread*.

Threads are implemented differently by individual operating systems(OS). In Solaris, for example, threads are defined and maintained in the user environment. The OS maintains responsibility over the process, regardless of what the process decides to do with itself. In a sense, the operating system treats the process as an object. The OS only cares about the interface to the process; how it starts up, shuts down, begins execution, and similar operations. It has no feelings whatsoever as to how the process executes information.

In fact, this is the fundamental concept of threads. Threads exist as a user-created and user-managed aspect of a program. The OS could care less if there are multiple threads in the executable object or if it is single threaded. Furthermore, the operating system will not help to resolve conflicts. All it cares about is the integrity of the process, not about what goes on inside of it.

HANDLING CONFLICTS

Let's say you have a couple of threads prancing along merrily within your application. Suddenly, they both access the same piece of data at the same time. This results in what is known as *concurrent access*. Concurrent access errors occur as a result of poor thread management.

Access errors occur in every day life, too. Let's say you've scheduled an appointment from eleven o'clock in the morning to one o'clock in the afternoon. Carelessly, you forgot your all-important staff meeting at twelve-thirty. Obviously, you can't be in two places at once! The end result is that you've placed yourself in two meetings. The threads within our applications have accessed identical data simultaneously.

When creating a thread, the first thing you must determine is what data that thread will touch. You then have to fence off that data so that only one possible thread can ever touch it at any given moment. In Solaris, this is done with a concept called *mutual exclusion*. A mutual exclusion lock that is placed around your data ensures that it will never be permitted to enter a concurrent access situation.

Imagine a relay team of four people competing at the Olympics in Sydney. The first runner on the relay team is given a baton that must be passed to a teammate before that teammate is allowed to run. If the teammate runs without the baton, she is disqualified. However, if the baton is passed properly, the next runner can continue running until she either arrives at the finish line or passes the baton to another teammate.

Likewise, different threads can lock around data *as long as the lock is available*. If the lock is unavailable, the thread must wait, effectively suspending itself, until the lock is available. There are specific settings to allow threads to continue without waiting, but these settings are beyond the scope of this book. If one thread grabs a lock but never lets go, it will have *deadlocked* the entire application. When your methods obtain a thread, make sure that they give it up somehow. Otherwise, the rest of your application will wait for a lock that will never come free.

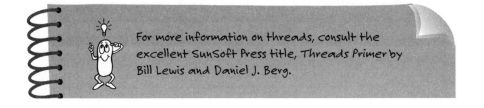

For more information on threads, consult the excellent SunSoft Press title, *Threads Primer* by Bill Lewis and Daniel J. Berg.

Threading in Java

Creating and debugging threads in Java is considerably simpler than doing so in C++. Deadlocks in Java are much easier to prevent, because the threads are a ton more intuitive. But MT applications in Java are not as robust or as powerful as their C++ counterparts. In short, there are trade-offs to threading in Java, for it is not an all-encompassing answer to the MT question.

Java treats threads as user-level entities as well. A Java applet or application runs within a process space defined in the Java Virtual Machine (JVM).

The JVM allocates processes and the resources for each process, and allows the applet or application to define how that process space is used. Java programs that implement threads must do so using the `Thread` class or a derivative thereof.

THE THREAD CLASS

Java's language hierarchy, which includes the likes of `Strings`, `Integers`, and so on, also contains a powerful, yet incredibly simple `Thread` object that can be implemented within your programs. The `Thread` class provides all of the functionality necessary for you to create fully multi-threaded and MT-safe applications using the Java language.

 Two approaches to spawning threads in Java are worth noting, as outlined in the following sections. Later on, many of our examples will make heavy use of either one or the other method. As always, there are trade-offs and benefits for each architectural decision you make.

USING THE ENTIRE CLASS AS A THREAD

The first method you could employ involves spawning threads in which an entire class can reside. For example, you spawn a thread, then create a *runnable* class and attach it to the thread. Now the entire class exists within the thread and the stream of execution for that class is maintained by the thread. If the thread is killed, the stream of execution is likewise destroyed.

The biggest advantage to this method is that the class need not know anything about how it is to be implemented. Take a look at the following example:

```
public class Animator extends Panel implements Runnable
{
    Animator() { ... }

    public void run() { ... }
}

public class AnimatorManager
{
    Animator animations[];
    Thread animationThreads[];

    AnimatorManager() { ... }

    public void createAnimation(
        Animator anim
    )
    {
        // first spawn a thread for the class

        // now let the thread continue...
    }
}
```

The `AnimatorManager` class is responsible for: creating a series of `Animator` objects; spawning a thread for the object to execute in; and shutting down, suspending, resuming, or inquiring about the status of the thread. Note how the `Animator` does not know or care whether it will be in a thread of execution or in an entire process. It is a runnable class, meaning that whatever is contained within the `run` function will be executed *if the parent process or thread allows.*

The object is created normally, and our `AnimatorManager` assumes that the object is already created. The thread is created, but the object is passed to it as a parameter. The corresponding constructor in the `Thread` class knows that the runnable object will reside solely within its thread of control:

```
public class AnimatorManager
{
    Animator animations[];
    Thread animationThreads[];

    AnimatorManager() { ... }

    public void createAnimation(
        Animator anim
    )
    {
        // first spawn a thread for the class
        animationThreads[currentThreadCount] = new Thread(anim);

        // now let the thread continue...
        animationThreads[currentThreadCount].start();
    }
}
```

 Remember that Java is inherently object-oriented, so this kind of thread creation is quite within the reach of the language. There is no funny business going on here. A thread is created and an object is told to live within it. It is actually quite intuitive in an object-oriented sense. The next method hearkens back to the days of structured programming.

INHERITING FROM THE THREAD CLASS

The second way to implement threads is to create a class that inherits from the Thread class. In the first method, you created an object that was a free-standing object in its own right. In this case, you will create an object that is a Thread object from the beginning. In essence, the JVM treats both methods as similar and reasonable means to spawning threaded objects, and both are acceptable from a style perspective. Using the entire class as a thread is more elegant, as you just saw, but either will suffice.

Inheriting from the Thread class is actually quite simple. Instead of extending from an applet or *Panel*, your class simply extends from Thread. In your `init` method or constructor, you must initialize the thread as well. Obviously, your class must be aware that it is running in a thread.

The thread code for a class that inherits from `Thread` is in the `run` method. As in a class that implements `Runnable`, inheriting from `Thread` automatically enables you to implement the run method. Any code that you want to manage the thread should be placed there. Also, place the thread there if you need to make it sleep or suspend.

The difference between extending `Thread` and implementing `Runnable` is that when you inherit from `Thread`, your entire class is a thread. The thread must be started and stopped from within the class, unlike the other method in which the thread controls are outside the class itself (see Figure 1.3).

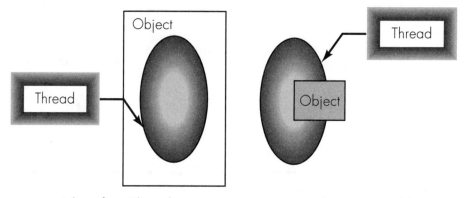

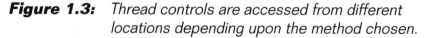

Inherit from Thread   Implement Runnable

Figure 1.3: *Thread controls are accessed from different locations depending upon the method chosen.*

Take a look at the following example, and notice how the constructor calls the `start` method or the thread:

```
public class Animator extends Thread
{
    Animator()
    {
        start();
```

```
    }
    public void run() { ... }
}
```

As you can see, the class is clearly a threaded class. What happens if you want to use the class' methodology without using threads? You'll either have to create a new class that doesn't use threads, or revert to the first method. Implementing `Runnable` and placing your thread controls outside the target class is the preferred way of using threads, but inheriting from threads can be particularly useful for highly modular code in which you want to package an entire object that does not rely on anything else.

THREAD CONTROLS

A thread has several control methods that affect its behavior. Simply starting and stopping a thread's execution are but two of the many tools available that manipulate how programs execute. For example, on several occasions, you will want to pause a thread's execution, and eventually resume it.

Let's say you had a stopwatch class. You want the counting to occur in a thread so that it doesn't impact any other classes or applets that will want to use it. In order to have complete control over the stopwatch, you must implement a few methods:

- Start

- Stop

- Suspend

- Resume

- Sleep

In fact, Java implements all five of these options for us in the `Thread` class. The `start` method does exactly what it says. It tells the thread that it may begin execution of all the steps contained in the `run` method. The `run` method itself may call any of the above thread controls, but obviously you will want to restart the thread somewhere if the `run` method decides to suspend it!

The `stop` routine terminates the thread and prevents the `run` method from executing any further steps. It does not, however, shut down any subthreads that it may have created. You must be careful and make sure that every thread you create either terminates on its own or is terminated by its parent. Otherwise, you could very well have several threads executing and consuming resources long after the applet or application has terminated.

The `suspend` and `resume` routines are pretty self-explanatory. When `suspend` is called, the thread ceases execution of its run method until `resume` is called somewhere down the line. If your parent thread needs to inquire about the current running status of a thread, it may call the `isAlive` method and find out if the thread is stopped. Obviously, if the thread isn't stopped, and it isn't running, it must be suspended.

Lastly, the `sleep` method tells the thread to pause for a given number of milliseconds. It is particularly useful for the clock because we want it to "tick" every second.

The state diagram in Figure 1.4 should make clear the thread timing you need to be aware of. Remember, before anything can be done to a thread, you must call `start` on it. Once you are finished with the thread of execution, you must call `stop`.

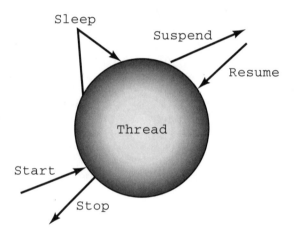

Figure 1.4: *The five control methods that affect a thread's behavior are start, stop, suspend, resume, and sleep.*

SYNCHRONIZED METHODS

Conflict handling within Java is implemented using method synchronization. If you have data that could potentially deadlock between two threads, you must declare the functions in which the data is modified as *synchronized*. Java prevents multiple threads from entering the synchronized methods and thereby eliminates the possibility of deadlock.

Creating a synchronized method is actually quite easy. It is simply a matter of declaring that the function will be synchronized in the method signature, as can be seen in the following snippet:

```
public class ThreadClass
{
    int data;
    ...
    public void synchronized addToData(
        int addend
    )
    {
        data += addend;
    }
    ...
}
```

There are a couple of important caveats to synchronized functions. Because multiple threads may require entry to a synchronized function, it is better to keep any function that is declared as synchronized short and sweet. When one thread enters a synchronized function, keeping its time spent in the function to a minimum will keep your programs running smoothly. After all, the idea behind threading is to get your programs to execute steps in parallel, not to spawn threads that end up waiting forever for each other to finish with the data.

NOTIFY, WAIT, AND YIELD

Often, in an application with multiple threads, you will have many threads competing with one another for resources. One way to allocate those resources effectively is to set the relative priorities of each thread. This will be discussed in a moment, but right now let's discuss some of the specific steps you can take within the thread itself. Remember that when threads execute, they all share the same process space in which the application resides. Like a bunch of kids forced to share a toy, the threads compete and vie for control of the process. However, like any good parent, you have several tools at your disposal to make sure the threads cooperate.

Sometimes you will want to control entry into a function and label the function as synchronized. Even though the function is long, you want to yield control of the function pretty early on. You can call the notify method to tell the parent thread that you are finished with the synchronized lock.

In order to make a thread stand by for a notify message, you must add the wait method to the thread's execution routines. The notify method is called somewhere in an executing thread. Once notify is called, any thread awaiting execution on a wait call automatically proceeds.

Another way to give up the process space in which a thread runs is to call the yield routine specifically. When yield is called within a thread, the thread gives up any scheduling priority, process space, or claim to its current turn in the sharing cycle.

THREAD PRIORITIES

In Java, threads may have one of three priorities: *minimum, normal,* and *maximum.*

> A more elegant, yet more confusing, way to control threads is by setting their priority. Obviously, when you set a thread to have a high priority, it gets first crack at any processing time and resources. You should be careful and judicious in setting thread priorities. Even with the best of intentions, setting every thread at a high priority could very well defeat the purpose of using threads.

You may set the priority using the `setPriority` method of the `Thread` class and retrieve the priority of any thread by using the `get-Priority` method, as shown:

```
Thread threadOne;
Thread threadTwo;
Thread threadThree;

threadOne.setPriority(Thread.MIN_PRIORITY);
threadTwo.setPriority(Thread.NORM_PRIORITY);
threadThree.setPriority(Thread.MAX_PRIORITY);
```

As threads are a powerful and underused aspect of most Java programs, thread scheduling and prioritizing are flexible and equally powerful ways to control how your applications behave and execute.

DAEMON THREADS

There are two kinds of threads. So far I have discussed application threads, which are tied to the process and directly contribute to the running of the application. Daemon threads, on the other hand, are used for background tasks that happen every so often within a thread's execution. Normally, an application will run until all the threads have finished their execution. However, if the only remaining threads are daemon threads, the application will exit anyway.

Java itself has several daemon threads running in the background of every application. Java's garbage collection is controlled by daemon threads known in computer science parlance as *reaper* threads, or threads that run through an application looking for *dead weight*. In the garbage collection thread's case, the dead weight happens to be unused but allocated memory.

If your application needs to set up a daemon thread, simply call the `setDaemon` method of the thread, as shown in the following snippet. The application in which the thread resides will know to ignore that thread if it needs to execute, and program execution will continue normally.

```
Thread t = new Thread(myClass);
t.setDaemon(true);
```

Thread Summary

Threads are one way in which you can affect the behavior of an object. Serialization is another. Serialization allows you to store your objects as strings. When we use threads, we do so in order to change how the object behaves while it is running. Serialization does not allow us to preserve this run-time behavior, only the class' static behavior and characteristics. Whenever you reconstruct a serialized class, only your class will be reconstituted correctly, not any of the threads. Therefore, it is important that your threads be as object-oriented as possible so that they can store their state when necessary.

Object Serialization

Serialization is a concept that enables you to store and retrieve objects, as well as to send full-fledged objects "over the wire" to other applications. The reason serialization is of such vital importance to Java should be clear: without it, distributed applications would not be able to send objects to each other. That means that only simple types such as `int` and `char` would be allowed in parameter signatures, and complex objects would be limited in what they could do. It's sort of like saying you would have to talk like a three-year-old whenever you spoke with your boss. You want to have a complex conversation, but you are limited in what you can say.

What is Serialization?

Without some form of object storage, Java objects can only be transient. There would be no way to maintain a persistent state in an object from one invocation to another. The serialization routines have been incorporated into the standard Java `Object` class with several routines to facilitate the writing and reading of a secured representation. There are several security concerns that you must be aware of, and those will be discussed in a moment. Without object serialization, Java could never truly be an effective Internet language.

Handling Object Relationships

An important consideration of the object serialization facilities is that the entire process is executed in a manner transparent to any APIs or user intervention. In other words, you need not write any code to utilize serialization routines. When writing an object, the serialization routines must allow full reconstruction of the object at a later time. Not only must the class structure be saved, but the values of each member of the structure must be saved as well. If you had a class with the following representation:

```
public class CuteBrownBear
{
    Color eyeColor;
    float heightInches;
    float weightPounds;
}
```

It must be saved so that the values of `eyeColor`, `heightInches`, and `weightPounds` are preserved and can be restored once the reading functions are invoked. Sometimes, however, things can become complicated when objects begin to refer to one another. For example, the following class contains `CuteBrownBear` as well as several other toy objects that we must save as well:

```
public class ToyBox
{
    CuteBrownBear bearArray[5];
    ActionFigure actionFigureArray[5];
}
```

The serialization routine must not only serialize the `ToyBox` object, but the `CuteBrownBear` objects and `ActionFigure` objects as well. To handle this kind of situation, the serialization routine traverses the objects it is asked to write or read. As it traverses an object representation, it serializes any new objects automatically. If, down the line, it finds another object of a type already serialized, it merely modifies the earlier serialized representation to refer to the new instance. In this manner, serialized objects are compact and efficient without much duplicated code.

For example, when you need to serialize the `ToyBox` object, the serialization routine first serializes `CuteBrownBear` in array position one.

Array positions two through five are not serialized on their own; rather the original serialized representation is modified to point to their locations and values. Therefore, the final serialized object has one reference to the `CuteBrownBear` object, plus five sets of data values.

The Output Streams

Serialization output is handled through the `ObjectOutputStream`. Serialization calls refer to the `writeObject` method contained within the stream, passing to it the instance of the object to be serialized. The stream first checks to see whether another instance of the same object type has been previously serialized. If it has, the routine handles it as discussed in the previous section, merely placing the new values alongside the representation. If, however, the object has yet to be serialized, the routine creates a new serialized representation and places the values next to it.

Most serialization is handled transparently. But, an object may at any time begin to handle its own serialization by reimplementing the `write-Object` method. The `writeObject` method is part of every `Object` class, and can be overridden on command. If you need a finer-grained serialized representation, or would like to include some kind of encryption or other technique between serialization endpoints, this is where and how to do it.

As an example, let us instantiate a `CuteBrownBear` object and serialize it:

```
// create the streams here…
FileOutputStream fileOut = new FileOutputStream("filename");
ObjectOutputStream objectOut = new ObjectOutputStream(fileOut);

// instantiate the new bear object
CuteBrownBear bear = new CuteBrownBear();

// serialize the bear
objectOut.writeObject(bear);
```

Handling Object Webs

An object web is a complex relationship between two or more objects in which objects refer to other objects that may eventually refer back to them. If you were to serialize such an object representation, you could potentially be caught in an infinite loop.

Let's say there is a system of roads between three cities, Seattle, Washington D.C., and San Francisco. You want to take an end-of-summer road trip and visit each city. The only instruction the auto association provided was, "If you hit one of these three roads, follow it until it ends." Following that logic, you would start at San Francisco, go to Seattle, visit the Redskins in Washington D.C., come back to the Golden Gate (San Francisco), and go to Seattle, and so on as shown in Figure 1.5.

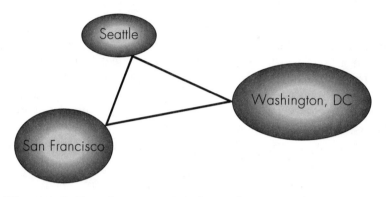

Figure 1.5: *An example of serialization in which stored objects are linked by a circuitous route.*

Likewise, if you were to serialize San Francisco, then Seattle, followed by Washington, and keep following the path back to San Francisco, you would end up following the same loop an infinite number of times. This lattice arrangement ensures that a simple tree-based algorithm will not suffice. Java's object serialization routine accounts for this kind of structure in the same manner that it handles multiple objects of the same type in the same stream.

Because of these object webs, any serialization must take into account those objects which have already been serialized. So, in addition to the serialization methods, Java's object serialization routines also keep track of the object's serialized state. Java also keeps track of whether object *types* have been serialized as well. In so doing, it can keep track of the data contained within the object, and not just the object itself.

Reading Objects

Reading objects is a matter of taking the serialized representation and reversing the process that created them in the first place. Remember to handle your deserialization in the same order as your serialization, traversing any trees in a similar fashion. The objective is to reconstruct the original object.

The deserialization routines are handled with a corresponding `ObjectInputStream` and the `readObject` method contained therein.

Once again, to obtain control over serialization routines for your object, you need to override and reimplement the `writeObject` and `readObject` routines.

Security and Fingerprinting

Sometimes objects can be serialized surreptitiously by other objects linked by your application. If your object does things that you would prefer to keep private and unknown to the world, then disable your objects. Serialization can be disabled for an object by adding the `private transient` tag to the class definition:

```
private transient class CuteBrownBear
{
    ...
}
```

Or, the object itself can override the serialization routines and return a `NoAccessException`. The `NoAccessException` tells any object that attempts to serialize your implementation that it may not do so. Furthermore, it gives a sufficient debugging warning to any applications that may reuse your object.

```
public class CuteBrownBear
{
    ... the rest of the CuteBrownBear class goes here ...

    public void writeObject(...) throws NoAccessException
    {
    }

    public void readObject(...) throws NoAccessException
    {
    }
}
```

Serialization Overview

Java automatically handles its own object serialization. However, you may reimplement the serialization routines within your own objects. You have been presented with several serialization concerns in this chapter. If you are going to handle the serialization for a given object, make sure you conform to the various restrictions we have supplied. If your objects do not handle their serialization properly, your entire object system may not be serializable.

The Java Event Model

In version 1.0 of the Java Developer's Kit, the Java event model was essentially thrown over the wall without regard to either the quick adoption of Java, or the subsequent use of Java in large, complex applications.

When you compose JavaBeans components, you begin to enter the realm of large, complex components. In order to support Beans and other non-Beans Java applications, the Java engineering team has devised a new delegation-based event model.

The Old Model

The old Abstract Window Toolkit (AWT) event model was based on inheritance and required that you subclass components that use the action method. From within the `action` method you could process the event as it was received. If you returned True from the `action` method, the event was consumed and not propagated back to other components. If you returned False, the event was passed back to all of the superclass' `action` methods (see Figure 1.6). You could still obtain the target and source of the event, so to say that it wasn't robust would be slightly incorrect. The old model did what it was intended to do, but it didn't do it properly.

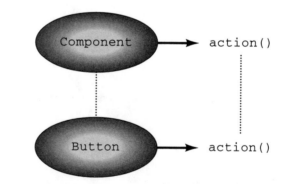

Figure 1.6: *Events were handled through inheritance of the action method.*

Inheritance should be reserved for when you want to extend the functionality of an object. Simply inheriting an object just to use an event goes against the tenets of object-oriented programming that we have all come to know and love. The old inheritance model prevented you from separating the Graphical User Interface (GUI) from the application since the GUI and the application were linked because of their need to subclass one another for events. Most smart developers choose to develop GUI components apart from their application components. The old model was also highly error prone since no complex filtering mechanism could be created within the `action` methods.

Delegation

The new AWT event model is based on a publish and subscribe system. Further chapters in this book will discuss the publish and subscribe system more thoroughly, but we will cover the basics now. If you were to suddenly fall in love with the sport of swimming and just had to have a newspaper dedicated to coverage of major and minor events, you would subscribe to *Swimmer's Ear*, the magazine for lovers of aquatic sport. *Swimmer's Ear*'s publisher has a subscription department that takes every subscriber and puts them in a list. When *Swimmer's Ear* has a new issue to publish, they send it out to all of the subscribers. *Swimmer's Ear*'s publisher also puts out several other magazines including *Athlete's Foot* and *Inline Skater's Scab*. People who wish to subscribe to those magazines will call up the same subscription department and subscribe to the appropriate magazine (see Figure 1.7).

Figure 1.7: *Publish and subscribe to magazines.*

Delegation works in a very similar manner. Objects wishing to provide events are called *publishers* or *sources*. Those objects that want events are *listeners* or *targets*. The listener simply waits for events to be *fired* on it, while the publisher will fire events when it chooses. The result is that the application can separate its event model from its object and GUIs and provide a seamless way for the two to interact.

TYPES OF EVENTS

All events inherit from `EventObject`. However, the new event model makes a slight distinction between types of events. The first type of event is called a *low-level event*. A low-level event is one that is tied to a visual element, like a GUI component. Typically, these events are of the focus, click, or key-pressed ilk. They represent the events that are triggered by buttons and other AWT components. The hierarchy of low-level events is displayed in Figure 1.8.

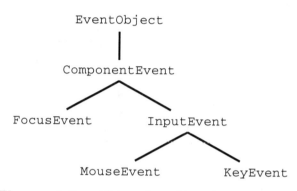

Figure 1.8: *Hierarchy of low-level events.*

The second type of event is the *semantic event*. A semantic event can be defined at a much higher level and allows you to customize how you want to represent your event. Java provides three basic semantic events, which you can go about subclassing and inheriting to your heart's content. The three rudimentary semantic events are listed in Figure 1.9.

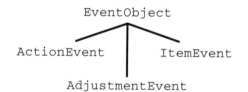

Figure 1.9: *Hierarchy of semantic events.*

LISTENERS

A listener sits around and waits for events. Generally, a listener should be named by prepending the type of event it listens for to the word *Listener*. In so doing, an `ActionEvent` is listened to by `ActionListener` objects. Likewise, `AdjustmentEvents` are listened to by `Adjust-mentListeners`. You should follow the same design pattern for your Java events.Chapter 3, *Bean Events*, covers how JavaBeans design patterns will impact the naming of your events and event listeners.

SOURCES

Sources are the location from which an event is fired. In order for your source to fire an event to a listener it must first be able to store the listeners locally within the object. If you create a `SwimmersEarEvent` and want to fire it to `SwimmersEarListener` objects, you will need a method through which listeners can register and unregister themselves with a source. Typically, these listener registration methods are named by prepending the words *add* and *remove* to the name of the listener object. For example, to add `SwimmersEarListener` objects to a source, you would more than likely create a method in the source object called `addSwimmersEarListener`. Once again, sources and listeners and how they pertain to JavaBeans will be discussed in Chapter 3.

Events are one of the fundamental aspects of Beans interoperability (discussed in Chapter 3). Another aspect of JavaBeans that warrants in depth discussion is *introspection*. Introspection is the act of looking into an object and determining its innards without having to refer to source code. Introspection uses low-level reflection to accomplish many of its tasks. In the next section, reflection and the special Java objects created by the reflection API are discussed.

Reflection

As will be discussed in Chapter 5, *Bean Introspection*, the single most important idea in JavaBeans is indeed introspection. Introspection allows classes to look into one another and determine their makeup. This is done without the use of any source code, only compiled bytecode. Support for this kind of object access was sorely lacking in version 1.0 of the Java Developer's Kit, but the latest revision revamps the support architecture for introspection with a series of objects referred to as *reflection* objects.

How Reflection Works

Using reflection, your objects can obtain instances, descriptions, and interfaces for other objects. You can determine all of the methods contained in an object, all of the variables in an object, and all of the exceptions and events thrown by an object. In order to support this kind of access into an object, a set of super objects is available for your use.

These objects comprise the various parts of a Java object, notably the Class, Array, Field, Method, and Constructor.

SIMPLE TYPES

By using an object and accessing its Field routines, you can get every kind of variable, as well as its modifiers (be they constant, abstract, or other), and its type. The types supported by the reflection API are Java complex types. Thus, in order to access simple types, the reflection API uses the standard Java wrapper classes depicted in Table 1.1.

Table 1.1: *Java's simple types are mapped to specific complex Java objects.*

Simple Type	Complex Type
Boolean	java.lang.Boolean
Char	java.lang.Character
Byte	java.lang.Byte
Short	java.lang.Short
Int	java.lang.Integer
Long	java.lang.Long
Double	java.lang.Double
Float	java.lang.Float

The type mapping also applies to Class objects that return simple types. If you were to invoke a Method operation that returned a simple integer on a Class object, you would end up with a complex type.

SECURITY

The biggest concern with reflection is how the Java security manager affects your ability to look into an object and see its innards. Reflection itself offers no new security restrictions or relaxations. Rather, it delegates to the system's security manager. When you run an applet within a browser, the browser's security manager is in effect, preventing the applet from modifying the local machine, and limiting the extent to which it can modify the remote machine from which the applet was received. Likewise, the reflection API defers to the security manager for the applet or application, and throws SecurityException errors should any reflection request be denied.

The system's security manager enforces three policies for untrusted, usually applet, code. The untrusted code is granted access only to public members of public classes that are loaded, public members of public system classes, as well as all declared members of all classes loaded by the class loader. Furthermore, all trusted applet code can access all members of the System classes. Lastly, all system code in applications (code accessible via the CLASSPATH environment setting) can have all access to all classes loaded by the class loader.

Reflection Objects

The most important reflection object is the Class object. The Class object contains all of the information about a class and gives you the ability to locate and reflect *into inner classes*, or classes contained within another class. Other classes contained in the reflection API include objects for retrieving methods, variables, and other Java constructs. Reflection should be used when you wish to apply a generic introspection algorithm to many objects of different types. Often, getting all of the methods in an object will be unnecessary, but for those applications that require the details of the inner classes of an object, reflection should be used.

GETTING A CLASS

Using the Class object allows your applications to manipulate a Java object while the program is running. For example, if we were to have two objects, a vending machine object and a soda object, we would be able to create a soda object and use reflection to determine what kind of object it is. You can do so using the Class object.

The Class object provides several routines for accessing the details of an object, whether it is an interface, a class, or a primitive type. The Class object will allow you to perform the same operations on either of the three constructs, giving you tremendous flexibility when using reflection. Often, reflection routines will be used as part of a grand scheme to introspect an object, and all of its member objects. Because the Class object is flexible in allowing classes, interfaces, and primitive types, you need not worry about encountering a strange member object in your introspection.

Constructor There are no public constructors for the Class object. Rather, the Java VM constructs the object for you when you require it. This prevents objects from creating malicious classes and further strengthens Java's security model.

Methods There are two methods to determine the nature of a Class. Remember, the type of a Class object cannot be used without some kind of conversion to a normal Java Object. To make this change, you will need the following two methods that convert a Class to an Object.

The `newInstance` and `isInstance` methods allow your `Class` to be cast to another, usable Java type. Without such a conversion, the `Class` object can never be used. The `newInstance` method accepts no parameters, but throws two exceptions. The first exception, an `InstantiationException`, is thrown when the type cast cannot be made, presumably because the object represented by the `Class` is not of the proper type. The second exception is thrown if the calling object cannot have access to the `Class`:

```
public Object newInstance() throws
    InstantiationException,
    IllegalAccessException
```

The `isInstance` method accepts one parameter, a Java `Object`. It returns true if the object represented by the `Class` is of the type represented by the `Object`:

```
public boolean isInstance(
    Object obj
)
```

Sometimes all you will want is the name of the class as it is written in the code. To get this information, use the `toString` method. At other times, you will know the name of the class you want, but need to get a handle on it. For those occasions, use the `forName` method to search for the class and return it to you. Most of the time, all you want is the name of the object, without any frills. Classes can also have modifiers associated with them, such as `final`, `protected`, or `public`. The `getModifiers` method can obtain those modifiers for you.

 The `toString` method accepts no parameters and returns a `String` whose value is the name of the class as it is written in code. If the value is a `class`, the word "class" is prepended to the name. If it is an `interface`, the word "interface" is prepended to the name. If it is a primitive type, only the name is returned:

```
public String toString()
```

The `forName` method attempts to locate and create a `Class` instance for the object whose name is `className`. The method throws a `ClassNotFoundException` if it cannot find the class, or if the security policy currently in effect for the application prohibits its instantiation:

```
public static Class forName(
    String className
) throws ClassNotFoundException
```

Unlike the `toString` method, the `getName` method simply returns the name of the class, without any prepending of types or constructs:

```
public String getName()
```

The `getModifiers` method returns an integer corresponding to the modifier encodings mentioned below. The encodings are constants whose value represents whether or not a class is `public`, `protected`, `private`, `final`, or simply an `interface`:

```
public int getModifiers()
```

■

You will also probably need methods that provide a clue as to what is contained within the `Class` object. Often during introspection, anything and everything becomes a `Class` object first, and is then narrowed down to the specific object that it really is. If you need to figure out if the `Class` is an interface, an array, or a primitive type, use one of three methods: `isInterface`, `is Array`, or `isPrimitive` .

The `isInterface` method returns true if the object represented by the `Class` object is an interface. Similarly, the `isArray` method returns true if the `Class` is an array, and the `isPrimitive` method returns true if the `Class` is a primitive type:

```
public boolean isInterface()
public boolean isArray()
public boolean isPrimitive()
```

■

Often times, a class will be composed of several inherited interfaces. If you truly want to know the make-up of a class, you will want to obtain these interfaces using the `getInterfaces` method. Sometimes, a class does not inherit from `Object` at all. In these instances, you will want to use the `getSuperclass` method to find out the ultimate superclass.

If an object is constructed by inheriting from several other objects or interfaces, those interfaces can be obtained via the `getInterfaces` method. The method returns an array of `Class` objects, on which the same APIs seen here may be used:

```
public Class[] getInterfaces()
```

Classes need not ultimately inherit from the Java-standard `Object` at all. In these instances, the superclass, or the class from which the class ultimately inherits, can be obtained using the `getSuperclass` method. The method returns one class, corresponding to the ultimate inherited class of the object:

```
public Class getSuperclass()
```
■

Classes also contain several methods, fields, and other classes as well. These may be obtained using the next few methods. The first of these methods concerns the need to obtain other classes contained within the `Class`, typically as variables. The second method merely obtains all of the `Fields` in the object. The next method returns all of the methods in the `Class`. Finally, the reflection API contains a method for obtaining the constructors for a `Class`.

 The `getClasses` method returns an array corresponding to all of the classes and interfaces contained within the object. The return value is null if there are no classes, or if the target class is a primitive type:

```
public Class[] getClasses()
```

The `getFields` method returns an array of `Field` objects corresponding to all of the public fields in the `Class`. The method returns both the public member fields of an object as well as the public hidden fields of the object. If there is an error in trying to obtain the fields, a `Security-Exception` is thrown:

```
public Field[] getFields() throws SecurityException
```

The `getMethods` method does exactly what it says and returns an array of `Method` objects whose value is all of the methods in the `Class`. If there is an error in trying to obtain the methods, a `SecurityException` is thrown:

```
public Method[] getMethods()
    throws SecurityException
```

The `getConstructors` method returns a list of `Constructor` objects and throws a `SecurityException` if there is an error in getting permission for the lookup:

```
public Constructor[] getConstructors()
    throws SecurityException
```
■

There are also specific accessors for the same four constructs. The `getField` method allows you to obtain a field by its simple string name, the `getMethod` method allows you to get a method by its name and parameters, and the `getConstructor` method lets you obtain a constructor for a class that accepts certain parameters.

 The `getField` method returns the `Field` object corresponding to the name of the field stored in `fieldName` or a `NoSuchFieldException` if the field does not exist. The method can also return a `SecurityException` if there was an error obtaining the field:

```
public Field getField(
    String fieldName)
    throws NoSuchFieldException, SecurityException
```

The `getMethod` method returns a `Method` object whose method name matches the value contained in `methodName` and whose parameter types match the value contained in `methodParameters`. The method can return a `NoSuchMethodException` if there is no method or a `SecurityException` if security policy prevents the method from executing:

```
public Method getMethod(
    String methodName,
    Class[] methodParameters)
    throws NoSuchMethodException, SecurityException
```

The `getConstructor` method returns a `Constructor` object whose parameter types correspond to the values contained in `constructorParameters`. Again, the method returns a `NoSuchMethodException` if the constructor does not exist, or a `SecurityException` if security policy prevents the method from executing:

```
public Constructor getConstructor(
    Class[] constructorParameters)
    throws NoSuchMethodException, SecurityException
```

■

DETERMINING MEMBERS OF AN OBJECT

The `Member` interface has no constructor and is used to determine information about a class, interface member, or constructor. Because it is an abstract base class, it must be implemented by other Java objects wishing to serve the member information. A member is, by definition, an element contained by the class. Thus, a member could be anything from a variable to a method to a constructor. It has two fields associated with it, `PUBLIC` and `DECLARED`, that are used by the security manager to determine the accessibility of the member.

The `Member` interface has two fields, `PUBLIC` and `DECLARED`, that are not necessarily intended for use by the programmer. Rather, they are used by the security manager to determine whether or not the member is accessible:

```
public final static int PUBLIC
public final static int DECLARED
```

The `Member` interface also has three methods that are used to determine some of the specifics of the object. The implementing object will choose how to go about providing this information based on the class or structure that the `Member` object points to.

 The `getDeclaringClass` method returns a `Class` object that represents the class or interface that owns the `Member` object:

```
public abstract Class getDeclaringClass()
```

The `getName` method returns a `String` representing the name of the `Member` object as it is declared in code:

```
public abstract String getName()
```

The `getModifiers` method returns an integer corresponding to values associated with `public`, `private`, or `protected`:

```
public abstract int getModifiers()
```

FINDING VARIABLES

The `Field` object implements the `Member` interface and adds a slew of functionality on top of it. A field is a variable or a data structure within the class itself. The programmer cannot create `Field` objects on his or her own. The Virtual Machine will create `Field` objects through methods such as the `getField` method which is, as shown in an earlier section, contained inside the `Class` object.

The first three methods in the `Field` object correspond directly to those in the `Member` interface. The `getDeclaringClass`, `getName`, and `getModifiers` methods are implemented here as they should be.

 The `getDeclaringClass` method returns a `Class` object that represents the class or interface that owns the `Field` object:

```
public abstract Class getDeclaringClass()
```

The getName method returns a String representing the name of the Field object as it is declared in code:

```
public abstract String getName()
```

The getModifiers method returns an integer corresponding to values associated with public, private, or protected:

```
public abstract int getModifiers()
```

■

The Field object also contains several means to obtain its value. The most primitive of these means is the simple get method. The get method has several, more specific, counterparts in getBoolean, get-Byte, and so on.

 The get method accepts one parameter, the target object to which we want to apply this method. Once the Field object is obtained from the Class, applying the get method to an existing object will determine the value of that particular field if it is located in the target object. If an instance of the Field object is not in the target object, an IllegalArgumentException is thrown. If the target object is null, a NullPointerException is thrown. If the Field is not accessible within the target object, an IllegalAccessException is thrown:

```
public Object get(
    Object targetObject)
throws NullPointerException,
       IllegalArgumentException,
       IllegalAccessException
```

There are also several more specific methods on the Field object that can obtain the properly typed object from the get method. These methods essentially wrap the generic get method and handle the type conversion for the user. All of the methods return the proper exceptions as just described.

```
public <primitive type> get<primitive type>(
    Object targetObject)
throws NullPointerException,
       IllegalArgumentException,
       IllegalAccessException
```

Where *<primitive type>* is one of the following:

- boolean
- byte
- char
- short
- int
- float
- double

■

Corresponding to the methods for accessing data, there are several methods you can use to set the value of the `Field` object. The simple `set` operation can handle the most complex of these operations, but there are more specific methods available that are directly related to their `get` counterparts.

The `set` method accepts two parameters, the target object on which to perform the operation, and the new value of the field being changed. The method returns on three exceptions. The `NullPointerException` occurs when the target object is null. The `IllegalArgumentException` is thrown when the type conversion cannot be made. And the `IllegalAccessException` is thrown if the target object's corresponding `Field` is inaccessible:

```
public void set(
    Object targetObject,
    Object newValue)
throws NullPointerException,
    IllegalArgumentException,
    IllegalAccessException
```

Just as with the generic `get` operation, there are several more specific `set` operations for primitive types:

```
public void set<primitive type>(
    Object targetObject,
    <primitive type> newValue)
throws NullPointerException,
    IllegalArgumentException,
    IllegalAccessException
```

Where <primitive type> is one of the following:

- boolean
- byte
- char
- short
- int
- float
- double

■

Constructor There are no public constructors for the Class object. Rather, the Java Virtual Machine constructs the object for you when you require it. This prevents objects from creating malicious classes and further strengthens Java's security model.

Methods There are two methods to determine the nature of a Class. Remember, the type of a Class object cannot be used without some kind of conversion to a normal Java Object. To make this change, you will need the following two methods that convert a Class to an Object.

 The newInstance and isInstance methods allow your Class to be cast to another, usable Java type. Without such a conversion, the Class object can never be used. The newInstance method accepts no parameters, but throws two exceptions. The first exception, an InstantiationException, is thrown when the type cast cannot be made, presumably because the object represented by the Class is not of the proper type. The second exception is thrown if the calling object cannot have access to the Class.

```
public Object newInstance() throws
    InstantiationException,
    IllegalAccessException
```

The isInstance method accepts one parameter, a Java Object. It returns true if the object represented by the Class is of the type represented by the Object.

```
public boolean isInstance(
    Object obj
)
```

■

Sometimes all you will want is the name of the class as it is written in the code. To get this information, you can use the `toString` method. At other times, you will know the name of the class you want, but you need to get a handle on it. For those occasions, you can use the `for-Name` method to search for the class and return it to you. And most of the time, all you want is the name of the object, without any frills. Classes can also have modifiers associated with them, such as `final`, `protected`, or `public`. The `getModifiers` method can obtain those modifiers for you.

 The `toString` method accepts no parameters and returns a `String` whose value is the name of the class as it is written in code. If the value is a `class`, the word *class* is prepended to the name. If it is an `interface`, the word *interface* is prepended to the name. And, if it is a primitive type, only the name is returned.

```
public String toString()
```

The `forName` method attempts to locate and create a `Class` instance for the object whose name is `className`. The method throws a `Class-NotFoundException` if it cannot find the class, or if the security policy currently in effect for the application prohibits its instantiation.

```
public static Class forName(
    String className
) throws ClassNotFoundException
```

Unlike the `toString` method, the `getName` method simply returns the name of the class, without any prepending of types or constructs.

```
public String getName()
```

The `getModifiers` method returns an integer corresponding to the following modifier encodings. The encodings are constants whose value represents whether or not a class is `public`, `protected`, `private`, `final`, or simply an `interface`.

```
public int getModifiers()
```
■

You more than likely need methods that give you a clue as to what is contained within the `Class` object. Often, during introspection anything and everything becomes a `Class` object first, and is then narrowed down to the specific object that it really is. So, if you need to figure out if the `Class` is an interface, an array, or a primitive type, you can use one of the following three methods.

The `isInterface` method returns true of the object represented by the `Class` object is an interface. Similarly, the `isArray` method returns true if the `Class` is an array, and the `isPrimitive` method returns true if the `Class` is a primitive type.

```
public boolean isInterface()
public boolean isArray()
public boolean isPrimitive()
```

■

Often times, a class will be composed of several inherited interfaces. If you truly want to know the make-up of a class, you will want to obtain these interfaces using the `getInterfaces` method. Sometimes, a class does not inherit from `Object` at all. In these instances, you will want to know the ultimate superclass using the `getSuperclass` method.

If an object is constructed by inheriting from several other objects or interfaces, those interfaces can be obtained via the `getInterfaces` method. The method returns an array of `Class` objects, on which the same APIs seen here may be used.

```
public Class[] getInterfaces()
```

Classes need not ultimately inherit from the Java-standard `Object` at all. In these instances, the superclass, or the class from which the class ultimately inherits, can be obtained using the `getSuperclass` method. The method returns one class, corresponding to the ultimate inherited class of the object.

```
public Class getSuperclass()
```

■

Classes also contain several methods, fields, and other classes. These may be obtained using the next few methods. The first of these methods concern the need to obtain other classes contained within the `Class`, typically as variables. The second method merely obtains all of the `Field`s in the object. The third method returns all of the methods in the `Class`. Finally, the reflection API contains a method for obtaining the constructors for a `Class` as well.

The `getClasses` method returns an array corresponding to all of the classes and interfaces contained within the object. The return value is null if there are no classes, or if the target class is a primitive type.

```
public Class[] getClasses()
```

The getFields method returns an array of Field objects corresponding to all of the public fields in the Class. The method returns both the public member fields of an object as well as the public hidden fields of the object. If there is an error in trying to obtain the fields, a SecurityException is thrown.

```
public Field[] getFields() throws SecurityException
```

The getMethods method does exactly what it says and returns an array of Method objects whose value is all of the methods in the Class. If there is an error in trying to obtain the methods, a SecurityException is thrown.

```
public Method[] getMethods()
    throws SecurityException
```

The getConstructors method returns a list of Constructor objects and throws a SecurityException if there is an error in getting permission for the lookup.

```
public Constructor[] getConstructors()
    throws SecurityException
```

■

There are also specific accessors for the same four constructs. The getField method allows you to obtain a field by its simple string name, the getMethod method allows you to get a method by its name and parameters, and similarly the getConstructor method lets you obtain a constructor for a class that accepts certain parameters.

 The getField method returns the Field object corresponding to the name of the field stored in fieldName or a NoSuchFieldException if the field does not exist. The method can also return a SecurityException if there was an error obtaining the field.

```
public Field getField(
    String fieldName)
    throws NoSuchFieldException, SecurityException
```

The getMethod method returns a Method object whose method name matches the value contained in methodName and whose parameter types match the value contained in methodParameters. The method can return a NoSuchMethodException if there is no method or a SecurityException if security policy prevents the method from executing.

```
public Method getMethod(
    String methodName,
    Class[] methodParameters)
    throws NoSuchMethodException, SecurityException
```

The `getConstructor` method returns a `Constructor` object whose parameter types correspond to the values contained in `constructor-Parameters`. Again, the method returns a `NoSuchMethodException` if the constructor does not exist, or a `SecurityException` if security policy prevents the method from executing.

```
public Constructor getConstructor(
    Class[] constructorParameters)
    throws NoSuchMethodException, SecurityException
```

■

DETERMINING MEMBERS OF AN OBJECT

The `Member` interface has no constructor and is used to determine information about a class, interface member, or constructor. Because it is an abstract base class, it must be implemented by other Java objects wishing to serve the member information. A member is, by definition, an element contained by the class. Thus, a member could be anything from a variable to a method to a constructor. It has two fields associated with it, `PUBLIC` and `DECLARED`, that are used by the security manager to determine the accessibility of the member.

The `Member` interface has two fields, `PUBLIC` and `DECLARED`, that are not necessarily intended for use by the programmer. Rather, they are used by the security manager to determine whether or not the member is accessible.

```
public final static int PUBLIC
public final static int DECLARED
```

■

The `Member` interface also has three methods that are used to determine some of the specifics of the object. The implementing object will choose how to go about providing this information based on the class or structure that the `Member` object points to.

The `getDeclaringClass` method returns a `Class` object that represents the class or interface that owns the `Member` object.

```
public abstract Class getDeclaringClass()
```

The getName method returns a String representing the name of the Member object as it is declared in code.

```
public abstract String getName()
```

The getModifiers method returns an integer corresponding to values associated with public, private, or protected.

```
public abstract int getModifiers()
```

■

FINDING VARIABLES

The Field object implements the Member interface and adds a slew of functionality on top of it. A field is a variable, or a data structure within the class itself. The programmer cannot create Field objects on his or her own. The Virtual Machine will create Field objects for you through methods such as the getField method which is, as you saw in an earlier section, contained inside the Class object.

The first three methods in the Field object correspond directly to those in the Member interface. The getDeclaringClass, getName, and getModifiers methods are implemented here as they should be.

The getDeclaringClass method returns a Class object that represents the class or interface that owns the Field object.

```
public abstract Class getDeclaringClass()
```

The getName method returns a String representing the name of the Field object as it is declared in code.

```
public abstract String getName()
```

The getModifiers method returns an integer corresponding to values associated with public, private, or protected.

```
public abstract int getModifiers()
```

■

The Field object also contains several means to obtain its value. The most primitive of these means is the simple get method. The get method has several, more specific, counterparts in getBoolean, get-Byte, and so on.

The `get` method accepts one parameter, the target object to which we want to apply this method. Once the `Field` object is obtained from the `Class`, applying the `get` method to an existing object will determine the value of that particular field if it is located in the target object. If an instance of the `Field` object is not in the target object, an `IllegalArgumentException` is thrown. If the target object is null, a `NullPointerException` is thrown. If the `Field` is not accessible within the target object, an `IllegalAccessException` is thrown.

```
public Object get(
    Object targetObject)
throws NullPointerException,
    IllegalArgumentException,
    IllegalAccessException
```

There are also several more specific methods on the `Field` object that can obtain the properly typed object from the `get` method. These methods essentially wrap the generic `get` method and handle the type conversion for the user. All of the return the proper exceptions as described before.

```
public <primitive type> get<primitive type>(
    Object targetObject)
throws NullPointerException,
    IllegalArgumentException,
    IllegalAccessException
```

Where *primitive type* is one of:

- boolean
- byte
- char
- short
- int
- float
- double

■

Corresponding to the methods for accessing data, there are several methods you can use to set the value of the `Field` object. The simple `set` operation can handle the most complex of these operations, but there are more specific methods available that are directly related to their `get` counterparts.

 The `set` method accepts two parameters, the target object on which to perform the operation, and the new value of the field being changed. The method returns on of three exceptions. The `NullPointerException` occurs when the target object is null. The `IllegalArgumentException` is thrown when the type conversion cannot be made. And the `IllegalAccessException` is thrown if the target object's corresponding `Field` is inaccessible.

```
public void set(
    Object targetObject,
    Object newValue)
throws NullPointerException,
    IllegalArgumentException,
    IllegalAccessException
```

Just as with the generic `get` operation, there are several more specific `set` operations for primitive types.

```
public void set<primitive type>(
    Object targetObject,
    <primitive type> newValue)
throws NullPointerException,
    IllegalArgumentException,
    IllegalAccessException
```

Where *<primitive type>* is one of:

- boolean
- byte
- char
- short
- int
- float
- double

■

INTROSPECTING FOR METHODS

The `Method` object also implements the `Member` interface and allows you to obtain information about methods within a class or interface. It also implements the base `Member` interface methods, but adds several more methods to obtain more specific information about a method within an object. The first of these methods is the standard group of `getDeclaringClass`, `getName`, `getModifiers` that you have seen earlier. In addition, you may also obtain the return type of the `Method` using the `getReturnType` method.

 The `getReturnType` method returns a `Class` object that contains the type of the value that will be returned by the `Method` object.

```
public Class getReturnType()
```

■

The `getParameterTypes` and `getExceptionTypes` methods return the formal parameter types, in the order that they are declared within the `Method` object, and the types of the exceptions that are thrown by the `Method`. If there are no parameters or exceptions, the appropriate function will return null.

 The `getParameterTypes` method and `getException-Types` method both return an array of `Class` objects corresponding to the types of the values in the parameter list or exception list, respectively.

```
public Class[] getParameterTypes()
public Class[] getExceptionTypes()
```

■

The `equals` method can be used to compare an `Object` to the `Method` object. The `hashCode` method should be used to obtain a hash code for the `Method` object. And the `toString` method will get you a string describing the `Method`.

 The `equals` method returns true if the `Method` and the specified `compareObject` are identical. The `hashCode` method returns an integer specifying a hash code for the `Method`. The `toString` method returns a `String` description of the `Method`.

```
public boolean equals(
    Object compareObject)
public int hashCode()
public String toString()
```

■

The most powerful of all the `Method` object's methods is the invoke operation. Using invoke, you can actually dynamically obtain a `Method` and then use it. The invoke method can be complicated at times, but it can also be a very powerful addition to your applications.

The `invoke` method invokes the operation specified by the `Method` object on the `targetObject` with the supplied `targetParameters`. The method throws a `NullPointerException` when a parameter conversion fails. It will throw an `IllegalArgumentException` if the `targetObject` does not contain a method as dictated by the `Method` object or if a parameter is not of the proper type. An `IllegalAccessException` occurs when the security manager determines that the method may not be executed on the `targetObject` (presumably because the method is declared as `private` within the `targetObject`).

```
public Object invoke(
    Object targetObject,
    Object[] targetParameters)
throws NullPointerException,
       IllegalArgumentException,
       IllegalAccessException,
       InvocationTargetException
```

∎

CONSTRUCTOR OBJECTS

The `Constructor` object looks exactly the same as the `Method` object, except instead of the `invoke` method, you use the `newInstance` method. The `newInstance` method will be described in detail shortly, but keep in mind that all of the functionality of the `Method` object still exists within the `Constructor`.

The `newInstance` method of the Constructor object returns a newly created and instantiated object to which the Constructor instance belongs given the targetParameters for the constructor. The `newInstance` method will return an `InstantiationException` if the Constructor represents an abstract class. It will return an `IllegalArgumentException` if the parameters are invalid. An `IllegalAccessException` is thrown if the security manager objects to the instantiation of the object, presumably if it is not public or is unloadable by the class loader. An `InvocationTargetException` is thrown for any errors caught during the execution of the constructor itself.

```
public Object newInstance(
    Object targetParameters[])
throws InstantiationException,
       IllegalArgumentException,
       IllegalAccessException,
       InvocationTargetException
```

∎

So, if you want to go about actually using the reflection objects that have been described thus far, you will need to first instantiate a `Class` for a given object name. In this case, you will be looking for the `Rainbow-Button` class. As you will see in the next chapter, the `RainbowButton` will be quite important for our further exploration into the magical world of Beans.

```
// get the class
Class myBean = Class.forName("RainbowButton");
System.out.println("my bean's name is: " +
    myBean.getName());
```

Once you have the `Class` object, you can go about invoking any of the reflection APIs that have been discussed thus far. As an example, let's get all the methods in the `RainbowButton` class and print them out one by one.

```
// get the class
Class myBean = Class.forName("RainbowButton");
System.out.println("my bean's name is: " +
    myBean.getName());

// get the methods
Method methods[] = myBean.getMethods();

// list all the methods
for(int x = 0; x < methods.length; x++)
{
    System.out.println("method [" + x + "]: " +
    methods[x].getName());
}
```

Summary

Now that you have a solid foundation in Java and understand the skills that will be required for your further exploration into Beans, you can go about outlining the different characteristics of Beans. As you will see in the next chapter, Beans makes heavy use of the reflection, event, and thread APIs that have been discussed in this chapter. Furthermore, because Beans is *nothing but 100 percent Pure Java*, you will find that Beans itself uses every single API seen here.

The History of Coffee

Every morning, you wake from a wonderful night dreaming about world peace and BMWs in every garage to the wonderful aroma of a freshly brewed cup of Java. Often, you'll take a moment from staring at your computer screen in order to head down to the break room and pour yourself a cup of steaming processed, rehydrated coffee. Without your caffeine injection, nary a moment would go by without a quivering hand reaching for a cup of water that's been washed through a pile of roasted arabica.

For much of us, coffee is more than a drink, it is the most important ingredient in a conflict-free, wholesome day. Ever since the early Arabians first discovered the importance of coffee to their social and economic well-being, the coffee bean has enjoyed much attention throughout some of history's greatest moments. In the early 17th century, the Pope made coffee a "truly Christian beverage" in an effort to protect the taste and aroma of the drink from the council of priests that had condemned it.

In 1699, on the island of Java, the Dutch had managed to be the first to transplant the coffee bean from its native Arabia. In 1706, the first test seedling was sent home to Amsterdam, where it quickly became the mommy for most of the coffee grown in the western world. In Germany around the same time, Johann Sebastian Bach composed the Coffee Cantata, poking fun at the political leadership that saw coffee as a threat to beer's place as the perfect drink.

Meanwhile, in the New World, Dorothy Jones became the first person to garner a license to sell coffee to Colonial Americans. Once the British began to tax the sale of tea, American revolutionaries fought back by drinking coffee, beginning a trend that would see the United States ending up becoming the world's largest consumer of coffee today.

Source: Kevin Knox and Julie Sheldon Huffaker, *Coffee Basics.* John Wiley and Sons, 1997.

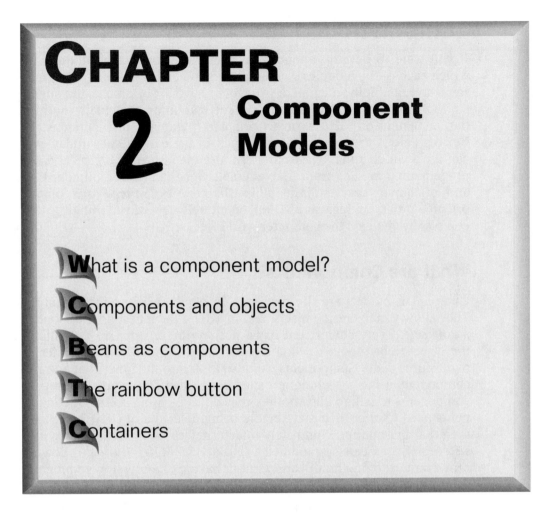

CHAPTER

2

Component Models

What is a component model?

Components and objects

Beans as components

The rainbow button

Containers

One of the many reasons behind the Java revolution is the promise the language holds for bringing the Internet and the capability to program the Internet to normal people who have little or no training in computer science. Indeed, as our industry progresses, programmers and coders will become commodities. The real power (and money) in the industry will shift towards architects and designers capable of putting together large systems of components. So, what exactly is a component, and why is it the future of this industry? This chapter will examine the intricacies of components, both in and out of the computer world, and show you why they are so important.

Component Models

If you were to develop applications that were completely modular, in which each of the modules were totally interchangeable, completely customizable, and fully integrated, you would have in your hands the mighty *component revolution*. The component revolution is actually nothing but an extension of the object-oriented paradigm first perfected in Xerox's Palo Alto Research Center back in the early 1980s. Today, you can use a variety of languages that espouse the virtues of object-oriented programming ranging from the venerable Smalltalk to the popular C++ and, of course, Java. As discussed in Chapter 1, *Advanced Java*, object-oriented programming was a vision, an entirely new way of thinking, that completely changed the computer world forever.

What are Components?

Component models are the next step in object-oriented programming. They allow you to create objects, and to extend them beyond the scope of a language. Every component has a notion of a *customizer* that allows the object to be modified when it is first used without having to alter its own source code. Components can also look into the innards of another component using a technique called *introspection*. If you want your components to talk to one another, they do so by firing *events*. If components need to alter their state before being deleted and come back later with that information completely intact, they can handle their own *persistence*. Beans can be modified using a *Bean GUI Builder*, allowing programmers to program Beans without having to know how to program source code.

Let's digress from the world of geekdom we currently inhabit, and take a look at that great example of automotive genius, the BMW Z3 Roadster. The Z3 is a beautiful piece of machinery, capable of great speed, possessing both head-turning looks and examples of sheer engineering brilliance. But, more than that, the Z3 is a Bean! Not literally, of course, but the Z3 Roadster is a component, as are all automobiles, and like all automobiles it is composed entirely of other components. This nested hierarchy of components enables the BMW engineers to plug and play various parts to make up the whole car as shown in Figure 2.1.

The Z3 has two different engine types. The first engine is a small 1.9 liter engine that limits the Z3 in terms of speed and power. The second engine is a 2.8 liter engine that greatly enhances the roadster and may actually make it more than just a pretty face. In order to add the new engine, the engineers need only to swap out the smaller 1.9 liter engine and add the larger 2.8 liter engine. No other modifications need to be made. Once the new engine is added, the hood is closed, and the car is

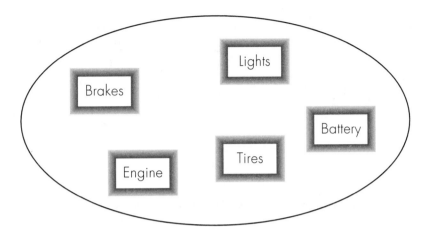

Figure 2.1: *Components can be nested in a hierarchical structure.*

shipped off to the dealer. When you arrive at the dealer to pick up your red convertible, you do not assemble the vehicle yourself, but simply drive home the whole car, engine and all, in one giant piece.

Component Customization

Just as you ask your salesman to give you a red car with black leather interior, components can be customized at design time. The color and interior style of the car have nothing to do with the inner workings of the car, they just happen to be how the car is represented. Components don't necessarily change their algorithms or inner workings because of customization, but they do allow you to change initialization states and other portions of the component. Customization is discussed in detail in Chapter 4, *Bean Properties*.

Component Introspection

When one component interacts with another, it should be allowed to peek inside the other object. Introspection allows one component to look at certain parts of a component, namely public methods and variables. The private or protected parts of the component are never made visible, so you can rest assured that components you create will always maintain their integrity. In order for introspection to work, components must be constructed properly. These techniques as well as introspection in general are discussed in Chapter 5, *Bean Introspection*.

For the time being, just understand that introspection allows your components to discover the methods and properties of another component *on the fly*. Say you add a new component to your system and your other components need to query it to find out if it is useful to them. If you were adding an engine to your car, your windows could query the component, discover that the engine has no bearing on them, and go about their business. However, your accelerator pedal component could discover the power property on the engine and attach itself to it. That way, if the engine ever changed its power property, the accelerator pedal would be notified.

Component Interaction

Somehow, these components need to interact with one another. After all, if the components in a car were just put together and not allowed to interact, then the car would be a collection of nuts, bolts, screws, and wires. There would be no cohesion between the components, and no way to get them to cooperate. Sort of like the United Nations.

Components can interact in one of two ways. The first way is the most obvious. Components can very easily tell one another what to do. The battery can tell the lights to turn on, or the accelerator pedal can tell the engine to apply more power. This is akin to objects directly invoking methods on one another. In Figure 2.2, the battery simply tells the lights, "light up my life baby," and magically the lights activate as you careen toward the deer caught in your headlights. Meanwhile, the brakes can tell the tires to stop spinning in the same manner.

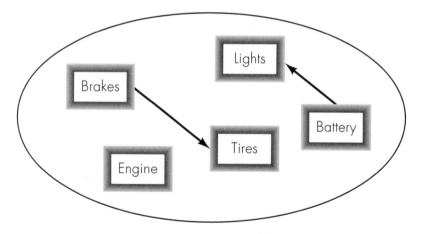

Figure 2.2: *Components can interact by calling one another directly.*

Direct component interaction has several advantages. First, it is simple to understand and equally simple to enact. Your components call one another in your source code just as they would if they were separate objects. Basically, there is no difference between your component and your objects. They are one and the same, and direct component interaction facilitates this method of communication. Unfortunately, components become wired together and lose their *plug-and-play* characteristics because they rely on the presence of other components.

A second way in which components can interact is through some sort of event mechanism. Events, as discussed in Chapter 1, are a robust means for components to broadcast their intentions. By taking your components event, wrapping it in some sort of event mechanism, and publishing it to the world, you can very easily communicate with a multitude of other components, both those you know of at design time and those you will discover later. After all, components were designed to be plugged in and out of many disparate systems. With only direct component interaction to work with, your component will be limited in the kinds of components it can play with.

Using an event-driven model, your component can simply publish an event, and subscribe to other events. The publish and subscribe paradigm are discussed in Chapter 4, but for now understand that events are both published and subscribed. A middleman needs to be present in this kind of communication in order to route published events to the appropriate subscriber. This event listener is responsible for keeping track of publishers and subscribers and for routing messages between the two. Typically, you will create a listener for each kind of event your components wish to generate. As you can see in Figure 2.3, this is definitely the preferred method for component interaction because it allows new components to be introduced without any additional coding.

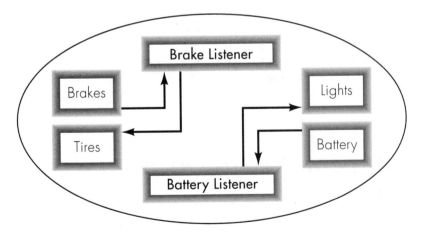

Figure 2.3: *Event-driven component interaction.*

Component Persistence

Components need a way to save and restore their state. Every component needs to manage its own state in a manner that allows it to save every component it touches. Generally this is done through some form of recursion in which components make sure they save all of their child components. In so doing, webs of components are saved and easily restored to their original state.

Component Construction

The great thing about components is that they can very easily be composed of many other components. In the BMW example, you can put a brand new engine in the car. If you were to create the engine, you would need to assemble various components, ranging from pistons to gears, in order to make up the big engine component. The engine component is then placed into the car as one giant blob. The car doesn't know or care about the pistons, only that the engine itself is functional and provides the power it says it will and accepts the oil and gasoline that is required.

Putting components together can be an arduous task. You need to create infrastructure for the components, stick them in a container, and link them by hand. Somehow the components must be made aware of one another. After all, when you bake a pizza crust you don't just throw the ingredients into a bowl and magically receive a slab of dough. You must do something to the components to connect them to one another. Often times, components can be constructed using a GUI-based component editor. Using the editor, you can drag and drop components and link them without ever once having to touch any code. These builders are discussed in great detail in Chapter 9, *Bean Integration*.

Throughout this book, you will be shown how to build your own basic components. There will be no skimping on the source code and you are intended to see as much guts as possible. However important it is to know how to develop components from scratch, you must still examine how to build components using other components. After all, that is the crux of the component revolution.

Components Versus Object-Oriented Programming

I've talked about how components are nothing more than a way to group objects together. In many ways, components accomplish nothing more than what is possible in object-oriented programming alone. In fact, skeptics of the component revolution often cite that everything that can be done with a component can be done using any object-oriented language. The skeptics are correct. But they're missing the point entirely.

Components are an extension of object-oriented programming, and in that sense do not necessarily evoke a comparison. Rather, you should look to object-oriented programming, and its excellent techniques and uses, to guide us as you develop components. After all, what makes a good object? Modularity, information hiding, and method implementations are all characteristics of well-designed objects. Because component programming is the next evolutionary step in object-oriented design, these are all smart and intelligent characteristics of good components.

Modularity in Components

When BMW makes a car, it does so with the notion that engines can be swapped at will. The car is, in essence, highly modular. In fact, if you wanted automatic windows as opposed to manual windows, you simply swap out the old windows and put in the new ones. Voila! You have the same car containing different modules.

Components should be designed in such a way that they can be plugged in and out of their container. They should be able to be called by other components in a strong object-oriented sense. Remember, the same principles of modularity found in great object-oriented implementations should be found in your components. If all else fails, remember these three all-important words: *plug and play*. Use them as your component design mantra.

In order to effectively create these kinds of plug and play components, you need to have some experience and foresight into object-oriented design. These principles, though beyond the scope of this book, will be discussed in a high-level manner as you proceed throughout the book. When you export methods in a component, how generic are those methods? Are the properties of your component applicable to different kinds of the same component? These are questions that we will help answer as we move on in our discussion of components.

Hiding Information in Components

Just as you build objects that hide their internal variables and data from outside users, you can create components that maintain their privacy. When you build components, you have full control over which data structures are exposed to the component consumer. Without this capability, components could never become popular since authors would have no incentive to build components whose internals were publicly known.

As you build components that are reused over and over again, you need to keep in mind the techniques necessary in traditional object-oriented programming: when to expose variables to the public, and when to maintain the privacy of your objects. In components, they are not called variables, rather they are referred to as *properties*. Properties are the internal information within a component.

Smart Methods in Components

Objects also expose methods that can change the state of the object's internal representation. In fact, rather than exposing variables, it's usually smart to expose *accessors* and *mutators* for the variable. An accessor is responsible for getting the information stored in a variable, while a mutator is responsible for changing the information in the variable. Components should use accessors and mutators not only because those methods can be invoked by other components, but because listeners can attach themselves to an accessor or a mutator quite easily. That way, components that fire events to a listener can indirectly change the internal representation of another component as shown in Figure 2.4.

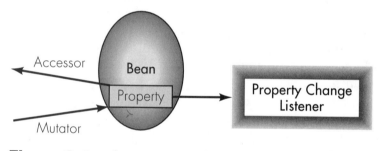

Figure 2.4: *Accessors and mutators can be attached to listeners.*

Remember, one of the principles of object-oriented design dictates that methods revolve around the data contained within an object. Every method you create should somehow change or affect the data in the object. Similarly, the methods in a component should revolve around the properties in the component.

Design Patterns

When you go to a fabric store and buy a dress pattern, you are purchasing a set of instructions, techniques, and suggestions for constructing an article of clothing. Contained within the design pattern is a set of guidelines for selecting fabric, cutting the fabric correctly, and putting it together properly. Similarly, components should be constructed so that they conform to certain design patterns. Otherwise, components may be incompatible with other components.

Design Patterns in Beans

Design patterns can range from certain functions that must be present with every public variable, to the name of the variable itself. In this book, Java is used. Because Java is a case sensitive language, it is very important that you match the case of the variables and functions as they are described in their design pattern. As you develop components throughout this book, *design patterns* will be pointed out, that you, as a component developer must follow. It is important to follow them as closely as possible.

Typically, these design patterns are syntactic descriptions of how your code should look. For every property you create in a Bean, you will need to create two methods to access the data contained in that property and to set the value of the property. The design pattern indicates what those methods should be named. In Chapter 4, you will outline exactly what these design patterns are for properties. In addition to those for properties, there are design patterns for events as well as the entire Bean as a whole.

Circumventing Design Patterns

JavaBeans engineers recognized that some developers will not want to follow the design patterns completely. Therefore, they created the `Bean-Info` object. Normally, when a Bean is introduced to a system, a series of introspection steps takes place that determines the methods, properties, and events of a Bean. The `BeanInfo` object allows you to basically handle the introspection of your object. However, by providing a `Bean-Info` object, you can bypass that introspection and determine your own methods, properties and events. The `BeanInfo` object is also flexible enough to allow you to handle only parts of your own introspection, leaving the rest for other objects. Introspection is discussed in great detail in Chapter 5.

Beans as Components

Up until now I have talked about components in a general sense. This is because for the most part, components transcend the language in which they are written. While this book concentrates solely on the Java implementation of a component model (with a brief look at Microsoft's ActiveX), many component designers will try the same techniques in other languages. You are encouraged to explore these alternatives on your own.

Components Using Beans

JavaBeans is a set of Java objects that provide the infrastructure for components to be written in Java. Beans include objects for customizers, introspection, and events. Some characteristics, like event handling, use the Java language itself. Others, such as customization, use special Java objects in conjunction with the Bean itself. As you can see, JavaBeans extends the object-oriented nature of Java itself. Between the language constructs and the objects constructed using the language, JavaBeans provides a strong component framework with which to build your own reusable Beans.

Special Beans Objects

JavaBeans has several added objects that support a component model. All of these objects are written entirely in Java, and therefore make Beans platform-independent and architecture-neutral. In so doing, Beans can easily be supported in Windows 32-bit platforms such as Windows NT and Windows 95. Many of these objects simply extend the functionality already present in the latest revision of the Java Developer's Kit (JDK). Because the new JDK introduces events and a new delegation-based event model (see Chapter 1), JavaBeans relies on the latest JDK (version 1.1 and higher).

While the JavaBeans architects made a *transitional Bean* specification available, in order to truly utilize the power and capability of JavaBeans you will need to upgrade to the latest JDK. The CD-ROM included with this book includes this new JDK, as well as JavaBeans.

Java and Components

Much of JavaBeans is built using the Java language only. While most of the framework for a Bean, including customizers and Bean information objects, are included as part of the `java.beans` package, there are several parts to JavaBeans that steal from the Java language itself. For example, rather than invent a new kind of event model, the JavaBeans architects chose to use much of the event system provided in the Java language. Beans components can also incorporate communication mechanisms such as Java RMI or Java IDL facilitating direct invocation across a network.

You surveyed the Java event model in Chapter 1, and JavaBeans does nothing different to it. It creates a bunch of classes that are based directly on the `EventListener` object, but for the most part the standard Java listener objects could just as easily be used in JavaBeans. JavaBeans makes a distinction between properties and events, thus requiring a certain dichotomy between listeners. However, the basic Java machinations of both a `PropertyChange` and an `Event` are pretty much the same.

Why Beans?

If you are not yet convinced of the value of JavaBeans, you are probably wondering what the big deal is anyway. Well, with JavaBeans you get all of the functionality of a normal class library, including reuse of modules and the ability to customize the object. Class libraries have been in existence since the dawn of objects, and companies such as Rogue Wave have been able to make quite a healthy living off of them.

CLASS LIBRARIES VERSUS JAVABEANS

JavaBeans takes class libraries and adds GUI extensions to them. Instead of fiddling with source code and typing out the code to use the class library, you can simply incorporate the object within a GUI builder and connect a bunch of them together *without once touching source code*. These GUI properties make JavaBeans an ideal programming construct for programmers and non-programmers alike.

VISUAL BASIC VERSUS JAVABEANS

Visual Basic allows you to use components, called Visual Basic Extensions (or VBXs) to put together a complex application based completely on its GUI interface.

You can drag and drop components and connect them together to form a very useful application. As you will see in Chapter 9, Visual Basic Extensions have been morphed into ActiveX controls and are now Internet-ready and aware. Visual Basic will be discussed in a little more depth then, but for now we offer only that JavaBeans can be used within Visual Basic itself.

The problem with Visual Basic was neither its design nor its ability to quickly and easily create a full-fledged application. On the contrary, Visual Basic is generally regarded to be one heck of a programmer tool. The problem with Visual Basic is the language underneath. Because it is not object-oriented, it has many limitations. Why not use Java for all of your development? In fact, with a JavaBeans to ActiveX bridge (see Chapter 9), there is no reason for you to develop Visual Basic components in their language. Instead, you can use Java to build a bunch of Beans and incorporate them directly into Visual Basic without much difficulty.

JavaBeans Versus Applets Versus Applications

Another important distinction to make between JavaBeans and other component models (such as ActiveX) is its easy integration with the programming constructs of the past. When Java first arrived bringing with it the notion of an applet, Web page developers became very excited at the prospect of dynamic content. Well, JavaBeans simply makes their life easier.

An *applet* is a Java object that is downloaded by a Web browser. In Figure 2.5, you can see how an applet is downloaded and executed. It remains within a security construct affectionately termed the *Java sandbox*. The sandbox prevents the downloaded Java applet from interacting with anything outside the browser. The browser will prevent the applet from accessing the local disk, and the applet in turn is quite secure. So, while you are surfing the Web and encountering Java applets, you can be assured that the applet will not pose a threat to your system because the Java sandbox strictly prevents the applet from interacting with your system. Rather, the Java applet interacts with the Virtual Machine in the browser and cannot go beyond the confines of the browser itself.

A *Java application*, on the other hand, is similar to a regular application written in any other language. It has no restrictions when it is being executed and has full reign over the system on which it is running. It can access files, sockets, and just about anything else it desires. You can see in Figure 2.6 how a Java application can interact with the Virtual Machine thereby allowing it to touch anything on the system itself.

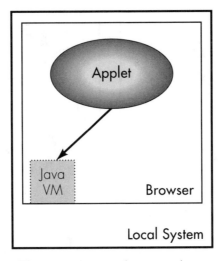

Figure 2.5: *Java applets.*

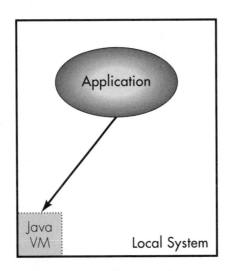

Figure 2.6: *Java applications.*

A JavaBean is slightly different from either of these constructs. Remember, a Bean is nothing but a set of Java classes used for building reusable components. Therefore, a bunch of Beans can be assembled to form an application or an applet (see Figure 2.7). A Bean is neither an applet nor an application. It has nothing to do with either. If you use Lego Bricks as an analogy, a Bean is a brick, while an applet or an application is the thing you build with a bunch of bricks.

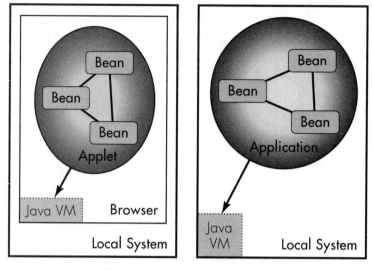

Figure 2.7: *JavaBeans.*

The important thing to remember is that Beans are completely flexible in how they can be used. One minute a Bean can be used within an applet, the next minute it can be used within an application.

When a Bean is used within an applet, it must conform to the security sandbox. These architectural issues are discussed throughout this book, but remember, if your Bean is doing extensive file manipulation, it may not be suited for incorporation within an applet.

Now that you have a good understanding of what a component is (and a Bean in particular), let's go about building a bunch of Beans. The next few sections outline the architecture to follow in building these simple Beans. As different aspects of JavaBeans are discussed in more detail than in this chapter, we will flesh out our architecture. In the end, we will wind up with a full-featured set of Beans that we can use to build an application without creating any additional code.

Introduction to the Rainbow Button

Throughout this chapter I've discussed how to go about creating a Bean that fires certain events, listens for other events, contains properties, and supports changes on those properties. In order to effectively create this kind of component, you will need to study the intricacies of events and properties, as well as how they can be determined from an outside source not privy to a code listing indicating how the component was built. The most practical application of this sort of component model is a graphical widget of some kind. For anyone who has used a Rapid Application Development (RAD) environment, the notion of picking up a component, plopping it in a GUI, and immediately being able to modify and configure it is very familiar.

A Button for All Seasons

To support the RAD concept, you will implement a simple button, which will be called the *Rainbow Button*, with two properties; its current color and the text it displays. The component you create will eventually be a full-fledged Bean that can be reused by applications at will. You will go about creating the events for the button, readying it for listeners to attach themselves to it, adding properties to it, and eventually you'll be able to store its properties persistently so that every time someone quits their application, the button will come back to life just as it was before it was terminated.

We could have built a more serious application, or even a more complex one. But to get you started with JavaBeans, and to show you how easy it is, we chose something lightweight and simple to implement.

In addition to the button, you will create a simple picture window that will display a different image whenever the button is pressed. This will allow us to show you how the interaction between components is managed and to explore the performance of JavaBeans objects. You will also develop a simple sound widget that will play a continuous sound whenever the picture is displayed. For example, if pressing the button triggers an event on the picture window causing an image of a rainforest to appear, then the sound widget will play a series of birdies chirping. Similarly, if our button event triggers the picture window to show an image of a BMW Z3 convertible, then the sound widget will play an audio file of the author of this book drooling.

Individual Components

Each of the components you design will be created with the idea that they can be easily reused in other applications. The RainbowButton can just as easily be used in a spreadsheet application as in our nifty example. The picture area could be used as a slide show for a presentation program, or it could be used as done here. You will endeavor to create widgets that have generic inputs and outputs that can easily be plugged into more complex applications.

For those programmers who simply want to experiment with JavaBeans and get started using more complex applications of Java, designing and building these little widgets is not only a great service to the Beans community, but an excellent way to learn how to program generic plug-and-play components.

In addition to our `RainbowButton`, you will also create a `PictureArea` and a `SoundMachine`. The `PictureArea` will simply change the picture on the screen given a certain kind of event. The picture it is currently displaying is a property of the widget. Meanwhile, the sound machine will loop through an audio clip. It will accept one event telling it to change the music, and the music it is playing is a property as well.

Properties

The `RainbowButton` has two properties; the current color of the button and the text that the button is displaying as shown in Figure 2.8. You will want to allow other Beans to subscribe to change events on the properties and will, in turn, publish any changes you get for the events. Properties are discussed in great detail in Chapter 4.

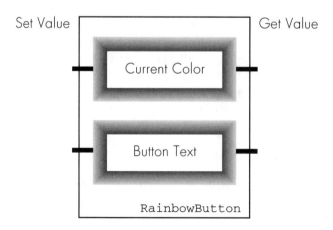

Figure 2.8: *The rainbow button has certain properties that you must fill in.*

The picture module will very simply display itself on the screen. Bean GUI issues are discussed in Chapter 8, *Bean GUI Issues*, but for now you will concentrate only on the properties of the module itself.

As illustrated in Figure 2.9, the current picture being displayed is definitely a property that you want others to be able to look into. You will not allow other Beans to set this property, but you will let them inquire as to what is currently being displayed.

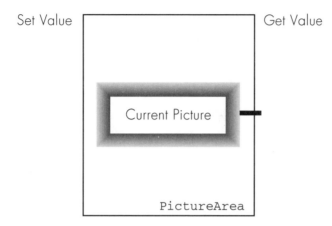

Figure 2.9: *The picture area has properties that may only be accessed, not changed.*

The `SoundMachine` is a simple, faceless Bean that exists only to play sound clips. It will do so in a platform-independent manner and will handle reading in the sound file, looping it without interfering with the platform on which it executes. It will also use a `MediaTracker` object to obtain the sound clip without pausing or disrupting the playback. It has only one property and, like the picture area, may only be accessed, not changed.

All of these components will be placed in a container of some kind and made to interact. As you will see in Part Three of this book, you may very easily use a GUI builder of some kind to drag and drop these components and connect them together.

Events

As shown in Chapter 1, events allow components to interact with one another without having to play with source code. Obviously, our button component is going to fire button push events to the picture area. The picture area will then respond to the event and change the picture on the screen. In doing so, it will alter its current picture property, triggering an event on all of its property listeners. The property listeners may then react to the event as they see fit. You will have two sound machine objects. The first sound machine object will attach itself to the picture area. Whenever the picture area changes its image, the first sound machine will change the music it is playing. The second sound machine will be attached to the button and will play a different *click* sound depending on the current color of the button.

At first, you will create this kind of component interaction by hand, using JavaBeans source code that we will generate on our own. However, in Part Three of this book, you will use a GUI builder to drag and drop components and link them together. In Figure 2.10, you can see how a change on the current color or button text properties will trigger a change event on the picture area.

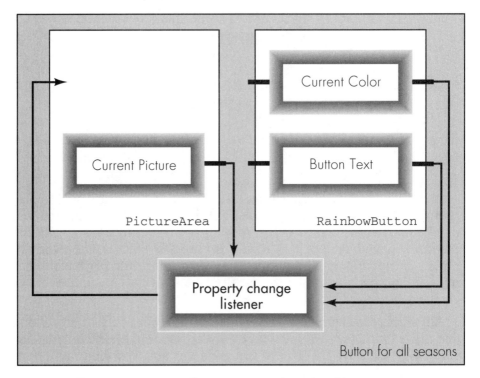

Figure 2.10: *Connecting a bunch of listeners.*

Graphical Representation

The button and picture area will have graphical interfaces, while the sound machine will not. Both the button and picture area will look differently based on the container in which they are placed. For example, if you had two containers, each with two different color schemes, then the button and picture area will look different in each container. However, the functionality and inner workings of the two widgets will remain the same. By the same token, the sound machine will still do its work regardless of the container in which it is placed. Even though you can't see the sound machine, you'll still be able to hear it!

How Beans display themselves is something of great concern to most developers. Indeed, a Bean does not necessarily need a GUI front end, but in most cases you will want to show off your work in some manner.

Beans Containers

Why do you need a container for your Beans? It's not like they're going to lose their flavor if you don't keep them sealed in a nice tight place. No, you need a container so that your Beans can fire events to something. A container is more than a hierarchical arrangement for Beans, it is also the place where listeners can be located, where events are passed, and a central place where Beans can be serialized. In the `RainbowButton`, all the components are placed within one container. That container will contain the listeners to which these other modules will talk. It will also dictate the rules for how components should display themselves.

Listeners

Typically, you will create your components within a container. Once the components are created, you can begin to attach them to listeners. If you were using a Bean GUI Builder, you would only have to drag and drop our components, and link them with a few mouse clicks. Since we are building our Beans by hand, our container will need to instantiate the components and link them together. The following code snippet illustrates how that is accomplished. Although the code is rather crude, it does illustrate how to go about creating and linking a component:

```
RainbowButton button = new RainbowButton();
button.instantiate();
PictureArea pictureArea = new PictureArea();
pictureArea.instantiate();
button.addEventListener(pictureArea);
```

In the example, you not only created two components, but you added the `pictureArea` components as a listener on the `button`.

Bean Hierarchy

Having a container also makes it easier to invoke serialization algorithms to store the state of your entire component system. Imagine a much more complex system than the one you are creating. The complex system will have not one button, but hundreds. There will be more than one target for each button. Almost certainly, the number of faceless objects will be rather huge. For these kinds of complex object systems, having a central location to begin your serialization is rather important. If you were to simply serialize the container, Java's own serialization mechanism, that was discussed in Chapter 1, will automatically traverse the entire tree, saving everything.

User Interfaces

Containers may also dictate the user interface properties of the entire object system. Those properties may range from something as simple and benign as a color scheme, to something drastically important as the format of buttons and the look and feel of an entire GUI. While user interface issues are discussed in great detail in Chapter 8, it is important to realize how the user interface of a Bean can affect its design.

 **Summary**

The JavaBeans component model is a smart, efficient use of the Java language. Providing the infrastructure for building reusable components, JavaBeans allows programmers to easily make the next step from simple object-oriented programming using Java to more complex objects capable of storing their state and communicating indirectly with other objects. These components make use of properties, of events, and of the notion of introspection to form a set of APIs that makes building a Bean a simple task. The next chapter will focus solely on the JavaBeans event model that allows Beans to communicate with one another without knowing the innards of the target Bean. From there, the discussions will move on to properties, introspection, and serialization of Beans.

All About Beans

Basically, there are two kinds of Beans in the world. *Coffee Robusta* is the most common and the easiest to produce, making it, therefore, the cheapest kind of coffee Bean on the market. Robusta is the blend typically used in your average grocery store brand. Robusta beans have substantially more caffeine than their counterparts, and are often used for that quick jolt of energy with which all coffee drinkers are familiar.

On the other hand, *Coffee Arabica* is the source of all great coffees. Arabica beans grow at higher altitudes than Robusta beans and are therefore more expensive to harvest and prepare for market. In addition, Arabica beans are significantly more plentiful than Robusta beans, but production problems often contribute to their high cost.

To further divide the Arabica category, another kind of bean, called the *specialty blend* is introduced. The specialty blend constitutes roughly 10 percent of the world's Arabica production. It is the combination of plant pedigree, altitude, microclimate, and cultivation that makes an Arabica bean a specialty blend.

Source: Kevin Knox and Julie Sheldon Huffaker, *Coffee Basics*. John Wiley and Sons, 1997.

PART TWO

Core Beans Technology

The following chapters delve straight into the meat of the Beans API. This part is intended to be a comprehensive journey through the wonders and intricacies of the JavaBeans technology. You'll start by studying the basic Bean interaction model known as events before moving on and taking a look at how Beans can represent their state and publish that state to other Beans. You'll also get a look at the customization and introspection routines that makes Beans powerful and truly *plug and play*. Part Two wraps up with an in-depth discussion into saving and restoring Beans and passing them as parameters across the wire.

CHAPTER 3

Bean Events

- **E**vents in Beans

- **E**vent listeners

- **F**iring events

- **I**mplementing events in an application

When last you played with events in Chapter 1, *Advanced Java*, you discovered the notion of passing events to event listeners. As you saw then, and as you will see once again in this chapter, passing events between objects is actually pretty simple and makes a whole lot of sense. Unlike early versions of Java which did not yet support this kind of event model, JavaBeans fully supports the publish/subscribe methodology that makes events so much easier to follow. As you examine this and other techniques of event handling in this chapter, you will find that much of what you have to learn in this subject is fairly straightforward.

The JavaBeans Event Model

JavaBeans makes no distinction between the events in the Java language and the events it creates for its own use. In the end, both kinds of events are handled in the same manner and are used similarly. Furthermore, the JavaBeans event model fully supports the publish and subscribe system already discussed. JavaBeans requires a generic event mechanism for its objects because Bean objects must be completely plug and play. In other words, Bean objects that you create today should be fully capable of working with Bean objects someone else creates tomorrow. By following the JavaBeans event model closely, you will be assured of such compatibility.

Publish and Subscribe System

When you telephone *Inline* magazine and subscribe to their product, you are telling them that whenever they publish an issue of their magazine, you wish to receive a copy. Whenever you get your annual *Publisher's Clearing House* mailing, you get a choice of several magazines to which you may subscribe. You are then able to select which magazines, if any at all, you wish to receive in your already cluttered mailbox.

Similarly, computer applications that conform to the publish and subscribe system are promising that, given the chance, they will publish a bunch of events. Other applications in the system may choose to subscribe to those events. As was discussed in Chapter 1, an event is merely a Java action of some kind. The event may be something obvious, like a mouse click or a key press, initiated by the user. Or, the event could be an application-defined entity that has nothing to do with a traditional user-driven action.

In JavaBeans, when we refer to a *publish and subscribe* system we are talking about the idea that an individual component Bean may at any time publish an event. Other Beans may then subscribe to those kinds of events and receive them whenever they are published.

Event Characteristics

The events created in your Beans need to have several things in common. Each of these characteristics ensure that Beans will be compatible across multiple implementations and will play well with one another. Beans that adhere to the methodology that you espouse in this chapter will be portable and ready for use with other Beans.

JAVA AND EVENTS

JavaBeans use the standard Java event model as its foundation. Because events are the single most important feature of Bean interaction, the architects of JavaBeans decided that they needed a simple and extensible means to facilitate interaction between Beans. In so doing, they decided that rather than create their own proprietary method for Bean interaction, they would use the regular Java event system. Because of this decision, they kept the Java feature of platform independence intact.

EVENTS AND SCRIPTING ENVIRONMENTS

Often, Java applications run in the same environment as some scripting languages such as JavaScript and VBScript. JavaScript has nothing really to do with Java. Rather, it is a simple language created by Netscape Communications Corporation to allow Web page programmers to create dynamic content on their HTML documents. JavaScript has other uses outside the web page realm, but that is the environment in which it is most familiar.

VBScript is a Microsoft Corporation language that acts extremely similarly to JavaScript. VBScript has many uses within the ActiveX environment, and can often provide the glue between ActiveX controls. Obviously, VBScript is also highly prevalent in the Visual Basic environment.

JavaBeans events must be able to send and receive events from the two major scripting environments as well. This special kind of Bean interaction is discussed in Chapter 9, *Bean Integration*, but for now you should be aware that your Beans can receive event requests from sources other than JavaBeans. In order to ready your Beans for such an eventuality (pun very much intended), you must be extremely careful to follow the event guidelines very carefully. If you do, you will need not do any additional work to plug your Beans into such esoteric mechanisms as scripting environments.

GUI BUILDER EVENT MANIPULATION

As is discussed throughout this book, the beauty of JavaBeans is not the wonderful extensions to object-oriented programming, or even the simplicity of Java itself, but the idea that your Beans can be used to construct more complex systems of Beans using a GUI Builder, or graphical Bean construction environment.

EVENT INTROSPECTION

During the introspection phase of Bean execution, the introspecting Bean must be made aware of what kinds of events are published and what kinds of events are to be subscribed to. When the Bean is placed within a GUI Builder, the GUI Builder will allow the graphical connection of Beans based on the events discovered during introspection. If you have two Beans, one a button Bean and the other a text field Bean, the button Bean's *push* event can be tied into the text field's *push* receiver. In the GUI Builder, this is done by dragging a rubber band line from the button Bean to the text field Bean.

In order to allow this kind of connection and graphical building ability, the introspecting Bean must be able to look into your Bean and discover the events contained within it. This is accomplished by following a few design patterns that the introspecting Bean can read and understand. These design patterns are discussed as you go about putting together several events.

Event Delivery

Events have more than simple characteristics; they have distinct behavioral patterns that are worth noting. By accounting for these intricacies, your applications can be developed to take better advantage of the event methodology in JavaBeans. Some of these behaviors center around the delivery of a large number of events, while others concern the delivery of one event to a large number of destinations. Nevertheless, knowing how the event model is constructed will assist you greatly.

UNICAST AND MULTICAST

Typically, events are delivered in a *multicast* format. Your Bean will store as many listeners as ask to be stored and will fire the event to each listener at the proper time. This multicast arrangement allows your Beans to communicate event notifications as if they were being broadcast widely (see Figure 3.1). If one listener throws an exception along the way, it is up to the Bean developer and the Bean's implementation details as to whether or not event delivery will continue to the remaining listeners.

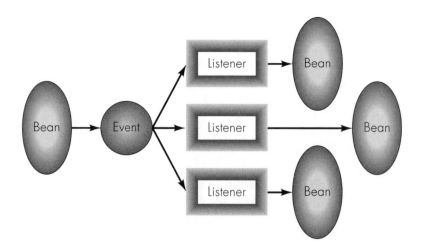

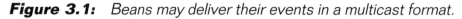
Figure 3.1: *Beans may deliver their events in a multicast format.*

Some Beans may require a *unicast* delivery mechanism in which the Bean may store only one listener, and only that listener will be notified of events (see Figure 3.2).

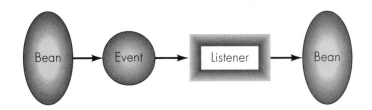

Figure 3.2: *Beans may also use a unicast method to deliver events.*

EVENTS AND THREADING

When you fire an event, Java does so as if it were a normal procedure call. That is to say that Java blocks the client's calling thread until the event invocation returns from the destination listener. The synchronous nature of event throwing and catching can be traced to the implementation of events in the Java core API. Unfortunately, asynchronous event firing is not yet supported.

When your multithreaded Bean throws an event to a listener, the listener's target object may, at the same time, be invoking similarly on the original Bean. In such cases, deadlock may occur as the original Bean is blocked because of the synchronous nature of event invocations. The original Bean cannot complete its invocation because its target Bean is also blocked by throwing its own event. Because the target Bean cannot complete its invocation on the original Bean, neither Bean will be able to extricate itself from this predicament (see Figure 3.3).

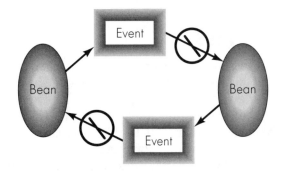

Figure 3.3: *Deadlock in simultaneous Bean events.*

For that reason, it is highly recommended that Bean event handlers *should not* be declared synchronized. Instead, the chunks of code responsible for events within the handlers should be surrounded by synchronized blocks.

Custom Events

JavaBeans also allow you to extend the capability of the Java event model by creating and defining your own types of events. Doing so allows great flexibility in the generation and proliferation of events throughout your Beans. Creating your own Bean event is as simple as extending the EventObject base class. Once you do that, you can name your event to something more familiar to you. In this case, use baseball as your theme and extend the base class with a PitchEvent:

```
public class PitchEvent extends EventObject
{
    String pitchType;

    PitchEvent()
    {
        pitchType = new String("curveball");
    }
}
```

Now that you know the Java representation of an event, and how to go about creating new events, you must turn your attention to the devices required to receive events. Event listeners allow you to receive events without the sender knowing anything about its destination. The sender can merely throw the event, and the listener will be waiting for it to arrive.

Event Listeners

As you saw in Chapter 1, whenever you want to receive events, you need to setup and configure an event listener. An event listener simply hangs around waiting for events and can then act on the events it receives. Part of the beauty of JavaBeans is the aforementioned GUI Builder. Beans can very easily be placed within a GUI Builder and can graphically be built along with other Beans. In order for these Beans to be linked with one another, you need to follow certain design patterns to ensure that other Beans can link to your Bean. First you must create the event listener itself.

Creating an Event Listener

In order to receive events, you must first create your own event listener. Chapter 1 showed how the Java language has two predefined event listeners, the `ActionListener` and the `EventListener`. The `Action-Listener` handles `ActionEvents` while the `EventListener` handles simple `EventObjects`. Similarly, you will create a `Pitch-Listener` for the `PitchEvent` created just a moment ago. While this kind of design pattern is not necessary for Beans to work, it is good design style. Typically, your custom event listeners will inherit from the `EventListener` base interface. Remember, you should define your custom listeners as interfaces, inheriting them later:

```
        import java.beans.*;
   public interface PitchListener extends EventListener
   {
        }
```

Now, you need to include some events within the pitch listener. Otherwise, it is simply a listener with no conceivable way to get events. In order to create event receiver methods, you need to follow a few very important design patterns for those methods.

Design Patterns for Events

There are two aspects of design patterns for event listeners. The first kind of design pattern revolves around the tracking and usage of event listeners. Those are discussed in an upcoming section on firing events. The other kind of design pattern involves the actual receiver method that will handle the event and provide a result based on it. In order for other Beans to be able to link to your receiver method, it must be declared with one, and only one, parameter whose type is the same as the kind of event you wish to receive.

 The design pattern for an event receiver method contains the name of the receiver method and one parameter whose type corresponds to the type of events that are to be received by the method:

```
void <event receiver name> (<event type> evt);
```

■

If you were to continue to model the baseball game, you would create a simple `receivePitch` method that receives one variable of type `PitchEvent`:

```
import java.beans.*;
public interface PitchListener extends EventListener
{
    public abstract void receivePitch(
        PitchEvent pitch
    );
}
```

Whenever you create a Bean that inherits from `PitchListener`, it will be able to listen for any kind of `PitchEvent` that is fired. When you place the Bean inside a GUI Builder and try to connect them using a graphical interface, any Bean that fires a `PitchEvent` will be allowed to connect to any Bean that implements the `PitchListener`; or any Bean that contains a method conforming to the design pattern for the `PitchListener`'s receive method.

Implementing the Listener

Once the `PitchListener` interface is complete, you need to create a Bean that receives pitch events. In baseball, the player who usually receives pitches is the catcher. Here, you will create a `Catcher` Bean that implements the `PitchListener`. Whenever the pitcher Bean fires a pitch event, your `Catcher` Bean will receive the event and do something with it:

```
import java.beans.*;
public class Catcher extends Beans implements PitchListener
{
    public void receivePitch(
        PitchEvent pitch
    )
    {
        // check the kind of pitch
        if(pitch.pitchType.equals("curveball");
        {
            // provide user feedback for the pitch type
            System.out.println("received a curveball!");
        }
    }
}
```

When your listener is invoked by the Bean that fired the event, the method that actually gets invoked is `receivePitch`. If you had several catchers on your squad, one pitcher could fire a ball to all of them if they were all registered as listeners to the pitcher. This form of multiplexed event handling is useful when you need to fire one event to several listeners. The listener that you design will need to handle the individual invocations.

Now you need to go about creating the infrastructure within a Bean that will allow you to attach a listener to it. In this case, you will be taking the Bean, creating methods to which you could pass listeners, and storing the listeners in a list to be used later.

Adding Listeners to Beans

Now that you've created the event and the listener for the event, you need to attach the listener to a Bean. Your Bean must be ready to accept listeners that wish to register themselves with it, and you must provide a facility to distribute events once they occur. In so doing, you must be careful not to sacrifice performance, for efficient event handling is at the heart of good Bean design.

Creating the Bean

The first task is to develop a Bean that maintains listeners inside it. For every type of listener you wish to support, you will need to create a data structure to store them all. Often, this will be done with a Java `Vector`, but it could just as easily be another data structure. The JavaBeans design patterns do not cover this aspect of listeners.

Here, you will create a `Pitcher` Bean. The `Pitcher` Bean has one event that it needs to throw. You will create a simple user interface for the `Pitcher` that creates a button and lets the user press it. Once the button is pressed, the `Pitcher` Bean will fire an event to all of its listeners. You will learn how to fire events in a moment, but for now you must concentrate on the listener portion of your Bean.

Your `Pitcher` Bean will include a `Vector` for a series of `Pitch-Listener` objects like those we created earlier. The Bean will keep track of the listeners and call each of them back when it is necessary to fire an event:

```
public class Pitcher extends Beans
{
    Vector myListeners;
}
```

Initializing the `myListeners` `Vector` is done the same way as any other Java object:

```
public class Pitcher extends Beans
{
    Vector myListeners;

    Pitcher()
    {
        myListeners = new Vector();
    }
}
```

Registering a Listener

When you create a registration area for listeners to come and inform your Bean of their existence, you need to do so while following a few more design patterns. Once again, design patterns will help other Beans introspect your Bean and discover the routines contained within it without having to see source code beforehand.

A listener registration method is added to a Bean by prepending the word *add* to the type of the event listener and passing a parameter whose type matches that of the event listener.

 In order for listener objects to register themselves with a Bean, the Bean must implement an addListener method that obtains an appropriately typed listener object as its one and only parameter:

```
public void add<listener type>(
    <listener type> listener);
```

■

In this case, a registration method for the PitchListener will be declared as addPitchListener, and the method will be passed a PitchListener object. You also need to add code to actually add the listener to the myListeners data structure:

```
public class Pitcher extends Beans
{
    Vector myListeners;

    Pitcher()
    {
        myListeners = new Vector();
    }

    public void addPitchListener(
        PitchListener listener
    )
    {
        myListeners.addElement(listener);
    }
}
```

Similarly, your Bean should support methods to remove a listener from its event list should the listener no longer wish to be served events. This method is created by prepending the word *remove* to the type of the listener.

 The remove listener method should be created by putting the word *remove* ahead of the type of the listener object and passing the method one parameter whose type corresponds to that of the listener object:

```
public void remove<listener type>(
    <listener type> listener);
```

■

With the baseball example, the remove listener method would be declared as `removePitchListener`, and the method will once again receive a `PitchListener` object. You will also include the code necessary to remove the listener from the `Vector`:

```
public class Pitcher extends Beans
{
    Vector myListeners;

    Pitcher()
    {
        myListeners = new Vector();
    }

    public void addPitchListener(
        PitchListener listener
    )
    {
        myListeners.addElement(listener);
    }

    public void removePitchListener(
        PitchListener listener
    )
    {
        myListeners.removeElement(listener);
    }
}
```

When registering the listener, keep in mind that in your baseball game you are preventing the multiple additions of identical listeners by using a Java `Vector`. The `Vector` object prevents you from being able to add the same object twice. This behavior is completely implementation-dependent. If, in your system of Beans, you wish to store identical listeners several times, you will need to add support for those cases yourself.

Registering a Unicast Listener

As mentioned earlier, you can create a unicast event distribution system within your Bean. Previously, you could have any number of listeners, and you needed to accommodate them all by creating a `Vector` data structure in which they resided. The only difference between the multicast distribution discussed before and the unicast distribution you are about to create is that here you may only have one listener for your Bean.

The design pattern for the remove listener portion of the unicast registration is the same as with multicast. You must simply prepend the word *remove* to the type of the listener object, passing one parameter whose type is the same as the listener. However, in registering the listener and adding one to the Bean, your design pattern is slightly different. We must still add the word *add* to the beginning of the listener type, and you must still pass one parameter. This time, though, you must also throw a `TooManyListenersException` exception at the add method.

 The design pattern for unicast event registration is identical to the remove method. However, the add method must be distinguished from its multicast counterpart by adding the `TooManyListenersException` exception to the throws clause of the method declaration. This lets introspecting Beans know that they are dealing with a Bean whose event handling is not capable of firing to multiple listeners:

```
public void add<listener type>(
    <listener type> listener)
throws TooManyListenersException
```

■

Because the presence of a unicast system also negates the need for a Vector data structure, you make the appropriate changes to your baseball game object. When you add, you will also need to check and see if a listener has already been set:

```
public class Pitcher extends Beans
{
    PitchListener myListener;

    Pitcher()
    {
        myListener = null;
    }

    public void addPitchListener(
        PitchListener listener
    ) throws TooManyListenersException
    {
```

```
        if(myListener != null)
            throw new TooManyListenersException();
        else
            myListener = listener;
    }

    public void removePitchListener(
        PitchListener listener
    )
    {
        myListener = null;
    }
}
```

Listener and Event Deadlocks

You must be careful in how you handle deadlocks of event firing and listener registration. Typically, an event will get fired by a Bean, and a listener on the other end will hear it and respond accordingly. Remember from our discussion on the details of event delivery that when an event is fired, it behaves like a normal Java method invocation, blocking the client's thread until the invocation returns, be it successfully or unsuccessfully. If the firing Bean were to subscribe to its own listener, a deadlock would occur because the firing Bean blocks upon firing an event, preventing the listener from receiving the Bean and finishing the invocation. How your Beans handle these cases is a matter of implementation. Java-Beans do nothing to prevent you from shooting yourself in the foot. If your Bean absolutely, positively must get its own events, you might want to fire events from within a separate thread.

Another form of deadlock that you must consider is the case where a listener is being added at the same time as an event is being fired. In light of this case, it is advisable that all of your listener registration methods be synchronized, preventing you from encountering this form of concurrent access:

```
public class Pitcher extends Beans
{
    PitchListener myListener;

    Pitcher()
    {
        myListener = null;
    }

    public synchronized void addPitchListener(
        PitchListener listener
    ) throws TooManyListenersException
    {
```

```
            if(myListener != null)
                throw new TooManyListenersException();
            else
                myListener = listener;
        }

        public synchronized void removePitchListener(
            PitchListener listener
        )
        {
            myListener = null;
        }
    }
```

Adding a `synchronized` tag merely prevents catastrophic concurrent access; not the implementation errors that may arise from allowing the list of listeners to be updated at the same time that an event is being fired to all the members of the list. Your Bean may choose to allow such an activity, firing events to listeners, no matter when they are added. Or, your Bean may choose to make a copy of the current list of listeners, and step down the copy to fire the event. The latter of these two cases is covered when you examine how to fire events.

Attaching Listeners to a Bean

Before listeners can receive events from a Bean, they must first be attached to a Bean. Since your `Catcher` object is a listener, you will need to tell the pitcher that it wishes to listen for certain kinds of events; in this case `PitchEvents`. This can be done in several ways. You could create your own container in which you create a `Pitcher` object, create a `Catcher` object, and pass the `Catcher` object to the `Pitcher` object's `addListener` method.

Here, you will create a `BaseballField` object, and in it you will need to create a `Pitcher` object and a `Catcher` object. You will then invoke the `addListener` method on the `Pitcher` passing it the `Catcher` object. In so doing, you will have created a very simple Bean interaction model in which the `Pitcher` knows of the `Catcher` listener object:

```
public class BaseballField
{
    Catcher catcher;
    Pitcher pitcher;

    BaseballField()
    {
        catcher = new Catcher();
```

```
            pitcher = new Pitcher();

            pitcher.addPitchListener(catcher);
        }
    }
```

As you will see in Chapter 7, *GUI Builders*, you can also use a GUI Builder to drag and drop the pitcher's `throwPitch` method onto the `Catcher` object, creating the exact same connection. For the time being, you will simply create the infrastructure for the individual containers.

Firing Events

Once your listener is attached to your Bean, you need to start firing events. Maybe the Pitcher Bean has a user interface of some kind with a button. When the button is pressed, you will fire a pitch off to your array of listeners. When the listeners receive the event, they will do something with it. Adding to your Pitcher code, you create the `action` method with a button-press event to handle:

```
public class Pitcher extends Beans
{
    Vector myListeners;

    Pitcher()
    {
        myListeners = new Vector();
    }

    public synchronized void addPitchListener(
        PitchListener listener
    )
    {
        myListeners.addElement(listener);
    }

    public synchronized void removePitchListener(
        PitchListener listener
    )
    {
        myListeners.removeElement(listener);
    }

    public boolean action(
        Event evt,
        Object obj
    )
    {
        if(evt.target == fastballButton)
```

```
        {
        }

        return true;
    }
}
```

You will now create an event to fire and walk down your list of listeners and invoke the `receivePitch` method that is contained in each one, passing the pitch event to it. As far as design patterns are concerned, the placement in your code of a function that passes an event to another object indicates to introspecting Beans that your Bean is capable of firing that kind of event. Furthermore, the object on which you are invoking is an `EventListener` or inherits from an `EventListener`, indicating once again that your object is capable of firing the proper event:

```
public class Pitcher extends Beans
{
    Vector myListeners;

    Pitcher()
    {
        myListeners = new Vector();
    }

    public synchronized void addPitchListener(
        PitchListener listener
    )
    {
        myListeners.addElement(listener);
    }

    public synchronized void removePitchListener(
        PitchListener listener
    )
    {
        myListeners.removeElement(listener);
    }

    public boolean action(
        Event evt,
        Object obj
    )
    {
        if(evt.target == fastballButton)
        {
            // create a pitch event
            PitchEvent pitchEvt = new PitchEvent("fastball");

            // walk down the list of listeners firing the event
```

```
        for(int x = 0; x < myListeners.size(); x++)
        {
                myListeners.elementAt(x).receive-
    Pitch(pitchEvt);
        }
    }

    return true;
    }
}
```

Underneath the covers, your invocation on an event listener allows your object to send information to another Bean as shown in Figure 3.4. The firing Bean simply lets loose an event, and the listener Bean grabs it and processes it. In our simple case, we are assuming that the listener Bean is the ultimate final destination. But in Beans, just as in the game of baseball, the `Catcher` listener could very easily fire the `PitchEvent` to any other Bean that is set up to accept it. You could even make the `Pitcher` itself a `PitchListener`, allowing the `Catcher` to fire the pitch right back at it.

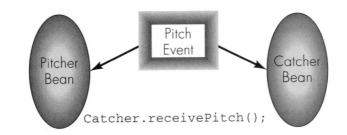

Figure 3.4:   *The Bean fires an event to the listener through a method invocation.*

This is a highly simplistic means of firing events between Beans. You will see in a moment how an event adapter, a sort of middleman in the whole event game, can handle events for us so that you don't have to resort to direct method invocations between Beans.

Listener Registration in a Nutshell

Once you have created a listener, you have to go about making the Bean aware of its existence. Indeed, one Bean may need to know of several listeners and you must be ready to handle those cases. Creating a listener and registering it is only the first step. From within the Bean you must now fire events to the listener. There is also room for an intermediary between the firing mechanism and the listener object. These event adapters make it easier to funnel information between Beans. Once an adapter sends it a request, the listener will have the freedom to do with the event as it pleases.

Event Adapters

In between the event firing mechanism and the event listener lies the event adapter. Typically, you will not code an event adapter by hand, instead the GUI Builder that you use to build and tie your Beans together will do the work for you. However, just to show you what an adapter is and how to create one on your own, you will devote this section to creating an adapter by hand. Hidden inside the mechanism for creating the adapter is the fundamentals of the event firing mechanism as well.

Firing Events

Earlier, when you fired an event from a Bean to a listener, you were really invoking a procedure call on the listener. There was nothing special about this at all because this is nothing but plain old Java. The event mechanism alone is boring and not exactly awe-inspiring. The interesting part of the procedure from a Beans point of view is the framework of the Bean. From design patterns for properties to actual predefined event interaction between Beans, this hard-wired, hand-written solution is interesting in and of itself.

Here, when you speak of firing events to a listener or another Bean, we are really talking about making a procedure call to an adapter. The adapter, as you will discover in a moment, is responsible for accepting the invocation and the event that comes with it and routing it to the appropriate listener. In so doing, the firing Bean is not required to block until completion of the event delivery. As was discussed earlier in this chapter, events are delivered synchronously, and are potential areas for Bean deadlock.

Let's examine the first method you employed. As you can see in Figure 3.5, the `Pitcher` Bean invokes the `receivePitch` method on its list of listeners. The end result of that invocation is a direct invocation on the target Bean's `receivePitch` method since the listeners are nothing but a series of instances of the `Catcher`.

Let's change the pitcher around so that the objects it actually stores are adapter objects. An adapter is a middle-man, a kind of go-between for the firing Bean to send its messages to. The adapter physically stores the location of the instances of target Beans. In this manner, the adapter can

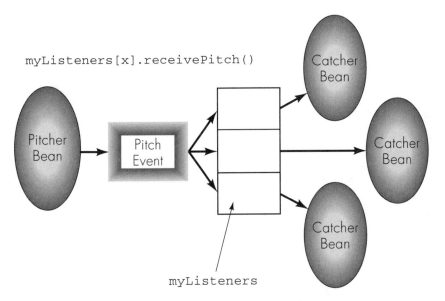

Figure 3.5: *Event delivery through direct invocation.*

get the request from the firing Bean and route it appropriately. Whether or not an adapter exists for every listener or simply for a group of listeners is an implementation detail.

Figure 3.6 shows the nature of this adapter scheme. The firing Bean invokes the `receivePitch` method on each element in its list of listeners. Thus, there are no changes to the firing Bean whatsoever. The code remains the same. Where originally you passed the target Bean to the `addListener` method, here you will actually pass only the adapters to the method. The end result is that the adapter is stored in the `myListeners` Vector rather than the target Bean.

The advantages of the adapter scheme are perhaps not as obvious as they could be. With an adapter, the delivery of the event is separated from the actual creation of the event. The firing Bean can create an event, pass it to the adapter, and resume its own execution without having to block for the delivery of the event. If the target Bean were a remote object, perhaps with a Remote Method Invocation (RMI) or Common Object Request Broker Architecture (CORBA) connection in between, then the firing Bean may have to wait a while for the event to be delivered across the network. With an adapter in between, the firing Bean does not have to wait (see Figure 3.7).

The adapter can also act as a queue for events, storing and delivering them as they arrive. Furthermore, the adapter can abstract the nature of the delivery from the firing Bean. Just as in the RMI example, you could have a system of Beans that reside on different machines or networks.

`myListeners[x].receivePitch()`

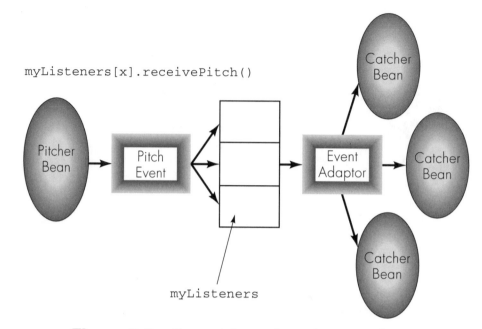

myListeners

Figure 3.6: *Event delivery through event adapters.*

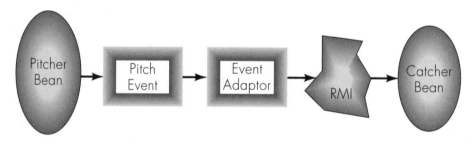

Figure 3.7: *Event delivery does not block the firing Bean when using adapters.*

With an adapter functioning as the visible listener to the firing Beans, the RMI, socket, or CORBA connection need not be of interest to the firing Bean.

Creating an Adapter

It is important to realize that the steps you are taking to use an adapter can be done by integrating the Pitcher and Catcher Beans in a GUI Builder. This is discussed in Chapter 7, but it should be somewhere in the back of your mind. When you use a GUI Builder to connect a bunch of Beans, the adapter is created for you automatically. Furthermore, the adapter created by a GUI Builder is more robust and is tailored for your Beans in a way that is not possible here through clever use of introspection and customization. Nevertheless, let's charge ahead in creating your own adapter by hand as an example

MODIFYING THE BEANS

Changing your baseball game to use adapters instead of direct invocation is fairly straightforward. First, you need to modify the `Catcher` object so that it is no longer a listener. This step is not required, indeed, you may want to leave it as is in case you want to revert to direct invocation at a later time without having to redo source code. However, for demonstration purposes you will change the code here:

```
import java.beans.*;
public class Catcher
{
    public void receivePitch(
        PitchEvent pitch
    )
    {
        // check the kind of pitch
        if(pitch.pitchType.equals("curveball");
        {
            // provide user feedback for the pitch type
            System.out.println("received a curveball!");
        }
    }
}
```

Equally important is the fact that you change absolutely nothing in your `Pitcher` implementation. After all, as far as the `Pitcher` is concerned, it is going to receive a listener of some kind. It could care less whether the listener is a Bean or an adapter.

BUILDING THE ADAPTER

Creating the adapter is as simple as creating an object that inherits from the listener base class that you implemented in your `Catcher`. So, you code a `BaseballGameAdapter` object that inherits from a `PitchListener` shown in the following example. The constructor to the adapter requires a `Catcher` object that will serve as the target to all requests:

```
public BaseballGameAdapter implements PitchListener
{
    Catcher catcherBean;

    BaseballGameAdapter(
        Catcher catcher
```

```
    )
    {
        catcherBean = catcher;
    }
}
```

ROUTING ADAPTER REQUESTS

Because you are implementing the `PitchListener` you must also implement the `receivePitch` method. Here, however, your `receivePitch` method will receive one `PitchEvent` and instead of processing it will simply call the `catcherBean`'s `receivePitch` method with the event that is passed in:

```
public BaseballGameAdapter implements PitchListener
{
    Catcher catcherBean;

    BaseballGameAdapter(
        Catcher catcher
    )
    {
        catcherBean = catcher;
    }

    public void receivePitch(
        PitchEvent pitchEvent
    )
    {
        catcherBean.receivePitch(pitchEvent);
    }
}
```

If you were using a GUI Builder of some kind, the introspection routines would first identify the receive method on the `Catcher` Bean and then the fire event statement on the `Pitcher` Bean. The GUI Builder would then create an adapter that would bridge the fire event statement and the receive method. Typically, the designer of the firing Bean will not know the exact name of the receive method on the other end. The adapter can translate the request from the firing Bean into the proper name on the target Bean. In Figure 3.8, a `Pitcher` Bean with a `throwPitch` method calls an adapter that calls the `receivePitch` method on the `Catcher`.

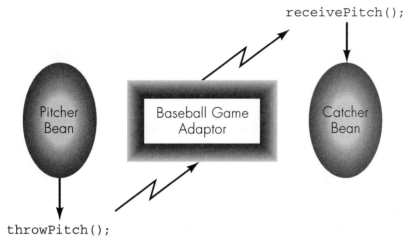

receivePitch();

throwPitch();

Figure 3.8: *Using adapters, Beans need not know the implementation details of the targets for their events.*

MODIFYING THE CONTAINER

In your original `BaseballField` container, you will now need to create the adapter specifying the `Catcher` instance. Furthermore, you will need to change the add and remove listener registration methods so that the `BaseballGameAdapter` is specified instead of the `Catcher`:

```
public class BaseballField
{
    Catcher catcher;
    Pitcher pitcher;
    BaseballGameAdapter adapter;

    BaseballField()
    {
        catcher = new Catcher();
        pitcher = new Pitcher();
        adapter = new BaseballGameAdapter(catcher);

        pitcher.addPitchListener(adapter);
    }
}
```

Complicated Adapters

Often times, your listener will receive the same event from multiple sources. For example, if you were to implement the `MouseListener` interface, your listener will receive mouse events from many sources, including all of the buttons, text areas, and widgets in your user interface. Similarly, when you implement a Bean event listener, it may have to field requests from multiple Bean sources. If you only intend to field the event and process it, no additional work is necessary and adapters are not required. If, however, you intend for events to be processed based on the source from which they came, then you will need to provide a more complicated adapter scheme.

In order to funnel identical events from disparate sources to the proper method action on the Bean end, you must create what is known as a *demultiplexing adapter*. A demultiplexing adapter should be created for every event source from which you expect to receive events. If you have two Beans, and each Bean is firing the same event to your listener, you should create two adapters, one for each Bean, and the adapter should receive the event, and subsequently invoke the proper method on the listener (see Figure 3.9).

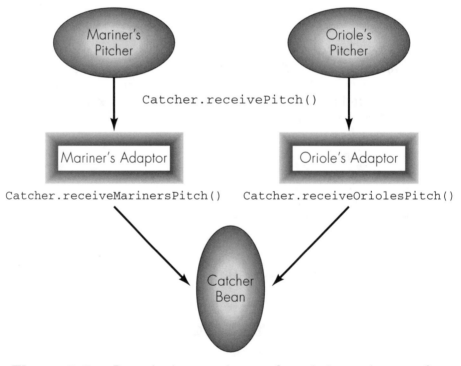

Figure 3.9: *Demultiplexing adapters funnel identical events from different sources to listeners.*

Once again, it is important to note that adapters are created by the GUI Builder or the container, not necessarily by you, the programmer. Indeed, one of the ways in which you will be able to determine which

GUI Builder is appropriate for your tasks is by the complexity and reliability of the adapters that it generates and its resulting ability to connect completely disparate Beans to one another.

Rainbow Button Events

Given the architectural description we gave for your Rainbow Button in Chapter 2, *Component Models*, you must now implement the event portion of the three components. As you will recall, the three Beans you need to create are the `RainbowButton` itself, the `PictureArea` that you will use to display an image based on a button press, and the `SoundMachine` that will continuously play a music clip. Both the `RainbowButton` and `PictureArea` have GUIs associated with them while the `SoundMachine` does not.

Creating Events

Your button will trigger one event, the aptly named `ButtonEvent`. Included as part of the `ButtonEvent` will be the text currently in the button as well as the new color of the button. This will enable any listener to respond based on what the current state of the button is. The `ButtonEvent` itself is rather simple. It inherits from the `EventObject` class we discussed earlier:

```
import java.util.event.EventObject;
public class ButtonEvent extends EventObject
{
    ButtonEvent(
        Object sourceObject
    )
    {
    }
}
```

Now, you need to add support for storing the button's text and color in the event. You will mark both variables as public for now, but the next chapter covers how you can go about making the variables full-fledged Bean properties, with their own accessors and mutators. You will also need to initialize the object by calling the `EventObject` superclass' constructor:

```
import java.util.event.EventObject;
public class ButtonEvent extends EventObject
{
    String buttonText;
```

```
Color buttonColor;

ButtonEvent(
    Object sourceObject
)
{
    super(sourceObject);
}
}
```

If you wanted to, you could initialize the variables as well. Now, you need to create a listener for the events. As was discussed earlier, a listener is an interface that must be implemented by other objects. The listener you will create here is an interface as well. It will inherit from the standard `EventListener` object, but you will add a method called `fireButtonEvent` that will accept a `ButtonEvent` object as a parameter:

```
import java.util.event.EventListener;
public class ButtonListener extends EventListener
{
    public void fireButtonEvent(
        ButtonEvent buttonEvent);
}
```

Your `PictureArea` and `SoundMachine` objects will both implement this interface, and therefore implement the `fireButtonEvent` method as well. This will enable your `RainbowButton` Bean to invoke events on other Beans that support the `ButtonListener` interface.

Creating the Button

When you create your `RainbowButton`, the first thing you need to realize is that it is a Java `Button` object in its own right. What this means is that the `RainbowButton` will inherit from the Java `Button` class, and therefore receive all of the cool little features such as labels, colors, and actions automatically. However, in order for your `RainbowButton` to receive mouse events, you will need to subscribe to the `MouseListener` interface. This is not at all unlike the example we showed in the events section of Chapter 1. This time you will make your button a full-fledged JavaBean:

```
import java.awt.*;
public class RainbowButton extends Button
                           implements MouseListener
{
    Color buttonColor;
```

```
    String buttonText;

    RainbowButton()
    {
        super();
    }
}
```

Once you create your shell, you need to create a place for your listeners to be stored. Once again, you will use the Java `Vector` object. The `Vector` gives us the flexibility and ease you need to store potentially large numbers of listeners. As was discussed in Chapter 2, a Bean is a Java object, but unlike typical Java objects, it should never handle its initialization in its constructor. Rather, it should implement an `instantiate` method and handle its initialization and instantiation there:

```
import java.awt.*;
public class RainbowButton extends Button
                           implements MouseListener
{
    Color buttonColor;
    String buttonText;

    Vector eventListeners;

    RainbowButton()
    {
        super();
    }

    public void instantiate()
    {
        // initialize the Vector
        eventListeners = new Vector();
    }
}
```

You will now include the add and remove listener methods. As you saw earlier, you must follow a certain design pattern for this. Specifically, you must prepend the words *add* and *remove* to the type of the listener. Since the type of the listener is called a `ButtonListener`, the methods are `addButtonListener` and `removeButtonListener`:

```
import java.awt.*;
public class RainbowButton extends Button
                           implements MouseListener
{
    Color buttonColor;
```

```
String buttonText;

Vector eventListeners;

RainbowButton()
{
    super();
}

public void instantiate()
{
    // initialize the Vector
    eventListeners = new Vector();
}

public void addButtonListener(
    ButtonListener listener
)
{
    eventListeners.addElement(listener);
}

public void removeButtonListener(
    ButtonListener listener
)
{
    eventListeners.removeElement(listener);
}
}
```

Now you will need to go about implementing the methods that are part of the `MouseListener` interface. Because you are implementing the interface, you must create all of the methods. However, the only method that really interests us is `mouseClicked`. The other methods, `mousePressed`, `mouseReleased`, `mouseEntered`, and `mouseExited`, do not need to be implemented. In your `mouseClicked` method, you will first create a new `ButtonEvent`, passing it the source Bean, in this case the `RainbowButton` instance, and then you will go about firing the change to every listener you have stored in `eventListeners`:

```
import java.awt.*;
public class RainbowButton extends Button
                            implements MouseListener
{
    Color buttonColor;
    String buttonText;

    Vector eventListeners;

    RainbowButton()
```

```
{
    super();
}

public void instantiate()
{
    // initialize the Vector
    eventListeners = new Vector();
}

public void addButtonListener(
    ButtonListener listener
)
{
    eventListeners.addElement(listener);
}

public void removeButtonListener(
    ButtonListener listener
)
{
    eventListeners.removeElement(listener);
}

public void mouseClicked(
    MouseEvent evt
)
{
    // first create a button event
    ButtonEvent buttonEvent = new ButtonEvent(this);

    // now notify all of the listeners of an event
    for(int x = 0; x < eventListeners.size(); x++)
    {
        // cast to proper type
        ButtonListener listener =
            (ButtonListener) eventListeners.elementAt(x);

        // invoke on the listener
        listener.fireButtonEvent(buttonEvent);
    }
}
}
```

You now have a working RainbowButton event mechanism. The ButtonListeners, which you will create in a moment, will call the addButtonListener method on the RainbowButton object and register themselves with the button. When the button gets a mouse click, it will go about firing a ButtonEvent to every one of the ButtonListeners.

This is a RainbowButton, not just an ordinary Button. Your RainbowButton needs to change colors whenever it gets a mouse click event. So, you need to modify your mouseClicked method slightly to change the color of the Button, and pass the current color and text of your button along with your ButtonEvent to the various ButtonListeners who are chiming in:

```
… code omitted for brevity …

    public void mouseClicked(
        MouseEvent evt
    )
    {
        // change the color of the button
        if(buttonColor == Color.red)
            buttonColor = Color.white;
        else if(buttonColor == Color.white)
            buttonColor = Color.blue;
        else
            buttonColor = Color.red;

        // first create a button event
        ButtonEvent buttonEvent = new ButtonEvent(this);
        buttonEvent.buttonColor = buttonColor;
        buttonEvent.buttonText = buttonText;

        // now notify all of the listeners of an event
        for(int x = 0; x < eventListeners.size(); x++)
        {
            // cast to proper type
            ButtonListener listener =
                (ButtonListener) eventListeners.elementAt(x);

            // invoke on the listener
            listener.fireButtonEvent(buttonEvent);
        }
    }
}
```

While you don't exactly use the buttonText here, you will in the next chapter. You will also implement a more robust color changing mechanism later as well, but for now you will stick with this most rudimentary red-white-blue changer.

Implementing the Picture Area

The PictureArea object has but one thing to do, display a pretty picture. In fact, it will display a sequence of pretty pictures, but will only change the picture when it receives a `ButtonEvent` from a source Bean. You created what could be used as a source Bean when you developed your `RainbowButton`, and now it is time to create a `ButtonListener`. The `PictureArea` object is nothing but a Java Panel object that inherits from a `ButtonListener` interface:

```
public class PictureArea extends Panel implements ButtonListener
{
    PictureArea()
    {
        super();
    }
}
```

Now you will need to implement a paint method for when you will get images to draw. You might also want to load all of the images in advance as well. As always, these routines should be performed in the `instantiate` method, not the constructor. JavaBeans should always be initialized in the `instantiate` method:

```
public class PictureArea extends Panel implements ButtonListener
{
    PictureArea()
    {
        super();
    }

    public void instantiate()
    {
    }

    public void fireButtonEvent(
        ButtonEvent buttonEvent
    )
    {
    }
}
```

For now, you will leave the rest of the `PictureArea` blank. When properties are discussed in the next chapter, you will have something intelligent to put inside the `PictureArea`.

Sounds From Afar

The `SoundMachine` is a Bean without any kind of user interface. As a result, the `SoundMachine` class only implements the `ButtonListener` and extends no User Interface (UI) component:

```
public class SoundMachine implements ButtonListener
{
    SoundMachine()
    {
    }

    public void instantiate()
    {
    }
}
```

There are a few properties in the `SoundMachine` that you will want to implement when properties are discussed in the next chapter. Once again, you will leave the object pretty much blank until that time. For now, you need only to fill in the `ButtonListener`'s `fireButton-Event` method:

```
public class SoundMachine implements ButtonListener
{
    SoundMachine()
    {
    }

    public void instantiate()
    {
    }

    public void fireButtonEvent(
        ButtonEvent buttonEvent
    )
    {
    }
}
```

Summary

Events are the means in the Beans component model that allow various components of varying and different breeds to communicate. While these components may be far-reaching and very different, the events with which they communicate allow them to speak a *common language*. This common language can then be used to incorporate even more disparate components so that, when intertwined, they can function like one large component. As you see in your daily lives, every component communicates somehow. In JavaBeans, you are pretty lucky to have such an easy mechanism to use.

Major Events in the History of Coffee

9th Century- An Abysinnian goat herd discovers that the boiling of coffee beans can help him stay alert during evening prayers.

1615 - Pope Clement VIII declares coffee a "Christian beverage."

1668 - Coffee makes it to the New World.

1699 - The Dutch plant the first coffee Bean outside Arabia in the island of Java!

1960s - The United States becomes the world's largest consumer of coffee.

1971 - Starbucks founded.

1994 - NBC television program Friends popularizes cafes as a place to socialize and generally bum around.

2002 President Howard Stern declares coffee National Drink.

2003 - Vice President Dick Clark assumes Presidency after President Stern's caffeine overdose.

2354 - Coffee plants replace evergreen trees.

Source: Kevin Knox and Julie Sheldon Huffaker, *Coffee Basics*. John Wiley and Sons, 1997.

CHAPTER 4

Bean Properties

▶ **V**ariables as properties

▶ **D**esign patterns for properties

▶ **I**nformation hiding

▶ **P**roperty listeners

▶ **C**ustomizers

▶ **I**mplementing properties in an application

JavaBeans has a notion of a property. A property is one of the characteristics of the Bean that should be available for other Beans to use. If you were to connect a group of Beans together, they would need to interact with one another by perhaps changing their properties. Beans also need a means to publicize the information contained within them. Furthermore, Beans may also need to store their internal state so that it can be serialized or even read by an external Bean serializer like a Bean capable of speaking with a back end data storage mechanism using Java Database Connectivity (JDBC). But, the distinction between a Bean property and an object's internal variable are very clear.

When to Use Properties

The big question you're probably asking is why on earth do you need a property when you can simply create a bunch of public variables within your object. In order to make the distinction between a property and a variable, there needs to be a more tightly focused definition of what a property is and how they can be used within Beans.

What is a Property?

As has been said, a property is a way for a component to maintain its state. When Beans have a property, that property can be modified at several moments. Let's say you go to *Jenny's House of Beans* and buy a component to interface with your television. Jenny has created a Bean that is fully customizable. The internal algorithms are hard-wired, so you don't ever have to program, but you can alter the kinds of televisions your Bean can communicate with, as well as the means it will use to communicate.

When you install and setup the Bean, the Bean will contain something called a *property sheet*. The Bean's property sheet will popup when you are ready to install the Bean. You can then edit the *television type* property in your television bean to *Toshiba* or *Sony* while the property sheet is up. When the Bean is then installed, it will be configured for the television you specified.

Why are Properties Important?

As you can see with the television Bean example, you don't ever have to recompile or edit any source code for your Bean. Your Bean's algorithm may be hardwired, but the data that it is configured with is not. These properties then become the means with which you can configure your Bean and pass it around. Your Bean can be completely plug and play. In fact, you can tie the value of a property on one Bean to the value of the property contained in another Bean and link them forever so that when one property changes, the other will be notified of the change and be allowed to change itself as shown in Figure 4.1.

Properties are an important quality of Bean development. It's important to realize that the overhead associated with creating a property is not on the creation side. For example, creating an integer that represents the current channel on the television is done as follows:

```
int currentChannel;
```

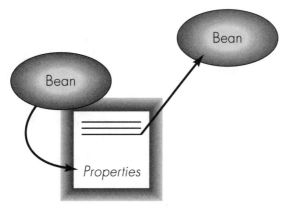

Figure 4.1: *Bean actions can be tied to properties.*

If, however, you were to create a property for the current channel, it is absolutely no different than the one just shown. For example:

```
int currentChannel;
```

The big deal with properties is not their definition or creation, but how they are managed. Properties can fire change events similar to the Java event model that we have espoused for the past two chapters. Indeed, when a property changes it can very easily tell anyone else who is interested in the property of the change. Our hypothetical television's current channel Bean can notify a tuner Bean to change its channel.

Design Patterns

In order for listeners and containers to be able to look into a Bean and access a property, the property must be defined in such a manner as to facilitate introspection. Introspection is a technique that will be discussed in great detail in Chapter 5, *Bean Introspection*, but for the time being all you need to understand about it is that every Bean is capable of looking into another Bean. This lets Beans find out information about another component without prior knowledge about either the contents of the Bean or the details of the source code. The design patterns required for the component's development allows you to ready a component for introspection later on.

Accessors

An *accessor* is a special function that allows us to get the value of a variable. Its return value is the value of the variable, and it accepts no parameters. The design pattern spoken so often of is not only the construction of the function itself, but its name as well. Indeed, because of the limited introspection algorithm in JavaBeans, the Beans infrastructure requires properties and their accessors to be named in a predescribed fashion with a predescribed capitalization. Without such a design pattern, there would be no way for a Bean to know the difference between an ordinary variable and a property.

Traditionally, the accepted style guidelines for a Java variable are pretty straightforward and easy to read. Hearken back to your old high school days when your Computer Science teacher told you that you should name variables so that they are easy to read and so that they describe the variable whose value they contain. If you had a string variable in which you want to store your sister's name, you would declare it thusly:

```
String sistersName;
```

In so doing, you can specify what the string represents. It is a whole bunch easier to tell what `sistersName` means than if you declared it obtusely like this:

```
String x;
```

What does `x` mean, and what does it talk about? Now, you need to declare a class object in which this string is going to reside. As was discussed in Chapter 2, *Component Models*, the class should extend the `java.beans.Beans` object:

```
import java.beans.*;

public class MySister extends Beans
{
    String sistersName;
}
```

Now you need to create the accessor for the `sistersName` variable. Remember, you haven't done a single thing to the variable to make it anything special yet. Right now, it is still a variable and not a property. A property has certain infrastructure associated with it, namely the accessor and, as you will discover in a few moments, the mutator and the customizer.

Creating the accessor involves taking the name of the variable, and prepending the word *get* to the front of it. Remember, the return type of the function *must* be the same as the type of the variable or you will get an `IntrospectionException` error once introspection begins. Remember to alter the capitalization appropriately:

```
import java.beans.*;

public class MySister extends Beans
{
    String sistersName;

    public String getSistersName()
    {
    }
}
```

 The proper way to name an accessor for a given variable is to prepend the word *get* to the name of the variable. You must alter capitalization appropriately:

```
<property type> <property name>;
<property type> get<property name>();
```

■

Now, you need to return the appropriate value. At this point, you may feel the need to protect access to the variable from thread-related problems. Some kind of synchronization or mutual exclusion may be required. Here, you take the simple approach, but you could just as easily wrap synchronization steps around the `return` statement:

```
import java.beans.*;

public class MySister extends Beans
{
    String sistersName;

    public String getSistersName()
    {
        return sistersName;
    }
}
```

Mutator

A *mutator* is a special function that allows you to edit the value of a property. Editing the property may cause a chain reaction of events firing change events to various listeners, but these are details that you will worry about in a moment. Nevertheless, the mutator function is vital to the success of a well-designed set of properties in your Bean.

Mutators are created similarly to their accessor counterparts. However, the mutator should have a `void` return value, but it should receive a parameter of the same type as the variable it is mutating. So, the `sistersName` variable that was declared earlier should have a `setSistersName` mutator that receives a string value as a parameter. Furthermore, the mutator should be prepended by the word *set* not *get* as you did with the accessor:

```
import java.beans.*;

public class MySister extends Beans
{
    String sistersName;

    public void setSistersName(
        String sistersName
    )
    {
    }
}
```

 The mutator for a given property should be named by prepending the word *set* to the property name and passing in one parameter whose type matches that of the property:

```
<property type> <property name>
void set<property name>(
    <property type> property
);
```

When you actually make the change, you may need to once again wrap synchronization steps around it, but for the time being ignore that eventuality:

```
import java.beans.*;

public class MySister extends Beans
{
    String sistersName;

    public void setSistersName(
        String sistersName
    )
    {
        this.sistersName = sistersName;
    }
}
```

Arrays and Indexed Properties

When your components contain indexed properties such as arrays, there are special design constraints that you must follow in your accessors and mutators. Most obvious of these design constraints is the need to include the index at which you are setting or getting a property. Let's say your `sistersName` variable from earlier is now an array of strings instead. You need to be able to set and get the values of this array:

```
import java.beans.*;

public class MySister extends Beans
{
    String sistersName[];
}
```

INDEXED ACCESSOR

If you had several sisters, and you wanted to be able to get the name of a particular sister, you would need to be able to specify which sister you wanted. This is done by specifying the index as the first parameter in the `get` method. For example, to get the name of our third sister, you would need to execute the following instruction:

```
String thirdSistersName = sis.getSistersName(3);
```

You should declare the indexed accessor as follows:

```
import java.beans.*;

public class MySister extends Beans
{
    String sistersName[];

    public String getSistersName(
        int index
    )
    {
    }
}
```

 In order to create an accessor for an indexed property, you must prepend the word *get* to the name of the property and pass in an integer indicating the index at which the property is to be accessed:

```
<property type> <property name> [<property length>]
<property type> get<property name>(
    int index
);
```

■

Then fill in the accessor by returning the proper value. Once again, the same caveat about mutual exclusion violations and other multithreading issues applies. Remember, your component will be used by people who could potentially know nothing about computers, or more probably people who don't want to know or can't be allowed to know the exact algorithms of the internals of the component:

```
import java.beans.*;

public class MySister extends Beans
{
    String sistersName[];

    public String getSistersName(
        int index
    )
    {
        return sistersName[index];
    }
}
```

INDEXED MUTATOR

The leap from accessors to mutators is not significantly large. In fact, you once again need to specify the index of the location that you want to set as the first parameter to the mutator. Once you receive the index, you will go about setting the value of the array just as you did with the non-indexed version:

```
import java.beans.*;

public class MySister extends Beans
{
    String sistersName[];

    public void setSistersName(
        int index,
        String sistersName
    )
    {
        this.sistersName[index] = sistersName;
    }
}
```

The mutator for an indexed property is named by prepending the word *set* to the property name and passing two parameters. The first parameter is the index at which you intend to modify the data, while the second parameter is the value to modify:

```
<property type> <property name> [<property length>]
void set<property name>(
    int index,
    <property type> propertyValue
);
```

■

INDEXED PROPERTIES

You also want to preserve your ability to get and set the entire property, indexed or not. Indeed, many of our applications may require the entire indexed property, not just an individual element. In order to keep our flexibility, you need to create parallel accessors and mutators. Once again, you use the `getSistersName` function, but since it is unnecessary to include the index since you want the entire property, you can omit the index and keep it independent from the indexed accessor:

```
import java.beans.*;

public class MySister extends Beans
{
    String sistersName[];

    public String getSistersName()
    {
        return sistersName;
    }
}
```

Similarly, you need to create a mutator for the entire indexed property. You do not require the index and can omit it in this instance so as to avoid conflict with the other mutator. The cool thing about this mutator is that you can use it to reset the size of the array. If your initial Bean setup creates an array with seven elements, you can come in here later and set a new array whose length is larger or smaller:

```
import java.beans.*;

public class MySister extends Beans
{
    String sistersName[];
```

```
    public void setSistersName(
        String sistersName
    )
    {

        this.sistersName = sistersName;

    }
}
```

EXCEPTION HANDLING

Because you are dealing with arrays, you always have the possibility of overstepping your bounds and accessing or setting an element at an index that is out of range. Java provides an exception handling mechanism that you too can take advantage of. Each of your indexed accessors and mutators can throw an `ArrayIndexOutOfBoundsException` any time it is asked to get or set an invalid index:

```
import java.beans.*;

public class MySister extends Beans
{
    String sistersName[];

    public void setSistersName(
        int index,
        String sistersName
    ) throws ArrayIndexOutOfBoundsException
    {
        this.sistersName[index] = sistersName;
    }
}
```

Boolean Properties

A boolean property is one whose value is either true or false and is implemented using the `boolean` simple type. There are two simple methods for a boolean property, that you should implement, an accessor and a mutator. The design pattern for these properties differs slightly from that of the other normal properties so that they may more easily be used in code.

ACCESSOR

The accessor for the boolean property asks the question, "is the value true?" In so doing, the accessor for the property is built by prepending the word "is" to the name of the property and adjusting the capitalization appropriately. For example, if you had a boolean property whose name was `turnip`, our accessor would be `isTurnip` and would return true if the property was true or, in English, if the property "is a turnip".

The accessor for a boolean property is constructed by prepending the word *is* to the name of the property. The accessor should return a boolean value corresponding to the data contained in the property:

```
public boolean is<property name>()
```

■

MUTATOR

The mutator for a boolean property is similar to that of its non-boolean counterparts. In order to construct it, you should prepend the word "set" to the name of the property and pass in one variable corresponding to the new value of the property. So, following the turnip example, the mutator should be `setTurnip`.

The mutator for a boolean property is built by prepending the word *set* to the name of the property and passing in one boolean parameter whose value will be stored in the property:

```
public void set<property name>(
    boolean newPropertyValue
)
```

■

Property Listeners

When you were examining the Java event model closely in Chapter 1, *Advanced Java* and Chapter 3, *Bean Events*, you discovered the notion of a publish and subscribe system. A publish and subscribe system divides objects into two categories: those objects that *want* information, and those objects that *provide* information. In between the two types of objects lies the listener, a sort of middleman that can exchange information between them. This ensures that as a provider of information, an object need only push events to the listener. As consumers of information, objects need only register themselves with a listener. In this chapter, you will create both producers and consumers.

Producers of Information

Your property objects may at times wish to notify others that they have changed. In this case, the property is the publisher, and those that it wishes to notify are the subscribers. In order to publish information about a property change, you must fire a `PropertyChangeEvent`. This special kind of event is associated only with properties, but is nothing more than an extension of the standard Event object.

In order to fire a property change, you must first know which property listeners you plan on supporting. To assist in this matter, JavaBeans provides us with a PropertyChangeSupport object. The PropertyChangeSupport object allows us to collect all our PropertyChangeListeners in one location and to access them when needed. In order to use the support object, you must first create it. You will then be able to add listeners to it and fire events based on its contents.

THE PROPERTY SUPPORT OBJECT

The PropertyChangeSupport object is a utility class provided to us by the Beans architecture that makes firing property change events simpler and more efficient. Instead of worrying about how to implement a storage mechanism for your listeners, or about how to fire an event to each individual listener, all you need to do is to simply implement the property support object (see Figure 4.2).

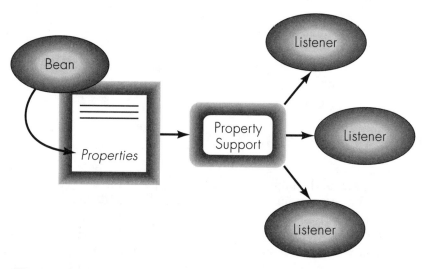

Figure 4.2: *Property support objects handle notifications for you.*

Constructor The constructor for the support object is fairly straightforward, accepting one parameter whose value is the source Bean in which the support object is contained and initialized.

The constructor for the PropertyChangeSupport object accepts one parameter, the sourceBean, whose value should be the Bean in which the support object is contained:

```
public PropertyChangeSupport(
    Object sourceBean
)
```

Methods The first two methods in the `PropertyChangeSup-`
`port` object are for adding and removing `PropertyChangeListen-`
`ers`. The `PropertyChangeListener` will be discussed in a moment,
but its internals are fairly unimportant here. These two methods merely
take a `PropertyChangeListener` object and add it to the array inside
the `PropertyChangeSupport` object.

Altering the listeners stored inside a `PropertyChange-`
`Support` object can be done using the following two
methods. Both methods take one parameter, a `Property-`
`ChangeListener` object, and do not return anything. To
protect against concurrent access or deadlock, both methods are tagged
as `synchronized`:

```
public synchronized void addPropertyChangeListener(
    PropertyChangeListener newListener
)
public synchronized void
removePropertyChangeListener(
    PropertyChangeListener removeListener
)
```

Once the listeners are stored, you can fire property change events (the
details of which will be discussed in a moment) to all of the listeners you
stored using the two previous methods.

The stored listeners can be fired upon using the `fireProp-`
`ertyChange` method. The method accepts three parameters, the name of the property being changed, the old value
of the property, and the new value of the property:

```
public void firePropertyChange(
    String propertyName,
    Object oldValue,
    Object newValue
)
```

CREATING THE SUPPORT OBJECT

To add support for property change events to our `MySister` Bean, you
would first need to declare and initialize the `PropertyChangeSup-`
`port` object in the constructor, passing it the sister Bean:

```
import java.beans.*;

public class MySister extends Beans
{
    String sistersName[];
    PropertyChangeSupport changeListeners;

    MySister()
    {
        // initialize the listener
        changeListeners = new PropertyChangeSupport(this);
    }

    public void setSistersName(
        int index,
        String sistersName
    )
    {
        this.sistersName[index] = sistersName;
    }
}
```

ADDING LISTENERS TO THE SUPPORT OBJECT

You must now add the methods required for property listeners to add
themselves to our property support object. These methods must follow
strict design patterns, since introspecting Beans must be able to find
them. In order to add a property listener to our Bean, you prepend the
word "add" to the type of the listener.

Adding property listeners to a Bean should be done using
the standard addPropertyChangeListener method.
The delete analog to the method is the removePropertyChangeListener method and should also be implemented within any Bean wishing to fire property change events:

```
public void addPropertyChangeListener(
    PropertyChangeListener listener);
public void removePropertyChangeListener(
    PropertyChangeListener listener);
```

■

In your case, you are only using PropertyChangeListeners. Support for the addition of listeners must be included in the addProperty-
ChangeListener method. Similarly, the removePropertyChange-
Listener method must also be implemented. Both methods should
simply add the listener to the support object:

```
import java.beans.*;

public class MySister extends Beans
{
    String sistersName[];
    PropertyChangeSupport changeListeners;

    MySister()
    {
        // initialize the listener
        changeListeners = new PropertyChangeSupport(this);
    }

    public void addPropertyChangeListener(
        PropertyChangeListener listener
    )
    {
        changeListeners.addPropertyChangeListener(listener);
    }

    public void removePropertyChangeListener(
        PropertyChangeListener listener
    )
    {
        changeListeners.removePropertyChangeListener
    (listener);
    }

    public void setSistersName(
        int index,
        String sistersName
    )
    {
        this.sistersName[index] = sistersName;
    }
}
```

ADDING LISTENERS FOR SPECIFIC PROPERTIES

As Figure 4.3 shows, JavaBeans will also let you add listeners for specific properties within your Bean. Once again, strict design patterns should be followed so that introspecting Beans may discover the existence of these special property listeners.

In order to allow the addition of property listeners for a specific Bean, you should create an addListener method for each property. This is done by prepending the word *add* to the name of the property and appending the word *Listener* to it. Support for the removal of a per-property listener can be had by simply prepending the word *remove* instead of *add*.

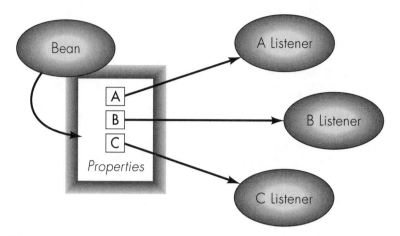

Figure 4.3: *Properties can have specific listeners also.*

 In order to create listeners on a per-property basis, every property that wants to publish events must have the following add listener method:

```
public void add<property name>Listener(
    PropertyChangeListener listener);
```

Similarly, every property should implement the following remove listener method:

```
public void remove<property name>Listener(
    PropertyChangeListener listener);
```

■

For example, if your `sistersName` property were to have an individual property listener, it would look like this:

```
import java.beans.*;

public class MySister extends Beans
{
    String sistersName[];
    PropertyChangeSupport sistersNameListeners;

    MySister()
    {
        // initialize the listener
        sistersNameListeners= new PropertyChangeSupport(this);
    }
```

```
public void addSistersNameListener(
    PropertyChangeListener listener
)
{

    sistersNameListeners.addPropertyChangeListener(
        listener);
}

public void removeSistersNameListener(
    PropertyChangeListener listener
)
{

    sistersNameListener.removePropertyChangeListener(
        listener);
}

public void setSistersName(
    int index,
    String sistersName
)
{

    this.sistersName[index] = sistersName;
}
}
```

 The use of listeners on a general basis or on a per-property basis is an either/or situation. You cannot combine the use of a general property listener and individual property listeners. If you want to create a listener for individual properties, you should do so for every property. Typically, per-property listeners are implemented as optimizing tools for Beans. Rather than firing events to every listener, your Bean will be able to fire events only to specific listeners that want information on that property alone.

FIRING THE CHANGE

Now, when you need to fire the property change event to the proper listeners, you will do so in the mutator for the sister Bean's `sistersName` property. Using the `PropertyChangeSupport` utility object, invoke the `firePropertyChange` method passing the name of the property as well as the old and new value for it:

```
import java.beans.*;

public class MySister extends Beans
{
    String sistersName[];
    PropertyChangeSupport changeListeners;
```

```
MySister()
{
    // initialize the listener
    changeListeners = new PropertyChangeSupport(this);
}

public void addPropertyChangeListener(
    PropertyChangeListener listener
)
{

    changeListeners.addPropertyChangeListener(listener);
}

public void removePropertyChangeListener(
    PropertyChangeListener listener
)
{

    changeListeners.removePropertyChangeListener(listener);
}

public void setSistersName(
    int index,
    String sistersName
)
{

    // what is the old value?
    String oldValue = sistersName;

    // make the change
    this.sistersName[index] = sistersName;

    // fire a property change event
    changeListeners.firePropertyChange(
        "sistersName",
        oldValue, sistersName);
}
}
```

 You should be aware and check for instances in which the new value that is to be assigned is the same as the old value. In such cases, loops may have been formed in the event firing mechanism as follows:

```
sister.setSistersName(sister.getSistersName());
```

This makes it dangerous to follow through with firing the property change. Ideally, you should check the old and new values beforehand and make the change and subsequently fire the event only if necessary.

Consumers of Information

Now that you've created the place for the events to be fired from, you need a place for those events to be sent to. This other Bean is the target, or consumer, Bean. The target Bean should be a place to where the original Bean's property changes are registered, or used. For example, every sister has a nagging mother. If you were to create a `NaggingMother` object that is a `PropertyChangeListener`, you would be able to later connect our sister Bean to it. The `NaggingMother` would be notified of any changes to the `MySister` Bean and would be able to respond accordingly.

THE PROPERTY LISTENER INTERFACE

The `PropertyChangeListener` is not an object, but an interface. Using the interface, you will be able to use the support object mentioned earlier in this section as long as you implement one very important method, the `propertyChange` method. This method is called whenever a bound property is changed. As discussed earlier in this section, a property change listener must first register itself with the Bean, and all subsequent changes to a given property will be fired back to the listener via the `propertyChange` method.

 The `PropertyChangeListener` interface's only method, `propertyChange`, is marked as `abstract` and therefore must be implemented by any subsequent inheriting objects. The method accepts one parameter, a `PropertyChange-Event` object corresponding to the event being fired:

```
public abstract void propertyChange(
    PropertyChangeEvent changeEvent
)
```

■

CREATING A LISTENER

Actually creating the listener is very similar to the listener you created in Chapter 3. In that chapter, you created an object that extends the `EventListener` object. By extending the standard Java event listener, you were able to implement some functions that could be called by Beans that fired events. Likewise, your `PropertyChangeListener` object will be extended by our `NaggingMother` object and you will then be able to connect our `MySister` Bean to the mom object:

```
import java.beans.*;
public class NaggingMother extends PropertyChangeListener
{
}
```

IMPLEMENTING THE LISTENER

Once you extend the `PropertyChangeListener` object, you are required to implement the `propertyChange` method. The `property-Change` method will be passed a `PropertyChangeEvent` object that you can use to determine the information about the property that has broadcasted its change results.

```
import java.beans.*;
public class NaggingMother extends PropertyChangeListener
{
    public void propertyChange(
        PropertyChangeEvent evt
    )
    {
    }
}
```

THE **PropertyChangeEvent** OBJECT

The `PropertyChangeEvent` object is delivered to the listener, via the `propertyChange` method, whenever a property is changed on a Bean to which the listener is subscribed. Using the object, you can determine the nature of the change as well as the originating Bean from which it came.

Constructor The constructor for the object is pretty straightforward and accepts parameters corresponding to the source of the event, the name of the property being changed, as well as the old and new values for the property.

The `PropertyChangeEvent` object's constructor allows you to create an event for property changes specifying information about a property change, including the new value, the old value, and the name of the property itself:

```
public PropertyChangeEvent(
    Object sourceBean,
    String propertyName,
    Object oldValue,
    Object newValue);
```

■

Methods You can also use the `getNewValue` and `getOldValue` methods on the event object. Both of the methods return a generic Java `Object`, allowing you to cast from complex data types if you so require.

The `getNewValue` and `getOldValue` methods return a Java `Object` so that properties composed of complex objects are still supported. The methods take no parameters, and simply return the values as set in the event object:

```
public Object getNewValue();
public Object getOldValue();
```

■

You may also use the `getPropertyName` method to obtain the name of the property. Your listeners may desire the information to filter, or possibly ignore, the event. It's kind of like going to a party and being ignored the whole time.

The `getPropertyName` method returns a `String` containing the name of the property as set by the firing Bean. Usually, this will correspond to the name of the property in code:

```
public String getPropertyName();
```

■

The JavaBeans 1.0 specification also mentions something called a propagation ID that can be set as part of the `PropertyChangeEvent` object. The propagation ID is not yet implemented or used, but will be in future releases of JavaBeans. Two methods, `getPropagationId` and `setPropagationId`, are included so that backwards compatibility will be possible.

The `getPropagationId` and `setPropagationId` methods are not implemented in JavaBeans 1.0, but will be in future revisions of the Beans architecture.

```
public Object getPropagationId()
public void setPropagationId(
    Object newPropagationId
)
```

■

Constrained Properties

What if you had a bunch of listeners that wanted to chime in and prevent the alteration of a property. In the United States Congress bills are proposed every day and sent to the President to sign into law. When Bill whips out his trusty pen, he has the option of accepting the pork-laden legislation or denying it with good judgement. In other words, the President has the option of vetoing legislation.

Similarly, property listeners have the option of vetoing a property change. In order to handle such cases, the Bean should use a vetoable listener instead of the normal property listener already discussed. The vetoable listener allows your Bean to fire property change events, letting the listener throw an exception if the change should not occur. Your Bean may then handle the exception and prevent the change from taking place in the Bean.

VETOABLE EXCEPTIONS

The `PropertyVetoException` is thrown by any listener that objects to a property change event. Included as part of the exception is a reason for the objection, as well as the original event to which the listener objects. The exception has a simple constructor that accepts the reason for the objection and the original event.

The `PropertyVetoException` is used to propagate objections to a change event back to the firing Bean. The firing Bean may then catch the exception and do with it as it pleases. Listeners that throw this exception are merely informing the Bean, whose property is being changed, that they object. Whether the Bean does anything or not with the objection is an implementation detail:

```
public PropertyVetoException(
    String reasonForVeto,
    PropertyChangeEvent propertyEventVetoed
)
```

The exception object also has one method that can be used to obtain the event. Note how constrained properties make use of the same `PropertyChangeEvent` as unconstrained properties.

The `getPropertyChangeEvent` method retrieves the event to which the exception objects. The reason for the objection may be obtained through normal exception mechanisms (`exception.toString()`):

```
public PropertyChangeEvent getPropertyChangeEvent()
```

VETOABLE LISTENERS

As with the `PropertyChangeListener`, the `VetoableChangeListener` is nothing but a normal Java interface that extends the normal

Java `EventListener` interface and that must, in turn, be implemented by those Beans wishing to be vetoable listeners. The listener contains one method, `vetoableChange` that throws the aforementioned `PropertyVetoException`.

The `vetoableChange` method accepts one parameter, the property change event, and throws a `PropertyVetoException` if it objects to the change. The firing Bean must then handle the exception as it sees fit. This interface, and the implementation of this interface, should not dictate to the firing Bean what it should do:

```
public abstract void vetoableChange(
    PropertyChangeEvent vetoablePropertyEvent
) throws PropertyVetoException
```

■

VETOABLE SUPPORT OBJECTS

Earlier, you had a `PropertyChangeSupport` object to help you out when you needed some infrastructure to handle our properties. Similarly, the `VetoableChangeSupport` object gives us the same means to fire events to multiple listeners without having to create our own Vectors or other storage mechanisms to keep track of them all. The only difference between this API and that of the `PropertyChangeSupport` object is that the vetoable support object supports the `PropertyVetoException` spoken of earlier.

It is important to recognize that using the support object forces your Bean to handle veto exceptions by reverting to the old value whenever an exception is encountered. There are some instances where you will want to customize how your Bean responds to a veto, and in those cases you should not use this support object. Instead, you should consider creating your own kind of support mechanism.

CONSTRUCTOR

The support object has one constructor that readies it for use. It accepts one parameter, the source Bean from which the events will be fired.

The `VetoableChangeSupport` object allows us to store our vetoable change listeners in a convenient location. The constructor for the object accepts one parameter, the `sourceBean`, that will be sent to every listener that receives an event:

```
public VetoableChangeSupport(
    Object sourceBean
)
```

■

Methods The `VetoableChangeSupport` object also has three methods that facilitate the addition, removal, and use of the listeners contained within it. The first two methods let you add and remove listeners from the data structure.

 The `addVetoableChangeListener` method accepts one parameter, a vetoable listener, and adds it to the internal data structure that is keeping track of listeners and objects. The `removeVetoableChangeListener` does the opposite:

```
public synchronized void addVetoableChangeListener(
    VetoableChangeListener listener
)
public synchronized void
removeVetoableChangeListener(
    VetoableChangeListener listener
)
```

■

The third method fires vetoable events to all of the listeners in the object. Unlike its `PropertyChangeSupport` analog, the `fireVetoableChange` also returns an exception if any of the listeners object. However, using the `VetoableChangeSupport` object forces you to handle that exception in a certain way. If any of the listeners object, then a new event is fired to all of the listeners forcing everyone to revert to the old value.

 The `fireVetoableChange` method is used to fire a property change event to every listener contained in the support object. If any of the listeners objects, then an event is fired to all of the listeners forcing them to revert to the old value. The method accepts three parameters, the name of the property being changed, the old value of the property, and the new value of the property:

```
public void fireVetoableChange(
    String propertyName,
    Object oldPropertyValue,
    Object newPropertyValue
) throws PropertyVetoException
```

■

MODIFYING THE BEAN

If you plan on using a vetoable listener, your Bean must support it in its property mutator. Earlier, you saw the design pattern for a standard property mutator. By simply prepending the word *set* to the name of the property and passing it the new value, you created a simple means for others to affect changes on our properties. However, with a vetoable property, you must also add support for the `PropertyVetoException`.

 The mutator function for a property whose changes can be vetoed must support the veto exceptions in the constrained property specification. The name and construction of the method is the same, but the function must be amended to also support the throwing of `PropertyVetoExceptions`:

```
<property type> <property name>
void set<property name>(
    <property type> property
) throws PropertyVetoException
```

■

USING A VETOABLE LISTENER

Actually implementing a vetoable listener is fairly easy and is a matter of implementing the `VetoableListener` interface. Let's create a `President` Bean that will veto changes when it feels necessary. Remember, you must also implement the `vetoableChange` method as specified in the API:

```
public class President implements VetoableChangeListener
{
    String name = "Bill Clinton the Pure";

    President()
    {
    }

    public void vetoableChange(
        PropertyChangeEvent evt
    ) throws PropertyVetoException
    {
    }
}
```

If the `President` receives something that is not to his liking, he can veto it. Otherwise, he may simply let the change proceed:

```
public class President implements VetoableChangeListener
{
    String name = "Bill Clinton the Pure";

    President()
    {
    }

    public void vetoableChange(
        PropertyChangeEvent evt
    ) throws PropertyVetoException
    {
        if(evt.getPropertyName().equals("Pork-Laden"))
        {
            // uh-oh!  Just got some pork-laden legislation
            throw new PropertyVetoException(
                "Newt, you can do better.", evt);
        }
        else
        {
            // we like it!
            System.out.println(
                "I feel your pain!  I'll sign it.");
        }
    }
}
```

As far as the firing Bean is concerned, you can create a simple Congress Bean that will fire property change events to the President whenever the property legislation is set. As discussed, when the property is set, it should be done by using the setLegislation mutator. Inside the mutator, you will fire an event to the listeners. If any listener objects, you will receive an exception from them; execution within the method will cease and the exception will be returned. That is why you need to place the code for setting the value of the property *after* firing the property change event. It is still our responsibility to set the value of the property, the support object merely notifies the listeners of the change and gives them the opportunity to object:

```
public class Congress
{
    String legislation;
    VetoableChangeSupport vetoableListeners;

    public void setLegislation(
        String newLegislation
    ) throws PropertyVetoException
    {
        // get the old value
```

```
    String oldLegislation = legislation;

    // now fire the change event
    vetoableListeners.fireVetoableChange(
        "legislation", oldLegislation, newLegislation);

    // no one vetoed!
    legislation = newLegislation;
    }
}
```

Customization

In order for your Bean to be truly plug and play, you will need a means for users of the Bean to customize it at design time. Design time is the period when a user can take an existing Bean and use it to design a system of his or her own consisting of several connected Beans. The key to a decent customization scheme is the use of the same techniques you would use in regular object-oriented programming. The decision to allow users to customize every one of your properties is a style decision. For example, if you were to publish a sister Bean to represent a loudmouthed younger sibling, you would allow users to customize the name, height, and weight properties. You would not, however, allow users to customize the gender property. After all, if it is a *sister* Bean, you are locked into one gender only.

Customization in Beans occurs with three distinct objects. These three objects work in concert to provide a GUI editor for a Bean. For example, the graphical representation of your sister Bean could very easily be a *blob* of some sort that, when clicked, pops up an editor inside of which you can edit the various properties. The `PropertySheet` and `PropertyEditor` objects are closely associated with the Bean and can control the representation of its editor. The `Customizer` is a more general object that allows `PropertySheets` and `PropertyEditors` to grab the customization information for a Bean and dynamically generates a GUI editor.

Property Sheets

Property sheets are generally a list of properties that, when clicked or otherwise activated, launch a property editor of some sort. The property editor is then used to modify the value of the property and to complete customization of the Bean. For those familiar with Rapid Application Development (RAD) tools such as Microsoft's Visual language products, property sheets are second nature. Typically, when you select a widget of some kind, a list of the widgets properties may appear as shown in Figure 4.4. You will then be able to edit those properties.

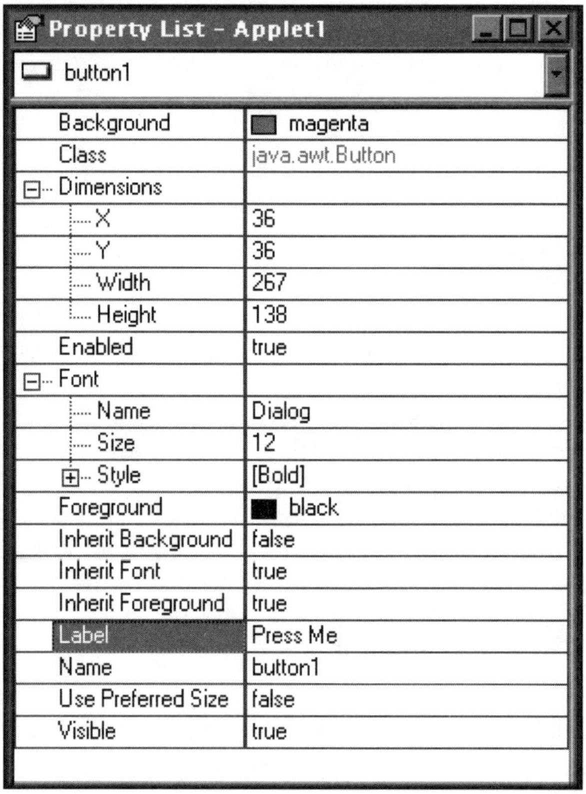

Property List – Applet1	
button1	
Background	■ magenta
Class	java.awt.Button
⊟ Dimensions	
X	36
Y	36
Width	267
Height	138
Enabled	true
⊟ Font	
Name	Dialog
Size	12
⊞ Style	[Bold]
Foreground	■ black
Inherit Background	false
Inherit Font	true
Inherit Foreground	true
Label	Press Me
Name	button1
Use Preferred Size	false
Visible	true

Figure 4.4: *Property sheets are used in Rapid Application Development tools.*

Property Editors

Imagine a user interface that asks you to specify your name within a text field. Your interface will also have *Cancel* and *OK* buttons. Pressing the Cancel button will erase any change you made to the text field, while the OK button will ensure that the changes you made will be put back into the variable that holds the value. The logic you setup for your text field editing can be done using the JavaBeans PropertyEditor interface. If you have an object that you would like to edit within a user interface, you will more than likely need to use a PropertyEditor to contain all of the logic for accepting changes and propagating them back to their variables.

WHY PROPERTY EDITORS?

Using the property listener objects, you can set up your property editors to pump changes back to the main variables that contain the properties. Furthermore, your property editor can be used by property sheets and allow you to create user interfaces to complex objects.

USING A PROPERTY EDITOR

Let's suppose for a moment that you have a complex object representing a street address that you would like to create a property editor for. What if you created a fancy property editor that allows you to use a graphical map and zoom in on the correct street? What if instead you wanted to create a simple set of text areas to represent the city, state, and ZIP code of a given address?

Remember, the representation of the property editor is irrelevant to the rest of the application. Indeed, the rest of the application could care less *how* the information is obtained, only that it is obtained and that it is correct. To use the `PropertyEditor`, you will need to create an object that inherits from the base class. Your property editor object will let you specify the listener to which you will send changes in the `addProperty-ChangeListener` method. In so doing, you can make sure that the `PropertyEditor` always sends change information to the proper listeners. The `removePropertyChangeListener` method should also be implemented if you plan on supporting property listeners with the editor:

```java
import java.beans.*;
public class StreetPropertyEditor implements PropertyEditor
{
    public void addPropertyChangeListener(
        PropertyChangeListener listener
    )
    {
    }

    public void removePropertyChangeListener(
        PropertyChangeListener listener
    )
    {
    }
}
```

You may also want to attach either the fancy graphical street address editor or the simple text area editors. You can do this by returning the fancy editor, which is a Java `Component` after all, in the `getCustomEditor` method. The method allows you to specify your own editor for a given property, and return it to any property sheet that needs to use it.

Part of the `PropertyEditor` interface specifies the `getCustomEditor` method. The `getCustomEditor` returns a Java `Component` object which can contain a user interface for the property editor. The `PropertyEditor` is responsible for hooking the custom component up to the `PropertyEditor`. Without doing so, your component will be unable to fire property change events. The custom editor should be responsible for walking down the list of listeners and invoking change events.

You will also want to implement and return true for the `supportsCustomEditor` method. The `supportsCustomEditor` method returns a boolean value which indicates to the calling object whether or not the property editor supports a custom GUI editor:

```
public abstract Component getCustomEditor()
public abstract boolean supportsCustomEditor()
```

■

Here, you extend our street property editor to include support for the custom editor objects:

```
import java.beans.*;
public class StreetPropertyEditor implements PropertyEditor
{
    public Component getCustomEditor()
    {
        StreetEditor editor = new StreetEditor();

        editor.setListeners(myListeners);
    }

    public boolean supportsCustomEditor()
    {
        return true;
    }
}
```

Your property editor will also need to implement methods to get and set values. The `getValue` method may be used by a peer object not associated with any kind of listener. The `setValue` method will probably be used in a similar fashion. The `getValue` and `setValue` methods act on complex Java objects. Two other methods, `getAsText` and `setAsText` send and receive strings representing the value of the object. Obviously, the string could easily be a serialized version of an object, or it could be a simple string representing a data type that requires manual parsing on both ends. In any event, your object and the calling object should be aware of the scheme being used.

Using the `getAsText` and `setAsText` methods, you can represent the value of your property, whether it is a fancy graphic or a simple primitive type, in a string format. No matter how you choose to represent the value, you should do so in a manner that allows the `setAsText` method to reset the property based on what it receives from the `getAsTextValue` method:

```
public abstract String getAsText()
public abstract void setAsText(
    String newValue
)
```

The `setValue` and `getValue` methods allow you to change and get the value of the property in its native Java Object format. Once you get the Object, you can cast it to the proper type. Using these methods, you need not convert your objects to a string format beforehand. These methods can be particularly useful for highly descriptive values, such as graphics or diagrams:

```
public abstract Object getValue()
public abstract void setValue(
    Object newValue
)
```

■

Your street editor will use these special `get` and `set` methods to store the value of the property if needed. If you were storing a Java Map Object, you could simply use the `getValue` method to obtain the value of the property. If, however, our object were simple enough to represent in a string format, you might as well use the `getAsText` method:

```
import java.beans.*;
public class StreetPropertyEditor implements PropertyEditor
{
    public Object getValue()
    {
    }

    public void setValue(
        Object obj
    )
    {
    }

    public String getAsText()
    {
    }
```

```
    public void setAsText(
        String text
    )
    {
    }
}
```

One of the more interesting portions of the `PropertyEditor` interface is the `getJavaInitializationString` method. This method allows you to specify a snippet of code that will be executed to initialize the value of the property. For example, if our street address were kept within an object called `StreetAddress`, you could very easily return the following Java code for a given set of data:

```
new StreetAddress("Prashant Sridharan", 95123);
```

 The `getJavaInitializationString` method allows you to specify Java code in a dynamic string form within compiled bytecode. The string code will then be executed as if it were part of the bytecode. With this method, you can pass an operation to be performed on a property, without having to know the exact operation at compile time:

```
public abstract String
getJavaInitializationString()
```

Therefore, the contents of the method would be as follows:

```
import java.beans.*;
public class StreetPropertyEditor implements PropertyEditor
{
    public String getJavaInitializationString()
    {
        return "new StreetAddress(\"Prashant Sridharan\",
95123)";
    }
}
```

Customizers

Sometimes your Beans will not need a `Customizer`. For extremely small Beans, or Beans that will not be passed around from person to person, customizers are not entirely necessary. You can very easily achieve the same functionality by just creating your own property sheets and property editors.

However, for large objects with several properties, or objects that could very easily be used by others, a customizer is very much required. Each person that uses your Bean may use a different Bean Machine. When your Bean is imported into a Bean Machine, the machine will more than likely introspect the Bean and then use its customizer object to generate a GUI editor or *wizard* for it. Therefore, it is important that you create a customizer for any object that will be used by others.

It is entirely possible that the customizer could be larger and more intricate than the Bean itself. The customizer should be built with the idea that its wizard-like interface will help the end-user configure and set up the Bean for use.

THE CUSTOMIZER INTERFACE

The Customizer interface is a simple abstract Java interface with three methods. Two of the methods concern the addition of listeners to the customizer object. The addPropertyChangeListener and removePropertyChangeListener methods should be implemented, and the object that implements the Customizer should plan on storing a series of listeners.

The following two methods allow the addition and removal of listener objects to the customizer. They should be implemented similar to normal property listener registration methods. The parameters should be valid Property-ChangeListener objects:

```
public abstract void addPropertyChangeListener(
    PropertyChangeListener listener
)
public abstract void removePropertyChangeListener(
    PropertyChangeListener listener
)
```

The third method, the setObject method simply accepts the Bean that is being customized and stores it internally. This allows the Customizer to perform whatever operations it requires on the Bean should it become necessary.

The setObject method allows the Customizer object to know of the Bean that it is customizing. It accepts one parameter; the source Bean:

```
public abstract void setObject(
    Object sourceBean
)
```

■

CREATING THE CUSTOMIZER

Normally, the customizer will be placed within the framework of the Bean Machine. When the machine launches the customizer it will place it inside a dialog box. The dialog box will be popped up and controlled by the machine, but everything inside the dialog box is owned by the customizer. In contrast, the property sheets are popped up and controlled by the Bean. In so doing, the look and feel of the machine's user interface will be lost because the Bean itself is controlling its own representation.

Creating a customizer is actually quite simple. Your object should implement the `java.beans.Customizer` object. In order for it to be placed within another GUI, the customizer should inherit from the AWT standard `java.awt.Component`:

```
import java.beans.*;

public class MySisterCustomizer extends Component
                                 implements Customizer
{
}
```

Because it inherits from the `Customizer` base class, your customizer must implement three methods. The first two involve property change listeners. Once again, your customizer should be sure to fire property change events for each property it is required to edit. Because the customizer's properties are not physically connected to the Bean they are from, in order to propagate changes back to the Bean you must fire property change events. The third method allows the customizer to get a target Bean with which it will work. Remember, for every Bean *class* there is one customizer. In order for the customizer to know which *instance* of the Bean it is editing, it must receive the Bean via the `setObject` call:

```
import java.beans.*;

public class MySisterCustomizer extends Component
                                 implements Customizer
{
    public void addPropertyChangeListener(
        PropertyChangeListener listener
    )
    {
    }
```

```
    public void removePropertyChangeListener(
        PropertyChangeListener listener
    )
    {
    }

    public void setObject(
        Object bean
    )
    {
    }
}
```

Every customizer should also have a constructor that sets up the GUI. This way, the customizer can be instantiated with ease by the Bean Machine as if it were an ordinary component (after all, the customizer is required to inherit from `Component`). The rest of the customizer's methods and operations are those that are required for the GUI to work. In this case you will simply create a text field within which we will edit our sister's name property. When the property is changed, you will fire a change event to all of the listeners, and change the property on the screen.

The `action` method shown here is the kind of property change event you will need to fire in your own customizer. In this case, whenever the user presses the OK button in the customizer's GUI, you will fire property change events to all of your listeners:

```
import java.beans.*;

public class MySisterCustomizer extends Component
                                implements Customizer
{
    public boolean action(
        Event evt,
        Object obj
    )
    {
        if(evt.target == okButton)
        {
        }
    }
}
```

If you wanted a more wizard-like look and feel to the customizer, you could create a series of panels that ask the user for information about the Bean. The Windows 95 operating system made the idea of a setup wizard very popular. The Microsoft operating system includes wizards for things as mundane as setting up a mouse, to more complicated matters such as activating the network. The point is that the wizard takes you through a series of easy-to-understand question and answer type screens after which the configuration is done automatically.

Once the customizer is completed, you need a way for the Bean to be attached to it. You can accomplish this by creating something called a `BeanInfo` class. The `BeanInfo` class will ensure that, during introspection, the Bean Machine will be aware that a customizer is present. Alternatively, the JavaBeans introspection mechanism will simply find the customizer for the Bean. If, however, you have several similar customizers floating around your environment, you will want to take the `BeanInfo` approach. `BeanInfo` objects are discussed in great detail in the next chapter on *Introspection*.

Properties in the Rainbow Button

When last you left your Rainbow Button, you had just finished developing the fundamental code and event mechanism for it. Using various `ButtonListeners` you were able to get our button to communicate with the picture area and sound machine rather easily. But, as you saw in Chapter 3, there was no way for us to include any kind of property or value within the Beans. Now that you have learned all about properties and the design patterns that are part of them, you can begin to develop our buttons and Beans into a more robust group of objects.

Button Properties

The `RainbowButton` is already a fairly robust object. Using the following code, you are able to invoke a GUI event to any number of listeners who desire information about your button Bean. One button push here will trigger an event on another Bean elsewhere via the event mechanism you have developed using `ButtonEvents` and `ButtonListeners`:

```
import java.awt.*;
public class RainbowButton extends Button
                          implements MouseListener
{
    private Color buttonColor;
    private String buttonText;

    Vector eventListeners;

    RainbowButton()
    {
        super();
```

```
    }

    public void instantiate()
    {
        // initialize the Vector
        eventListeners = new Vector();
    }

    public void addButtonListener(
        ButtonListener listener
    )
    {

        eventListeners.addElement(listener);
    }

    public void removeButtonListener(
        ButtonListener listener
    )
    {

        eventListeners.removeElement(listener);
    }

    public void mouseClicked(
        MouseEvent evt
    )
    {
        // first create a button event
        ButtonEvent buttonEvent = new ButtonEvent(this);

        // now notify all of the listeners of an event
        for(int x = 0; x < eventListeners.size(); x++)
        {
            // cast to proper type
            ButtonListener listener =
                (ButtonListener) eventListeners.elementAt(x);

            // invoke on the listener
            listener.fireButtonEvent(buttonEvent);
        }
    }
}
```

Now you want to introduce a PropertyChangeSupport object into our Bean. You will also need to create add and remove listener methods for our PropertyChangeListener objects to connect to. Looking briefly at our architectural design from Chapter 2, you see that you will not be using PropertyChangeListener objects at all. However, in order to ready this Bean for more uses beyond that of just this simple application, you will include the add and remove methods here:

```
import java.awt.*;
public class RainbowButton extends Button
                          implements MouseListener
{
    private Color buttonColor;
    private String buttonText;

    Vector eventListeners;
    PropertyChangeSupport propertyListeners;

    RainbowButton()
    {
        super();
    }

    public void instantiate()
    {
        // initialize the Vector
        eventListeners = new Vector();

        // initialize the property change support
        propertyListeners = new PropertyChangeSupport(this);
    }

    public void addButtonListener(
        ButtonListener listener
    )
    {
        eventListeners.addElement(listener);
    }

    public void removeButtonListener(
        ButtonListener listener
    )
    {
        eventListeners.removeElement(listener);
    }

    public void addPropertyChangeListener(
        PropertyChangeListener listener
    )
    {
        propertyListeners.addPropertyChangeListener(listener);
    }

    public void removePropertyChangeListener(
        PropertyChangeListener listener
    )
    {
        propertyListeners.removePropertyChangeListener(
            listener);
    }
```

```
public void mouseClicked(
    MouseEvent evt
)
{
    // first create a button event
    ButtonEvent buttonEvent = new ButtonEvent(this);

    // now notify all of the listeners of an event
    for(int x = 0; x < eventListeners.size(); x++)
    {
        // cast to proper type
        ButtonListener listener =
            (ButtonListener) eventListeners.elementAt(x);

        // invoke on the listener
        listener.fireButtonEvent(buttonEvent);
    }
}
}
```

This `RainbowButton` Bean has two properties that you want to make public. The first of these properties is the current color of the button, known as `buttonColor`. The second property is the text currently displayed on the button, the `buttonText`. You will also need to create accessors and mutators for these properties. In the mutator for the `buttonColor`, you will first obtain the old button color, fire a property change event to the various listeners, and change the button's color to the new color. You will need to make similar adjustments to the `buttonText` property's mutator. The accessors for both properties are straightforward and simply return the value as it is currently set for the property:

```
import java.awt.*;
public class RainbowButton extends Button
                        implements MouseListener
{
    private Color buttonColor;
    private String buttonText;

    public Color getButtonColor()
    {
        return buttonColor;
    }

    public void setButtonColor(
        Color newColor
    )
    {
```

```
        // get the old color
        Color oldColor = buttonColor;

        // fire the property change event
        propertyListeners.firePropertyChangeEvent(
            "buttonColor", oldColor, newColor);

        // set the old color
        buttonColor = newColor;
    }
… ommitted for brevity …
```

Picture Properties

The `PictureArea` object's only properties are the current image being displayed. You want other Beans to be able to see which `Image` is being displayed, but you don't want them to be able to set the `Image`. So, following our design pattern, you create a property called `currentImage` and a method called `getCurrentImage`. By omitting the `set-CurrentImage` method, you are telling any introspecting Beans that this property is for reading only:

```
public class PictureArea extends Panel implements ButtonListener
{
    private Image currentImage;

    PictureArea()
    {
        super();
    }

    public void instantiate()
    {
    }

    public void fireButtonEvent(
        ButtonEvent buttonEvent
    )
    {
    }

    public Image getCurrentImage()
    {
        return currentImage;
    }
}
```

The `SoundMachine` has but one property, the current `AudioClip` being played. You want users of the `SoundMachine` Bean to be able to find out what is playing, but not be able to set the property. Thus, like the `PictureArea` object, you must create an accessor-only property for the `currentSound`:

```
public class SoundMachine implements ButtonListener
{
    AudioClip currentSound;
    SoundMachine()
    {
    }

    public void instantiate()
    {
    }

    public AudioClip getCurrentSound()
    {
        return currentSound;
    }
    ... omitted for brevity ...
}
```

Creating a Wizard for the Rainbow Button

Now you will go about creating a simple setup wizard for the Rainbow-Button. The wizard will have three panels. The first panel will ask for the initial color of the button. Remember, the cool thing about our `RainbowButton` is that it changes its color at random. But, you still want users to be able to customize the initial color if they so choose. The second panel will ask for the text to be contained in the button. Finally, the third panel will show the selections that the user has made, and give them a place to finish their configuration.

BUILDING WIZARD PANELS

Basically, you want to create a simple card layout type interface. At the bottom of the interface, you will include *Next*, *Previous*, and *Cancel* buttons. When you reach the final panel, you will add a *Finish* button. The buttons will be grayed out or removed when they should not be used as shown in Figure 4.5.

The actual user interface is very simple. You will start with a simple `Panel`, and insert another `Panel` within it. The new panel's layout manager will be set to `CardLayout`, allowing us to add the various screens

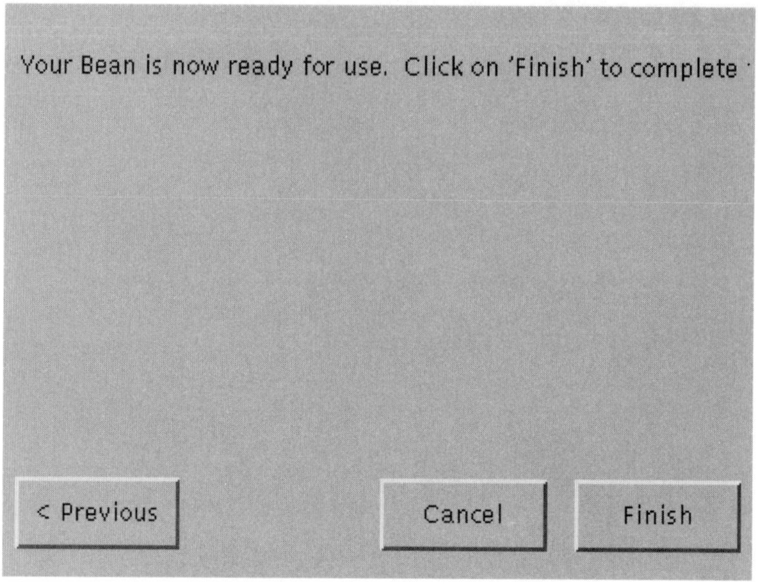

Your Bean is now ready for use. Click on 'Finish' to complete

| < Previous | | Cancel | Finish |

Figure 4.5: *Rainbow button wizard.*

for the wizard to the same panel. Meanwhile, the first panel will contain four buttons, which, depending on the moment, will be either active or inactive. The `finishButton`, for example, will not be active unless the final screen is showing.

IMPLEMENTING THE WIZARD

The design and infrastructure of the wizard is left to you, for this is not a user interface book. However, in your `action` method, you must still handle the button press for the `finishButton`. The following code snippet illustrates what must be done when the wizard is complete:

```
public boolean action(
    Event evt,
    Object obj
)
{
    if(evt.target == finishButton)
    {
        // create a property change event
        PropertyChangeEvent propertyEvent =
            New PropertyChangeEvent(
                oldButtonColor,
                "buttonColor",
                newButtonColor);

        // go through the list of listeners and fire the event
```

```
            propertyListeners.firePropertyChange(propertyEvent);
        }
    }
```

INTEGRATING THE WIZARD

Simply declaring a `RainbowButtonCustomizer` object and placing it where it can be obtained via the Bean Machine's class loader will integrate the wizard with the Bean. The Bean Machine's introspection algorithm will be able to locate and load the `customizer` object. Once the object is obtained, the machine will place it in a window and allow it to execute when it is time to customize the Bean. The next chapter discusses Bean introspection in great detail. For more information on how Bean Machines work and use introspection, consult Part 3 of this book, and Chapter 7, *GUI Builders,* in particular.

Summary

Without properties, Beans would not be able to have any public state. It is important to recognize when and where to use a property, and hopefully this chapter does a good job of explaining that to you. Once you have a collection of properties and events inside your Bean, you need a means for other Beans to inquire and discover those properties and events. Introspection is a powerful tool that can be used by all Beans to determine the nature of those objects with which they communicate. The next chapter discusses the Introspection API and how to implement Beans using it.

Kinds of Beans

When you go out to buy your next bag of beans, you may be slightly perplexed at the various labels placed on your selection. Is it a blend, or a dark roast, or a varietal?

A blend is a mixture of many Beans, all from different countries. Often, the word blend appears after the creative name of the mixture. As an even further side note, the coffee industry employs many marketing types whose only business it is to come up with names for blends. This is somewhat akin to being in charge of naming the breakfast combos at Denny's.

A dark roast is a strange label that can mean all sorts of things. If the roast is termed a Vienna, the coffee will have a medium-brown color with very little acidity. It should be noted that Starbucks coffee is often of the Vienna variety. An Italian or French roast, on the other hand, is almost totally black with a flavor that is more indicative of the time the Beans spend under the fire than the origin of the plant from which it came.

Meanwhile, the varietal roast means that the entire bag of Beans come from one single country of origin. In their exceptional book, *Coffee Basics*, Kevin Knox and Julie Sheldon Huffaker refer to the varietal roast as single-origin since all the Beans share the same origin.

CHAPTER 5

Bean Introspection

An overview of introspection?

Introspection APIs

Introspecting another Bean

Using introspection

One of the really interesting aspects of JavaBeans development is that you can create your Beans to interact with one another without ever knowing the specifics of the other Beans in your system. At runtime, a process called *introspection* is used to allow a Bean to discover the properties, methods, and events of another Bean. This enables you to build your Beans without knowing the internal arrangement of the other Bean. This chapter examines the nature of introspection in the Java language and how it is implemented in Beans. You will see how to introspect other Beans, as well as how to prepare your own Beans for introspection by other Beans. This is perhaps one of the most important chapters in this book because, using the techniques described here, your Beans can be truly plug-and-play.

What is Introspection?

The definition of what introspection is has been briefly outlined, but let's get more into the details here. This, like the JavaBeans event model, would never have been possible without the latest revision of the Java Developer's Kit (JDK). The new JDK supports a notion called *reflection* which was discussed in Chapter 1, *Advanced Java*. Reflection is the fundamental means used by the Beans introspection routines to get information about an object. JavaBeans also supports its own kind of introspection with which it can determine Beans properties, events, methods, and parameters by using reflection in concert with the design patterns that have been discussed in the previous chapters.

Introspection and Java

The driving force behind allowing introspection in JavaBeans is that when you choose to write Beans, you want people to use only the Java language. It may seem odd, but you could very easily intersperse Beans written in other languages with your JavaBeans. This can be done using any number of techniques ranging from native method calls to an external construct like CORBA. However, in giving your Beans an introspective capability, the engineers behind JavaBeans allowed you to build entirely in Java if you so choose.

Handling Your Own Introspection

Introspection is available for both simple Beans and complex Beans. Simple Beans need not provide any unnecessary overhead to support introspection since it is ingrained in both the Java language as well as the many design patterns that have been pointed out as you go along. So long as your Beans follow the design pattern and are written in Java, they will be able to be introspected by other Beans (see Figure 5.1). You, as a Bean developer, will not need to do any additional work.

But, JavaBeans is flexible enough to allow you to handle your own introspection. Perhaps your Beans do not wish to make everything public, and in those cases they may provide a simple `BeanInfo` object to funnel back its properties, methods, and events. The `BeanInfo` object was briefly touched on in Chapter 4, *Bean Properties*, but will be explored in detail in a moment.

Design Patterns for Properties

Many of the design patterns for properties were discussed in Chapter 4. While you won't read about each and every one of them once again in

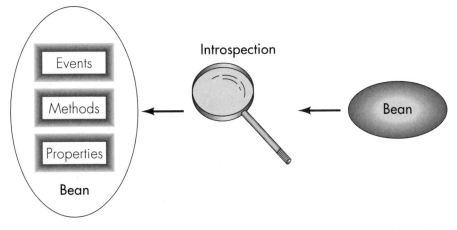

Figure 5.1: *Introspection gives you insight into an object's construction.*

this section, you will be directed to Chapter 4 in order to gain a better understanding of them. The design patterns for properties do not concern the names of the properties themselves, but dictate the names of the accessors and mutators for each property. As discussed then, an accessor is a special function that you may use to obtain the value stored in the property. Meanwhile, a mutator is a special function that you may use to set the value stored in the property. Alternatively, they are referred to as *getters* and *setters*.

Design Patterns for Events

The design patterns for events are discussed in great detail in Chapter 3, *Bean Events*. Once again, you will be directed to this chapter so that you can get a good grasp on how events are constructed in JavaBeans. Usually, the design patterns for events do not concern the names of the events, but rather how the listeners and firing methods for those events are built.

The facilities that make all of this possible are included as part of the `java.beans` package supplied on the CD-ROM that accompanies this book.

As part of the JavaBeans infrastructure, the introspection objects provided with JavaBeans is easy to use, extend, and implement in your applications. While the documentation is somewhat lacking, the following section should outline the APIs associated with introspection.

Beans and Introspection APIs

Introspection is a valuable resource that is available for all Java objects, not simply Beans classes. JavaBeans simply builds on top of the low-level reflection classes in the JDK and gives you a better interface to Bean objects retrieved or discovered through introspection. You've taken a look at a few of these objects in Chapter 4 when the `Customizer` object was covered, but now you'll get a closer look at how these objects work.

Bean Descriptors

A `BeanDescriptor` allows you to get information about a Bean's structure. Using it, you may obtain the name of the Bean's class, its customizer class, and its display name. A Bean descriptor can be retrieved using the `BeanInfo` object.

CONSTRUCTORS

There are two separate constructors for the Bean descriptor. The first constructor is for Bean classes without a customizer, while the second is for Beans with customizers. Both constructors throw `Introspection-Exceptions` if the required parameters are invalid or if the constructor cannot introspect them.

 The first constructor is for Beans without a customizer and accepts one parameter, the Bean that is to be described:

```
public BeanDescriptor(
    Class bean
)
```

The second constructor is for Beans with a customizer and accepts a parameter for the Bean to be described as well as that Bean's customizer object:

```
public BeanDescriptor(
    Class bean,
    Class customizer
)
```

■

There are three methods that are available for Bean descriptors. The first of these methods merely returns the Bean that is being described. The second method is for the retrieval of the Bean's customizer. The last method is used to retrieve and specify a more descriptive name for the Bean than simply the type that it is called in code.

 All three of these methods can be invoked on a `Bean-Descriptor` object. None of them accept parameters, and none can throw exceptions.

```
public Class getBeanClass()
```

The `getBeanClass` method returns an instance of the Bean being described by the `BeanDescriptor` object.

```
public Class getCustomizerClass()
```

The `getCustomizerClass` method returns an instance of the customizer belonging to the Bean being described in the `BeanDescriptor` object.

```
public Class getDisplayName()
```

Beans may have a *display name* that is different from the name given to it in code. For example, you could have a pitcher Bean as you did in Chapter 3, and give it a slightly more descriptive name such *as Pitcher Bean by Jenny's House of Beans*. Leaving this method null will return the name of the Bean as it is referred to in code.

■

Bean Information

A `BeanInfo` class is optional, but any Bean that wishes to provide information to any introspecting Bean may want to implement one of these objects. Typically, introspection will get all information pertaining to a given Bean. However, in some instances, a developer may want to restrict or control what information is provided about a Bean. In order to control the information about a Bean's methods, properties, or events, you may want to construct a `BeanInfo` class to go along with your Bean.

It's important to note that when you construct a `BeanInfo` object for your Bean, you need not implement every method. Indeed, those methods not implemented in a `BeanInfo` object will be determined through low-level reflection and normal introspection routines. This way, you can pick and choose which parts of introspection you wish to override. In concert with the `SimpleBeanInfo` object that will be discussed in a moment, you can get very fine-grained control over the introspection of your Bean components.

The BeanInfo interface contains only abstract methods. You will need to extend it yourself or use the SimpleBeanInfo object. The SimpleBeanInfo object implements all of the abstract methods in the BeanInfo interface. You can then override the methods that you choose.

CONSTRUCTORS

There are no special constructors for the BeanInfo object. It is a simple, parameterless method that does minimal initialization of the object.

The constructor for the BeanInfo object:

```
public BeanInfo()
```

■

METHODS

The first method to examine is the BeanDescriptor method. As has been discussed, a BeanDescriptor allows you to get specific information about the structure of a Bean, not necessarily its innards. Using the BeanInfo object, you can return the BeanDescriptor to any object that desires it.

The getBeanDescriptor method may return null if it wishes for the BeanDescriptor to be determined through low-level reflection or normal Bean introspection:

```
public abstract BeanDescriptor getBeanDescriptor()
```

■

Sometimes Beans may have a default event that will more than likely be used by other Beans. More often than not, this event will be fired by the Bean, and is therefore the *default* event for the Bean. The getDefaultEventIndex method returns the index in the event set for this event.

If you wish to provide a default event at all, you must specify it in the BeanInfo object. There is no way for normal Bean introspection using low-level reflection to discover a default event. The method returns an integer referring to the index in the EventSetDescriptor for the default event. You may also return −1 if there is no default event:

```
public abstract int getDefaultEventIndex()
```

■

Similarly, the Bean may have a default property. The default property, like the default event, is the property most likely to be updated or changed by the Bean or by an event triggered on the Bean.

Like its event counterpart, the default property cannot be discovered through normal introspection. Therefore, if you wish to specify a default property, you must specify it here. The returned value is that of the index of the property in the `PropertySetDescriptor`. You may also return –1 if there is no default property:

```
public abstract int getDefaultPropertyIndex()
```

■

The `EventSetDescriptor` will be discussed in a moment, but to summarize its purpose, the `EventSetDescriptor` is a sequence of events that can be triggered by the Bean.

The `EventSetDescriptor` is a list of all events that can be fired by the Bean. You must construct the event descriptor array to be returned. Note that since you have control over how the event set array is built, you can use that information to specify correct values in the `getDefaultEventIndex` method. The method returns an array of `EventSetDescriptors`:

```
public abstract EventSetDescriptor[]

getEventSetDescriptors()
```

■

Often, Beans can specify an icon that is to be used to represent it in a GUI builder as shown in Figure 5.2.

The `getIcon` method returns an `Image` object. The `getIcon` method is not required since Beans are not required to have icons. If you wish to support icons, you may choose one of four different kinds of icons (16×16 pixels, 32×32 pixels, either black and white or color). It is recommended, should you choose to implement only one kind of icon rather than all four, that you implement 16×16 color. Typically, your icons should contain a transparent background so that they do not interfere with the GUI of the builder or toolbox in which they are used.

The `getIcon` method is not required. If you wish to implement icons at all, however, you should specify them here. There is no way for normal introspection to determine or obtain icons for a Bean. The method may return null if icons are not to be supported. The `pixelFormat` parameter should be one of the four constants:

```
public abstract Image getIcon(
    int pixelFormat
)
```

■

Figure 5.2: *Beans can have icons that are used in a GUI builder.*

MethodDescriptors are discussed in a moment, but in short, they are a list of methods that can be invoked on a Bean. The `getMethodDescriptors` method returns an array of `MethodDescriptors` specifying each method available in the Bean. Note that during normal introspection, all of the methods available in a Bean can be retrieved. However, by using a `BeanInfo` class and overriding this method, you can explicitly list only those methods that you desire to be made available.

 The `getMethodDescriptors` method is optional. Regular Bean introspection can obtain the information concerning the methods available in a Bean without much difficulty. If you wish to implement the method, you should do so merely to control which methods are made available to other Beans.

However, if you wish to implement the method for completeness' sake, you may return null here if the information is to be obtained by automatic introspection:

```
public abstract MethodDescriptor[]
getMethodDescriptors()
```

■

A property descriptor, like its method and event counterparts, is used to obtain a list of properties available for changing or updating in a Bean. Once again, overriding this method in the `BeanInfo` class can give you control over which properties are exposed to introspecting Beans.

 The `getPropertyDescriptors` method need not be implemented. Properties can also be determined through regular Bean introspection, but you may choose to implement the method here to control which properties are exposed. The method may return null and the information will be obtained through normal introspection routines:

```
public abstract PropertyDescriptor[]
getPropertyDescriptors()
```

■

CONSTANTS

There are four constants in the `BeanInfo` object definition, all pertaining to the use of icons. They should be used with the `getIcon` method.

 The four constants are integers with fairly obvious names. They represent the pixel dimensions of the icon as well as whether the icon is in color or black and white (monochromatic):

```
public final static int ICON_COLOR_16x16
public final static int ICON_COLOR_32x32
public final static int ICON_MONO_16x16
public final static int ICON_MONO_32x32
```

■

Simple Bean Information

Because every method in the `BeanInfo` object is marked as abstract, they must be reimplemented somewhere else. This can be tedious for those authors who wish to implement only some of their own introspection, not all of it. For this reason, a `SimpleBeanInfo` object is provided. The `SimpleBeanInfo` object implements every method in the `BeanInfo` object, but with default null or no-op values (see Figure 5.3).

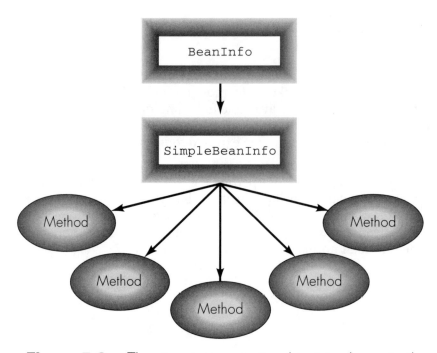

Figure 5.3:   The `SimpleBeanInfo` *object implements the* `BeanInfo` *object so you don't have to.*

In so doing, it allows you to create your own `BeanInfo` objects for your Beans without having to go through the same trouble. The next section shows how implement your own `SimpleBeanInfo` object and you will discover that extending the `SimpleBeanInfo` object and choosing which functions to implement is much easier than implementing the entire `BeanInfo` interface.

Feature Descriptors

A feature descriptor is the common base class for all of the descriptor objects that will be discussed in a moment. Since descriptors are used very frequently in Beans introspection, let's take a moment to see how the feature descriptor is constructed, and the various methods and variables contained within it that facilitate introspection of various forms.

When you speak of a feature, you are talking about a method, an event, a property, or a parameter for a Bean class. For example, a `MethodDescriptor` is a specialized `FeatureDescriptor` that concerns the various methods in a given Bean. Similarly, a `PropertyDe-scriptor` refers to property features, a `ParameterDescriptor` refers to parameter features, and an `EventDescriptor` refers to event features. Because these other descriptors inherit from the `FeatureDe-scriptor`, all of the methods in this section are available for use by other descriptor objects.

CONSTRUCTOR

There is only one constructor for the `FeatureDescriptor` object. It is a fairly nondescript method that accepts no parameters and initializes all the data contained in the object.

The `FeatureDescriptor` object has one simple constructor that accepts no parameters:

```
public FeatureDescriptor()
```

■

METHODS

The first major method in the `FeatureDescriptor` object is one that returns an `Enumeration` of all the attribute names in the feature. An attribute is a tag of sorts for a Bean. It is neither a variable nor a property, but is instead a simple means to label a Bean. For example, if you had a suite of Beans that implemented buttons, sliders, and text areas, you could tag them all with a certain attribute. The attribute could say something like *3-D widgets* or represent a number for its revision like *3*. The attribute can also be a full-fledged Java object in its own right.

The `attributeNames` method returns an `Enumeration`, a Java construct that lists all of the names of attributes set with the `setValue` method:

```
public Enumeration attributeNames()
```

■

The `setValue` and `getValue` methods are accessors and mutators for a given attribute. The `setValue` method accepts two parameters, the name of the attribute as well as the value that will be associated with the attribute's name. The `getValue` method accepts one parameter, the name of the attribute, and returns the value associated with it.

The `setValue` and `getValue` methods allow you to associate a name and a value for the name with the feature described in the descriptor. The `attributeName` is the Java variable name for the attribute, and the `initial-Value` is the value that the attribute will take initially:

```
public Object getValue(
    String attributeName
)
public void setValue(
    String attributeName,
    Object initialValue
)
```

■

The `getName` method gives you a means to pass back the name of the Bean as it is referred to in code. For instance, you may have a spreadsheet Bean whose class name is `MicrosoftExcelMiscalculation-Bean`. You can pass back that value in the `getName` method.

The `getName` method returns the name of the feature as it is referred to in code:

```
public String getName()
```

■

The `getDisplayName` method allows you to specify a different name for a feature than the name given to it in code. For example, you may have a button Bean whose programmatic name is `ButtonBean`, but whose name you want it to be known to the outside world as being `Pete's Wicked Button`. Using the display name attribute, you can set the feature to be referred to as something different than in its code.

The `getDisplayName` method allows you to refer to a feature's name as something more descriptive than that which is available in code. If this function is not implemented, a call to it will result in the return of the value specified by `getName`:

```
public String getDisplayName()
```

■

To further enable you to customize the representation of your Bean, you can specify a short description for it. For example, instead of referring to `ButtonBean` as `Pete's Wicked Button`, you can have this method return the value `Pete's Wicked Button by Beans R Us, Inc.`

The `getShortDescription` method returns a string corresponding to a more robust description of a feature. If you choose not to implement this method, it will default to returning the value of the `getDisplayName` method:

```
public String getShortDescription()
```

■

There are also a couple of flags that you can set that give you slightly more control over how a feature is used. An expert flag can help you distinguish those features that should be used by expert users and those that are for more general use. JavaBeans itself does not enforce that particular flag, but a given GUI builder or Bean Machine may wish to display only certain features.

In addition, you can specify a feature as hidden or not hidden. Once again, JavaBeans itself does not enforce this flag, and simply specifying a feature as hidden will in no way affect its introspection; it will still be available to introspecting Beans. However, Bean Machines will be able to determine whether a feature should be made visible or not by checking this flag.

 Two flags, hidden and expert, give you some control over how Beans will be represented in Bean Machines. The `isExpert` and `setExpert` methods can get and set the value of the expert flag, respectively. The `setExpert` method accepts one parameter specifying the new value of the flag:

```
public boolean isExpert()
public void setExpert(
    boolean newExpertValue
)
```

The hidden flag is accessed and mutated using the `isHidden` and `set-Hidden` methods. Once again, the `setHidden` method accepts one parameter specifying the new value of the flag:

```
public boolean isHidden()
public void setHidden(
    boolean newHiddenValue
)
```

■

Event Set Descriptors

An event set descriptor describes the events that a Bean can fire. As discussed in Chapter 3, an event is delivered as a method call on a listener. Registration is handled through `EventListener` objects, and the events themselves are `EventObjects`. The `EventSetDescriptor` object inherits from `FeatureDescriptor` and is the means required to group events together.

CONSTRUCTOR

There are four constructors to the EventSetDescriptor object, each offering a different amount of control over the initialization of the object. The first constructor handles the simplest case of event handling and firing, when you have a single event triggered on a single class of event listener.

 The first argument to this constructor is the class from which the event will be invoked. Then, you need to specify the stringified name of the event. In other words, if the event is called a pitchEvent, the string you must pass is pitchEvent. Be careful to capitalize properly.

You should also specify the interface for the target class to which events will be fired. You must also pass the stringified name of the method that is called on the listener end. In other words, if the method that is called by the firing of the event is called receivePitch, the string that should be passed is receivePitch.

Using this constructor, you assume that the registration methods for adding and removing a listener on the sourceClass are constructed using the design patterns discussed in Chapter 3:

```
public EventSetDescriptor(
    Class sourceClass,
    String eventName,
    Class listenerInterface,
    String listenerMethodName
)
```

■

The second constructor is for a slightly more complex case when there are several methods that can be invoked by an event on a listener and when you want control over the add and remove registration methods on the listener itself.

 This constructor is oodles more complicated than the first one. The source class, name of the event, and listener interface parameters should all be specified once again. However, three new parameters must be included to use this constructor.

The first of these new parameters is an array of strings consisting of the names of methods on the listener interface that can accept the kind of event specified in the event name parameter. Unlike the first constructor, here you can specify more than one listener method.

Additionally, the constructor accepts two strings corresponding to the names of the add and remove registration methods. In the first constructor, assume that the add and remove registration methods follow accepted design patterns by prepending the words *add* and *remove*, respectively, to the name of the listener interface. Here, you can obtain control over how the add and remove methods are defined:

```
public EventSetDescriptor(
    Class sourceClass,
    String eventName,
    Class listenerInterface,
    String listenerMethodNames[],
    String addListenerRegistrationMethodName,
    String removeListenerRegistrationMethodName)
```

■

METHODS

There are several methods that can be invoked on the `EventSet-Descriptor` object to obtain the information that is set either through further introspection by the object or through the constructors specified earlier above. The first few of these methods are fairly obvious from their names and correspond directly to data set in some of the constructors.

 This method retrieves the `Method` to be used on the source class for add or remove registration of a listener for the kind of event represented in the object:

```
public Method getAddListenerMethod()
public Method getRemoveListenerMethod()
```

The first method gets an array of `MethodDescriptors` corresponding to the methods that are invoked by firing the event in this object. The second method returns an array of Method objects instead of `MethodDescriptor` objects:.

```
public MethodDescriptor[]
getListenerMethodDescriptors()
public Method[] getListenerMethods()
```

This method returns the `Class` for the listener interface:

```
public Class getListenerType()
```

■

The next few methods in the `EventSetDescriptor` object are slightly different and offer information on the kinds of events and event listeners contained in the object itself. The first two of these methods is the `isInDefaultEventSet` method and its analog `setInDefault-`

`EventSet` method. A default event set is the basic set of events that can be fired by a Bean.

 The method returns true if the event set represented by the `EventSetDescriptor` object is part of the default event set. It defaults to true if it is not implemented:

```
public boolean isInDefaultEventSet()
```

The `setInDefaultEventSet` method allows you to specify whether or not the events represented by the `EventSetDescriptor` object are part of the default event set. As mentioned, the events are, by default, part of the default event set. This method affords you some control over this characteristic.

```
public void setInDefaultEventSet(
    boolean partOfDefaultSet
)
```

■

The `setUnicast` and `isUnicast` methods allow you to set the nature of the listener registration method. As discussed in Chapter 3, a unicast event is one that only allows one listener at a time, whereas a multicast event allows several listeners. You can set and get that characteristic using these methods.

 The `setUnicast` method accepts one parameter that specifies, as a `boolean` value, whether or not the event set is unicast. You can obtain the unicast status of the event through the `getUnicast` method:

```
public boolean getUnicast()
public void setUnicast(
    boolean isUnicast
)
```

■

Property Descriptors

A property descriptor is the fundamental unit in JavaBeans for representing properties for introspection. Using the object, your Beans can handle their own introspection for given properties. Furthermore, you can control the exposure of certain properties, even though they may be publicly readable. Often, your Bean may wish to prevent other Beans from introspecting and discovering all the properties it contains. In such cases, you will want to handle your own introspection.

The first constructor for the `PropertyDescriptor` object assumes that the accessor and mutator methods follow standard JavaBeans design patterns. For example, if the name of the property is `jennyButton`, then the accessor and mutator should be `getJennyButton` and `setJenny-Button`, respectively. The constructor takes two arguments, the name of the property and the class within which the property exists.

 The constructor for the `PropertyDescriptor` object accepts two parameters, the name of the property and the class in which the accessor and mutator for the property may be found. The accessor and mutator are then discovered by using JavaBeans design patterns. An `IntrospectionException` is thrown on any errors:

```
public PropertyDescriptor(
    String propertyName,
    Class sourceClass
) throws IntrospectionException
```

■

The second constructor allows you to specify the names of the accessor and mutator methods yourself by passing in Java `Method` objects.

 This constructor accepts two new parameters, the names of the accessor and mutator methods. The methods corresponding to the names must be present in the `source-Class` variable. In this case, no introspection of the sourceClass will be done since you already have a handle on the accessor and mutator. An `IntrospectionException` is thrown on any errors:

```
public PropertyDescriptor(
    String propertyName,
    Class sourceClass,
    String accessorName,
    String mutatorName
) throws IntrospectionException
```

■

This third constructor lets you specify the actual methods for the accessor and mutator. The target class is omitted because it is only used to determine the class for the accessor and mutator methods. Here, since you are actually getting the methods themselves, you need not specify the class.

In this constructor you accept two parameters for the actual accessor and mutator `Methods`. Once again, no further introspection will be done, mainly because no source class is present to introspect. The accessor and mutator methods should exist, otherwise an `IntrospectionException` will be thrown:

```
public PropertyDescriptor(
    String propertyName,
    Method accessorMethod,
    Method mutatorMethod
) throws IntrospectionException
```

■

METHODS

The first two methods in the `PropertyDescriptor` object concern a property editor. I spoke in detail of property editors and property sheets in Chapter 4. Normal introspection can determine only the qualities of a property, not whether it has an editor associated with it. Usually, the first method will return null indicating that no property editor has been created for this specific property. You can use the second method to set up a property editor for a given property.

The property editor may be set and retrieved using these two variables. The first method sets the property editor to the value contained in `editorClass`. The second method returns that editor if it exists. It may return null if no property editor exists for the property:

```
public void setPropertyEditorClass(
    Class editorClass
)
public Class getPropertyEditorClass()
```

■

This method allows you to retrieve the type for the given property. The value is returned as a Java `Class` object, and can very easily represent simple types like `int` and `char`.

The type of the property can be anything from a simple type to a complex Java object. Using this method, the type of a property can be easily returned to introspecting Beans:

```
public Class getPropertyType()
```

■

The next two methods allow you to retrieve the accessor and mutator methods for the property. They are returned as Java `Method` objects, and may at times return null.

 The accessor and mutator for a property handle the retrieval and storage of values for the property. Using these two methods, the accessor and mutator of the property can be returned:

```
public Method getReadMethod()
public Method getWriteMethod()
```

■

As you saw in Chapter 4, a property is considered bound, sometimes referred to as *constrained* or *vetoable*, when it fires a change event upon being modified. Using these two methods, you can set or get the bound quality of the property.

 By setting the bound quality of the property using the `set-Bound` method, the property will fire change events whenever it is modified. The current state of the bound quality may be retrieved using the `isBound` accessor:

```
public boolean isBound()
public void setBound(
    boolean newBoundValue
)
```

■

A property is considered to be constrained when it fires a vetoable change event upon being modified. Unlike a bound property, a constrained property may have its modification overridden by another Bean. When the property is modified, it first fires a vetoable change event to everyone listening to it. Any listener may then object to the change and cause the change to not happen. These two methods set the constrained characteristic of the property.

 A constrained property allows other Beans to object and override to changes in a property. Using these two methods, the constrained quality of a Bean may be obtained and changed. A property may be marked as constrained using the `setConstrained` method, while the value may be retrieved using the `isConstrained` accessor:

```
public boolean is Constrained()
public void setConstrained(
    boolean newConstrainedValue
)
```

■

Indexed Property Descriptors

In Chapter 4 you learned about the notion of an indexed property. An indexed property is a property whose representation is that of an array. Its accessors get the value of the property at a specific location, or index. Its mutators modify the value of the property at a specific index of its own. As was discussed, indexed properties also provide simple non-indexed accessors and mutators to get the property as a whole. This `IndexedPropertyDescriptor` object inherits from the `Property-Descriptor` object, so you can use all of the methods from the `PropertyDescriptor` section as well.

CONSTRUCTORS

The three constructors for the `IndexedPropertyDescriptor` object set various portions of the `IndexedPropertyDescriptor` object. The first constructor sets an object with default accessor and mutator methods that follow the standard JavaBeans design patterns. As discussed in Chapter 4, the standard JavaBeans design pattern for an accessor is to prepend the word *get* to the name of the property.

This constructor for the `IndexedPropertyDescriptor` object gets simply the property name and the class to which the property belongs. The `IntrospectionException` must be caught:

```
public IndexedPropertyDescriptor(
    String propertyName,
    Class sourceClass
) throws IntrospectionException
```

■

The second constructor for the `IndexedPropertyDescriptor` object allows you to specify the accessors and mutators by hand. It also gives you the opportunity to specify the name for the accessors and mutators of the property as a whole.

This constructor gives you the ability to specify the accessor and mutator methods in addition to the name of the property and the class to which the property belongs. Once again, the `IntrospectionException` must be caught. The accessor and mutator names may be set null, if desired. Typically, the `set` methods will be set to null if the property is read-only. In addition, the accessor and mutator for setting the property as a whole can be null if the property must be indexed:

```
public IndexedPropertyDescriptor(
    String propertyName,
```

```
    Class sourceClass,
    String getPropertyAsAWholeMethodName,
    String setPropertyAsAWholeMethodName,
    String getPropertyByIndexMethodName,
    String setPropertyByIndexMethodName
) throws IntrospectionException
```

∎

If you already have a handle on the methods you wish to use for accessors and mutators, you may specify the Method object in the constructor's signature using the third constructor for the IndexedProperty-Descriptor object.

 Once again, this constructor takes the name of the property, but this time it omits the source class for the property. However, the accessors and mutators are set using Java Method objects. Typically, this constructor will be used after you have done some kind of introspection on your own. Those Methods that you do not wish to be implemented may be set to null:

```
public IndexedPropertyDescriptor(
    String propertyName,
    Method getPropertyAsAWholeMethod,
    Method setPropertyAsAWholeMethod,
    Method getPropertyByIndexMethod,
    Method setPropertyByIndexMethod
) throws IntrospectionException
```

∎

METHODS

The three methods available to the IndexedPropertyDescriptor object allow you to get information about how the property is stored, read, and written. Typically, you will use these methods to read and write your properties and cast them to the appropriate type. The first of these methods simply returns the Java Class whose type the parameter is, enabling you to cast your property more efficiently.

 The getIndexedPropertyType method allows you to get the type of the indexed property described in this object:

```
public Class getIndexedPropertyType()
```

∎

The last two methods allow you to retrieve the indexed accessors and mutators. To obtain the other accessor and mutator, use the routines described in the PropertyDescriptor object section.

These methods allow you to get the indexed read and write methods for the property in the object:

```
public Method getIndexedReadMethod()
public Method getIndexedWriteMethod()
```

■

Method Descriptors

A method descriptor describes the construction of a method in a Bean that can be used by other Beans for direct invocation. Typically, these things can be discovered using JavaBeans' own introspection, but should you desire control over how and when methods are exposed, implementing a `MethodDescriptor` object would be in your best interest.

CONSTRUCTORS

There are two constructors for a method descriptor object. The first of these constructors merely initializes the object for later use given a simple Java `Method` object. The `Method` object represents the method that will be stored in the descriptor. The second constructor accepts a parameter descriptor as well. The `ParameterDescriptor` will be discussed object in a moment, but as its name implies its purpose is to list and describe the parameters in a method.

The first constructor for the `MethodDescriptor` object simply initializes the object with a method:

```
public MethodDescriptor(
    Method method
)
```

The second constructor also adds a `ParameterDescriptor` object:

```
public MethodDescriptor(
    Method method,
    ParameterDescriptor parameters
)
```

■

METHODS

The `MethodDescriptor` object has only two methods, both of which retrieve the values set in the constructor. Using these methods, you can get the value of the method represented by the descriptor as well as the parameters that go with it.

 The two methods for retrieving the `Method` and `ParameterDescriptor` object are fairly straightforward. Unfortunately, the JavaBeans specification does not call for accessor methods to set the same variables. This is an oversight that should be corrected by the JavaBeans developers:

```
public Method getMethod()
public ParameterDescriptor[]
getParameterDescriptors()
```

■

Parameter Descriptors

The `ParameterDescriptor` is, in name only an object in its own right. In fact, the `ParameterDescriptor` object is nothing but an inherited `FeatureDescriptor`. No new state or methods are added to it. In the future, the JavaBeans development team may wish to make the `ParameterDescriptor` more robust, but for the time being your applications should use it for parameters rather than the functional equivalent parent class, `FeatureDescriptor`.

Introspectors

As its name suggests, the `Introspector` object is the heart and soul of Bean introspection. The `Introspector` object will first look into the `BeanInfo` object for a corresponding Bean. Failing to find a `BeanInfo` object in either the local search path or the defined `CLASSPATH`, the `Introspector` object will do its own low level introspection on a Bean and return the proper `BeanInfo` and related information.

CONSTRUCTOR
The constructor is a simple constructor that initializes the `Introspector` object and readies it for invocations.

 The Introspector object's constructor accepts no parameters and is extremely easy to use:

```
public Introspector()
```

■

JavaBeans Developer's Resource

METHODS

So far, many of your introspection methods have held the caveat that you should check for capitalization. The first method in the `Introspector` object does this for you automatically. After being passed a string, the method will return another string whose capitalization follows accepted JavaBeans guidelines.

Most notable of these guidelines is that the initial letter of the string should be lowercase, while the remaining letters of the string should be capitalized only if they mark the start of a new *virtual* word. For example, the variable `jennysbuttonbar` should be capitalized as `jennys-ButtonBar`. While the method will not intelligently determine this capitalization, it will handle the initial conversion of the first letter to a lowercase letter. It will, however, leave the capitalization intact if the entire variable is capitalized, presuming that the variable represents the name of a constant.

The `decapitalize` utility method will convert the capitalization of a string to that of accepted JavaBeans guidelines:

```
public static String decapitalize(
    String featureName
)
```

■

The second method returns the `BeanInfo` for the given object. If a `BeanInfo` object is not found to exist, regular Beans introspection will create one and return it to you by using the low-level reflection routines that are part of the Java language.

The `getBeanInfo` method returns the `BeanInfo` object for the specified class object. For objects that do not specify their own `BeanInfo` object explicitly, low-level reflection is used to determine the `BeanInfo` object. For those classes that implement some, but not all, of the `BeanInfo` methods, reflection will be used to fill in the gaps. An `IntrospectionException` is thrown if an error is produced:

```
public static BeanInfo getBeanInfo(
    Class sourceClass
) throws IntrospectionException
```

■

The second version of the method above adds a unique identifier. Sometimes, you will want Beans to introspect *up to a point*. For these cases, a stop class can specified in the `getBeanInfo` method to cease introspection at a certain class. Once a class of the specified type is found, introspection stops and the `BeanInfo` object is returned incomplete. This can be a real time saver if all you want to use introspection for is to determine the basic makeup of an object.

 This version of the `getBeanInfo` method also specifies a stop class which, upon encountering, introspection will stop and return an incomplete `BeanInfo`. An `IntrospectionException` will be thrown on any errors:

```
public static BeanInfo(
    Class sourceClass,
    Class stopClass
) throws IntrospectionException
```

■

The next two methods allow you to get or set the search path for a `BeanInfo` object. Usually, the `BeanInfo` object will be obtained using the externally set `CLASSPATH` variable. However, you may specify your own search path here. Be forewarned, your search path must conform to security restrictions placed on your JavaBeans applet or application.

 The `setBeanInfoSearchPath` method and its friendly little cousin the `getBeanInfoSearchPath` method help you determine the locations to look in for a `BeanInfo` object. Your search path should conform to the security restrictions placed on your Bean:

```
public static String[] getBeanInfoSearchPath()
public static void setBeanInfoSearchPath(
    String newSearchPath[]
)
```

■

Now that you've examined the API closely, you need to go about actually implementing it. You can do so by creating a `BeanInfo` object for your `RainbowButton`. You will need to create and initialize descriptors for the events and properties contained within your Bean, and you must be sure to effectively defer out introspection to the automatic Bean introspection algorithm. Remember, handling your own introspection is entirely optional if you have chosen to follow the design patterns for JavaBeans. It is only required if you choose to deviate from the design patterns and create events and properties that do not conform to the standard JavaBeans syntax.

Introspecting Another Bean

Now, let's go about creating a simple `BeanInfo` object and exploring how you will implement each of the APIs discussed so far. As you've seen, a `BeanInfo` object acts on a Bean, so you will first create a simple Bean. This Bean will be the same `RainbowButton` you have created earlier, a small button whose colors change with every press. After you create the `RainbowButton`, you will go about creating the `SimpleBeanInfo` object for it, and implement your own introspection routines in the process. The code for the `RainbowButton` can be seen throughout this book. The events for it are designed in Chapter 3, and the properties for it are designed in Chapter 4. Here, in Chapter 5, you add support for handling your own introspection.

Creating a Bean

Before you move on, let's take a look at what your `RainbowButton` looks like so far. Its properties include the button's current color (`buttonColor`) and the text that is within the button itself (the `buttonText`). The properties use the standard get and set accessors and mutators, with standardized names. Since the properties conform to the proper design patterns, you need not create additional property descriptor information for it, though you will as an example.

The `RainbowButton` also fires an event, a `ButtonEvent`, to a listener, a `ButtonListener`, using the action method called `fireButtonEvent`. Once again, the event system for your Bean conforms to normal design patterns. However, we will go ahead and implement the `EventSetDescriptor` for it as well.

Even though it is not required, we will create the `BeanInfo` object for your Bean anyway. This will let us show a concrete example of how to use it correctly.

Creating the Bean Information

When you create your Bean information class, you will extend `SimpleBeanInfo`, as is recommended. But, the nice thing about the `SimpleBeanInfo` object is that you do not have to implement every method. For the sake of completeness, you will, however, implement all of its methods, but the idea behind the special object is that you could choose which parts of introspection to handle on your own.

CREATING THE BEAN DESCRIPTOR

The first thing you need to do in the Bean information object is to obtain Java `Class` objects for the various classes you will use in the information object. For the `RainbowButton`, that means you need the `Rainbow-Button` class itself, the `RainbowButtonCustomizer` class, and the listener class for the `ButtonEvents`. It's important to realize that these are *classes*, not objects. You cannot instantiate these classes, rather you will use them to signify to the users of the descriptor object the types of the objects you are returning:

```
public class RainbowButtonBeanInfo extends SimpleBeanInfo
{
    private final static Class rainbowButtonClass =
        RainbowButton.class;
    private final static Class rainbowButtonCustomizerClass =
        RainbowButtonCustomizer.class;
    private final static Class buttonListenerClass =
        ButtonListener.class;

    RainbowButtonBeanInfo()
    {
        super();
    }
}
```

You choose to place these `Class` objects in private variables because it will be easier to pass them around later. They are declared `final` so that if any other object inherits from the information object, they will not get the `Class` objects. The `static` tag simply ensures that multiple instances of the `Class` object refer to the same variables. The constructor for the descriptor merely calls the super class', `SimpleBeanInfo`, constructor.

GETTING A DESCRIPTOR

You will now go about supplying a `BeanDescriptor` object and filling in its detail. As you will recall from earlier in this chapter, a `BeanDescriptor` takes two arguments as its constructor, the `Class` representing the Bean, and a `Class` representing the Bean's customizer. Here, you create the `BeanDescriptor` and pass it back:

```
public class RainbowButtonBeanInfo extends SimpleBeanInfo
{
    private final static Class rainbowButtonClass =
        RainbowButton.class;
    private final static Class rainbowButtonCustomizerClass =
        RainbowButtonCustomizer.class;
    private final static Class buttonListenerClass =
        ButtonListener.class;

    RainbowButtonBeanInfo()
```

```
    {
        super();
    }

    public BeanDescriptor getBeanDescriptor()
    {
        // create the bean descriptor
        BeanDescriptor descriptor = new BeanDescriptor(
            rainbowButtonClass, rainbowButtonCustomizerClass);

        // send it back
        return descriptor;
    }
}
```

SPECIFYING EVENTS

Now, you must create an `EventSetDescriptor` and pass it back.
When you create it, you will have to create an array of descriptors. You
will then need to fill in each event by hand. It's a somewhat long-winded
process, but it accomplishes the task and provides the requisite information:

```
public class RainbowButtonBeanInfo extends SimpleBeanInfo
{
    private final static Class rainbowButtonClass =
        RainbowButton.class;
    private final static Class rainbowButtonCustomizerClass =
        RainbowButtonCustomizer.class;
    private final static Class buttonListenerClass =
        ButtonListener.class;

    RainbowButtonBeanInfo()
    {
        super();
    }

    public BeanDescriptor getBeanDescriptor()
    {
        // create the bean descriptor
        BeanDescriptor descriptor = new BeanDescriptor(
            rainbowButtonClass, rainbowButtonCustomizerClass);

        // send it back
        return descriptor;
    }

    public EventSetDescriptor[] getEventSetDescriptors()
    {
        // declare the event array
        EventSetDescriptor events[] = null;
```

```
        try
        {
            // create the array
            events = new EventSetDescriptor[1];

            // set each event
            events[0] = new EventSetDescriptor(
                rainbowButtonClass, "ButtonEvent",
                buttonListenerClass, "fireButtonEvent");
            events[0].setUnicast(false);
        }
        catch(IntrospectionException exc)
        {...}

        // return it
        return events;
    }
}
```

You will also need to implement the `getDefaultEventIndex` method and have it return –1, signifying that there is no default event.

SPECIFYING PROPERTIES

Properties are completed similarly, with the creation of an array of `PropertyDescriptor` objects and the individual completion of each element. Once again, you can imagine how tedious this could be for complex Beans with several properties. But, if you choose to implement your own introspection, this is the best way to do so:

```
public class RainbowButtonBeanInfo extends SimpleBeanInfo
{
    private final static Class rainbowButtonClass =
        RainbowButton.class;
    private final static Class rainbowButtonCustomizerClass =
        RainbowButtonCustomizer.class;
    private final static Class buttonListenerClass =
        ButtonListener.class;

    RainbowButtonBeanInfo()
    {
        super();
    }

    public BeanDescriptor getBeanDescriptor()
    {
        // create the bean descriptor
        BeanDescriptor descriptor = new BeanDescriptor(
            rainbowButtonClass, rainbowButtonCustomizerClass);
```

```
            // send it back
            return descriptor;
        }

        public PropertyDescriptor[] getPropertyDescriptors()
        {
            PropertyDescriptor properties[] = null;

            // set each property
            try
            {
                properties[0] = new PropertyDescriptor(
                    "buttonColor", rainbowButtonClass);
                properties[0].setConstrained(false);
                properties[0].setPropertyEditorClass(
                    ColorSelector.class);

                properties[1] = new PropertyDescriptor(
                    "buttonText", rainbowButtonClass);
                properties[1].setConstrained(false);
                properties[1].setPropertyEditorClass(
                    TextSelector.class);
            }
            catch
            {...}

            return properties;
        }
    }
```

Just as you did with the event descriptors, you will also implement the `getDefaultPropertyIndex` method, forcing it to return –1, once again signifying that there is no default property.

DEFERRING INTROSPECTION

The `BeanInfo` object also allows you to specify the methods that can be performed on a Bean. By implementing the `getMethodDescriptors` method, you can handle the introspection of any methods on your Bean. Here, you will implement the `getMethodDescriptors` method but force it to return null. When introspection encounters a null return value from a `BeanInfo` method, it automatically reverts to low-level reflection to determine the specified characteristic of the Bean. When introspecting Beans obtain a null value for the `getMethodDescriptors` object, they will know to use low-level reflection to get the methods for the Bean:

```
public class RainbowButtonBeanInfo extends SimpleBeanInfo
{
    private final static Class rainbowButtonClass =
        RainbowButton.class;
```

```
private final static Class rainbowButtonCustomizerClass =
    RainbowButtonCustomizer.class;
private final static Class buttonListenerClass =
    ButtonListener.class;

RainbowButtonBeanInfo()
{
    super();
}

public BeanDescriptor getBeanDescriptor()
{
    // create the bean descriptor
    BeanDescriptor descriptor = new BeanDescriptor(
        rainbowButtonClass, rainbowButtonCustomizerClass);

    // send it back
    return descriptor;
}

public MethodDescriptor[] getMethodDescriptors()
{
    return null;
}
}
```

Now that you've examined how the `BeanInfo` object is constructed, let's take a look at how to use it. Your `BeanInfo` object is a means for you to handle your own introspection. It ensures that introspecting Beans will know only what you want them to know about your Bean. But, as with the `getMethodDescriptors` implementation, there are instances when the introspecting Bean should just do the work on its own. The next section examines both of these cases from the perspective of an introspecting Bean.

Rainbow Button Introspection

Once you complete the `BeanInfo` object for the `RainbowButton`, you can go about using it. Typically, only Bean Machines, or GUI builders of the same ilk, will use the `BeanInfo` object in this manner. For that matter, typically Beans will not do introspection on their own either. However, for the sake of completeness, I will show you how to get the `BeanInfo` object for a Bean, and use it to determine the innards of the Bean itself. I will also take this opportunity to show you how to use the low-level reflection algorithms to accomplish the task in the event that the `BeanInfo` object defers introspection to the automatic Beans facility.

Using the Bean Information Object

Once you've created the Bean Information object, the Bean Machine will more than likely use it to determine the properties and methods of a Bean. In doing so, the Bean Machine will circumvent normal introspection for those cases in which the Bean Information object specifies the details of the Bean. Here, you will use the Bean Information object to grab the events and properties of a Bean and display them on the screen. This is a simple example, Bean Machines will more than likely do something much more complex with the Bean Information object.

GETTING THE BEAN

The first thing you will do is get the Bean Information object and print out the specifics of the Bean including its name, the name of its customizer class, if it has one, and the name of any other descriptor classes associated with it. You may choose to use this example in the future to handle your own Bean debugging:

```
public class BeanInfoTest
{
    RainbowButtonBeanInfo beanInfo;

    BeanInfoTest()
    {
        beanInfo = new RainbowButtonBeanInfo();

        // get the descriptor for the bean info
        BeanDescriptor descriptor =
            beanInfo.getBeanDescriptor();

        // get the Bean
        Class myBean = descriptor.getBeanClass();
        System.out.println("my bean's name is: " +
            myBean.getName());

        // get the customizer
        Class myCustomizer = descriptor.getCustomizerClass();
        System.out.println("my customizer's name is: " +
            myCustomizer.getName());
    }
}
```

The output for that simple set of invocations should be:

```
my bean's name is: RainbowButton
my bean's customizer's name is: RainbowButtonCustomizer
```

Getting the Events

Now you want to get the set of event descriptors from the Bean. You will then go through the array of events and print out the specifics for each event. With your `RainbowButton`, there should only be one event to display.

Getting the Properties

Similarly, you will go to the `BeanInfo` object and get all of the properties contained within your Beans. You will display the details of each property you receive. With your `RainbowButton`, there should be only two events to display, and neither of them should be constrained.

Using Reflection Instead

You may also use low-level reflection to obtain the events and properties in your Bean. An example of using reflection to obtain the same information for the `RainbowButton` is available in the Chapter 1 section on reflection. That example bypasses the need for introspection altogether. However, it is important to stress once again that reflection is used by the Bean introspection algorithm.

Summary

Introspection is the key to how JavaBeans functions. Without it, the GUI builders that will be discussed in Chapter 7, *GUI Builders*, cannot function. Without some kind of ability for Beans to discover things about one another at runtime, the true plug and play ability of Beans would be severely hampered. Once Beans can dynamically make connections and attach themselves to one another, the cost of customizing chunks of code for one another is greatly minimized and Beans becomes a truly powerful programming tool. The next chapter covers more Beans-related technologies that allow Beans to be packaged and distributed. Furthermore, you will find that the security features built into Beans and Java in general make it a better alternative than any other component model on the market.

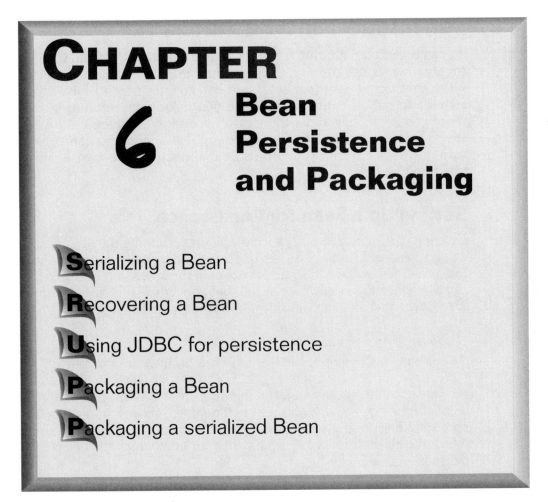

CHAPTER 6

Bean Persistence and Packaging

- **S**erializing a Bean
- **R**ecovering a Bean
- **U**sing JDBC for persistence
- **P**ackaging a Bean
- **P**ackaging a serialized Bean

Serialization allows you to save your Java objects as strings. You can then take those strings and store a Java object in a file and recover it later. This is what is known as persistence. When you serialize an object, you are not only storing the makeup of a class, but the data stored in that class as well. JavaBeans uses the normal serialization mechanisms in Java to handle its own persistence. In this chapter, you will examine how to use serialization to make a Bean persistent. You will also take a brief look at Java's Database Connectivity (JDBC) and how to use a database to store our Bean. Once you have created a bunch of Beans, you need a means to group them all together, along with their serialized state. This chapter will also cover the techniques for packaging a Bean for later use.

Serialization and Beans

As mentioned, serialization is the act of taking a Java object and converting it into a string. You examined the built-in Java serialization mechanisms in Chapter 1, *Advanced Java,* but now it's time to look at the serialization of an entire Bean. When you talk about *handling persistence* you are talking about the means necessary for taking a Bean and saving it into a file for later use. Here you will see how to handle your own persistence within your Beans by implementing the Java serialization routines.

Setting Up a Bean for Persistence

Creating persistent Beans is as simple as implementing the `Serializable` interface. The `Serializable` interface contains a few methods that must then be filled in so that the data in the object can be stored in a *.ser* file. Once the Bean is serialized and converted to a passable string form, it can then be placed inside a Java Archive (JAR) file.

THE SERIALIZABLE INTERFACE

As you saw in Chapter 1, the `Serializable` interface consists of two methods, `writeObject` and `readObject`. Both of these methods must be implemented by any object inheriting from `Serializable`. The `writeObject` and `readObject` methods each receive one parameter corresponding to the appropriate object stream (input or output) to which the object is intended to be written or from which the object is to be read.

 The `Serializable` interface is a public Java interface consisting of two methods, `writeObject` and `readObjects`. Both methods receive an object stream as a parameter:

```
public void writeObject(
    ObjectOutputStream outputStream)
public void readObject(
    ObjectInputStream inputStream)
```

■

OBJECT STREAMS

Object streams abstract the file storage mechanism so that it can remain platform independent. By obtaining an object stream for a given file stream, you need not worry about formatting details of the string. Indeed, since all Java objects consist of one or more base Java type, serialization is pretty much handled for you all the time. Java has built-in serialization mechanisms for all of the core JDK classes, so you will never have to worry about the exact format of the serialization output.

Another important reason to use the object stream is that the target or source of the stream may vary from time to time. For example, much of the serialization talked about refers to storing a persistent state in a file. However, you could just as easily obtain an object stream from a network connection or a socket stream. By using the object streams, your serialization code will not change, only the code that initially obtains the object stream will change (see Figure 6.1).

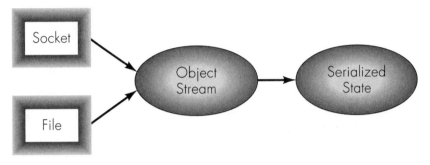

Figure 6.1: _Object stream sources and targets may vary._

AUTOMATIC BEAN SERIALIZATION

It's been mentioned that serialization is automatic in JavaBeans. Indeed, serialization is automatic in Java itself. However, you must invoke the algorithm. The automatic part of the whole thing refers not to a magical incantation that converts an object to a string, but the fact that the formatting of the serialized state and the makeup of the resulting string is handled for you by Java. Note that, in Figure 6.2, the `Goober` Bean consists of an `Integer`, a `String`, and a `Vector`. In order to serialize the entire tree, you will need to first invoke `writeObject` on the candy-Object. The `candyObject`'s `writeObject` method will then go about serializing its internal state by calling `writeObject` on every member variable. One of the member variables is the instance of the `Goober` object. That's how the `writeObject` finally percolates down to the `Goober` object.

Once the `Goober` object's `writeObject` method is invoked, you can store the `Integer`, the `String`, and the `Vector`. You need not explicitly declare how it is done; you simply call `writeObject` on each variable and Java handles it for us.

You cannot explicitly call the `writeObject` on primitive types because primitive types do not have methods. To serialize primitive types, you need not do anything. Java will automatically include any primitive types contained in an object as part of the serialization output stream.

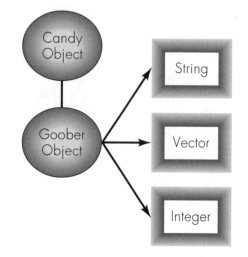

Figure 6.2: *Serialization of trees of objects can be made automatic.*

Invoking a Serialization Algorithm

In order to actually serialize a Bean, you must implement the `writeOb-ject` method that is inherited with the `Serializable` interface. Once completed, the `writeObject` method will be the central point from which you save the rest of the Bean. Simply invoking the `writeObject` method on any constituent object of your Bean will serialize it along with your current Bean. For example, invoking the `writeObject` method on the `DaddyBean` object shown in Figure 6.3 should trigger the serialization steps in the `SonBean` and the `DaughterBean`. Note that both the `SonBean` and `DaughterBean` should implement the `Serializable` interface as well.

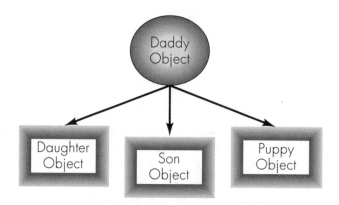

Figure 6.3: *Serialization of a tree of objects.*

For more information on serialization and the serialization techniques described in the serialization specification, see the section on serialization in Chapter 1.

Saving Serialization Files

Let's say you wanted to save the family tree in Figure 6.3. You would have to obtain an object output stream for the parent object, and begin to serialize from there. The following example illustrates how the DaddyBean is created and initialized, and how it is further serialized. Typically, serialization will be started by the GUI builder in which the Bean application is assembled. More than likely, you will not have to make the initial call for serialization.

CREATING AN OBJECT

Normally, you will create an instance of the DaddyBean by invoking the new operation on it. Nothing special, the new operation simply allocates a chunk of memory and fills it with the DaddyBean data structure. Once the DaddyBean is allocated and ready to go, you must go about serializing it and writing its data to a file. The following code snippet shows the creation of the DaddyBean from within an application main method:

```
public class TestDaddyBean
{
    public static void main(
        String args[]
    )
    {
        DaddyBean daddy = new DaddyBean();
    }
}
```

OBTAINING AN OBJECT STREAM

Getting an ObjectOutputStream to write your DaddyBean to involves first getting another stream of some kind. An ObjectOutputStream can be created only with the help of another stream. You write to your ObjectOutputStream as if it were a base stream of some kind (see Figure 6.1). For example, here you will get a FileStream object, specifying a file name to which the FileStream will be written. Using the FileStream, you will obtain an ObjectOutputStream. Writing to the ObjectOutputStream will subsequently result in writing to the FileStream:

```
public class TestDaddyBean
{
    public static void main(
```

```
        String args[]
    )
    {
        DaddyBean daddy = new DaddyBean();

        // get a file stream
        FileStream fileOut = new FileStream("/tmp/daddy.ser");
        ObjectOutputStream objectOut =
            new ObjectOutputStream(fileOut);
    }
}
```

SAVING THE OBJECT

Now that you have an object stream to write to, you can go ahead and call the `writeObject` method on the `DaddyBean` passing in the `ObjectOutputStream` as a parameter. The `DaddyBean` instance will then need to call `writeObject` on each of its constituent objects in order for the serialization to take place completely:

```
public class TestDaddyBean
{
    public static void main(
        String args[]
    )
    {
        DaddyBean daddy = new DaddyBean();

        // get a file stream
        FileStream fileOut = new FileStream("/tmp/daddy.ser");
        ObjectOutputStream objectOut =
            new ObjectOutputStream(fileOut);

        // write the object
        daddy.writeObject(objectOut);
    }
}
```

How the Java Sandbox Affects Serialization

Serialization saves into an `ObjectOutputStream`. In order to obtain a valid `ObjectOutputStream`, you must obtain it from another stream of some kind. Because Java applets cannot obtain file streams on either the local machine or socket streams to any machine other than the machine from which the applet was downloaded, the Java sandbox prevents you from saving to files. In these cases, you will more than likely want to serialize an object, pass it via a network connection to a server, and have the server save the string. Remember, the Java sandbox will limit your ability to save and restore a persistent state. By their very nature, applets were intended to be transient objects, ones that do not store any kind of state. Serialization of Beans that are used within an applet will be difficult at best.

Deserialization and Beans

Now, let's say you have a serialization file. You must now be able to look into that file and restore the Bean as it is written. Using the Java serialization routines, you can revert to a saved state quite easily. You will need to implement those serialization routines and look into the serialization file.

In this example, you are using files. It is entirely possible that your application will use another source for the serialization data. It could be a socket, a remote object using Remote Method Invocation (see Chapter 10, *Bean Networking*), or another construct. Once you obtain a stream for the construct, the rest of the steps are exactly the same.

Opening the Serialization File

You must first open the file that contains the serialized state for the Bean. In the DaddyBean example, you used the filename /tmp/daddy.ser. Once you open the file you can obtain an ObjectInputStream for it. The ObjectInputStream will allow us to read in objects that have been serialized via the ObjectOutputStream:

```
public class TestDaddyBean
{
    public static void main(
        String args[]
    )
    {
        // get the object stream
        FileStream fileIn = new FileStream("/tmp/daddy.ser");
        ObjectInputStream objectIn =
            new ObjectInputStream(fileIn);
    }
}
```

Setting Up a Bean for Restoration

In order to deserialize a Bean, you must first know the type of the class you are deserializing. If you do not know the class that you are reading, you can always revert to the generic `Object` datatype and cast later on. However, there is no way to obtain the details about a serialized state from the serialized state itself. You cannot obtain the data structure from the serialized state, only the data contained in the data structure. In our case, you don't have to worry about this because you know that you are deserializing a `DaddyBean`:

```
public class TestDaddyBean
{
    public static void main(
        String args[]
    )
    {

        // get the object stream
        FileStream fileIn = new FileStream("/tmp/daddy.ser");
        ObjectInputStream objectIn =
            new ObjectInputStream(fileIn);

        // get the object that we want to deserialize
        DaddyBean daddyBean = null;
    }
}
```

Recovering a State

Now that you have the object and an object stream, you can go about reading the object from the stream. The `ObjectInputStream` has a method called `readObject` that is analogous to the `writeObject` method found in the `ObjectOutputStream` that you saw earlier. Applying the `readObject` method, you will obtain a Java `Object`. You must then cast that Java `Object` to the appropriate type. Once the execution has finished and all casting is complete, the object will be reconstituted and ready for use, just as before:

```
public class TestDaddyBean
{
    public static void main(
        String args[]
    )
    {

        // get the object stream
        FileStream fileIn = new FileStream("/tmp/daddy.ser");
        ObjectInputStream objectIn =
            new ObjectInputStream(fileIn);

        // get the object that we want to deserialize
        DaddyBean daddyBean = null;
```

```
// get the object from the stream
Object obj = objectIn.readObject();
daddyBean = (DaddyBean) obj;

// go about invoking just as before
daddyBean.invoke_a_method_on_me();
    }
}
```

Object serialization is a wonderful tool that's been discussed in general in Chapter 1, and one that you have used specifically for Beans here. Since JavaBeans is nothing more than a set of Java objects, object serialization becomes a trivial task to carry over to the Beans environment, fulfilling one of the key design goals of the Beans environment.

As wonderful as object serialization is, some folks will still want another means to save and restore object states. For them, the JDBC package may be the answer. JDBC allows Java objects to connect and manipulate databases using nothing more complex than Structured Query Language (SQL) statements. As you will see later in Chapter 10, Beans can connect to a variety of networking mechanisms with much ease, and JDBC certainly follows along the same path.

Using Another Form of Persistence

The Java serialization mechanism alone is a fantastic way to handle your persistence. It is quick and efficient, easily available, and simple to implement. But, for those Beans that require a more complex state storage mechanism, you can push off Bean persistence to a database. The database, be it Oracle, Sybase, or something else, can safely store the information with security safeguards of its own.

Introduction to JDBC

As the Java revolution moves on, there remains an extraordinarily large camp of people who require access to legacy systems and legacy databases in particular. While Java Interface Definition Language (IDL), which will be discussed in some detail in Chapter 10, provides a robust set of Java objects to connect legacy applications with the Internet applications of today, a coherent methodology for accessing databases directly from within a Java object is lacking.

Java Database Connectivity was created for just such a case. Knowing full well that there are a plethora of databases in existence today, the architectural challenge for JDBC was to provide a simple front-end interface for connecting with even the most complex of databases. To the programmer, the interface to a database should be the same regardless of the kind of database to which you want to connect.

Database Drivers

In the desktop world, a driver enables a particular piece of hardware to interface with the rest of the machine. Similarly, a database driver gives JDBC a means to communicate with a database. Perhaps written in some form of native code but usually written in Java itself, the database drivers available for JDBC are wide and varied, addressing several different kinds of databases.

Typically, the JDBC core API is available for users to download and use as a development tool. Then, the programmer has to acquire one of the many database drivers that fits the database best. With the API and driver, the application has the tools necessary to exchange information between Java objects and databases.

The guidelines for creating the JDBC architecture all center on one very important characteristic: simplicity. Databases are complex beasts, and companies that rely on them generally have an army of personnel ready to administer and program them. As a result, transferring that complexity to Java via JDBC would violate the ethos of the language. Therefore, the JDBC architects developed the specification with the idea that database access would not require advanced degrees and years of training to accomplish.

THE DRIVERMANAGER OBJECT

At the heart of JDBC lies the `DriverManager`. Once a driver is installed, you need to load it into your Java object by using the `Driver-Manager`. It groups drivers together so that multiple databases can be accessed from within the same Java object. It provides a common interface to a JDBC `Driver` object without having to delve into the internals of the database itself.

The `Driver` is responsible for creating and implementing the `Connection`, `Statement`, and `ResultSet` objects for the specific database, and the `DriverManager` then is able to acquire those object implementations for itself. In so doing, applications that are written using the `DriverManager` are isolated from the implementation details of databases, as well as from future enhancements and changes to the implementation itself, as you can see in Figure 6.4.

DATABASE CONNECTION INTERFACE

The `Connection` object is responsible for establishing the link between the Database Management System and the Java application. By abstracting it from the `DriverManager`, the `Driver` can isolate the database

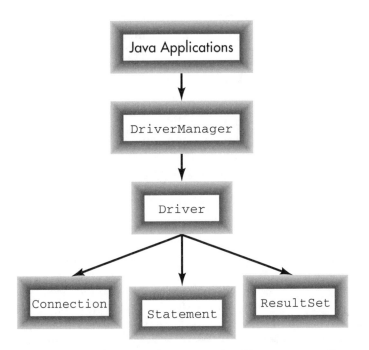

Figure 6.4: *The Driver abstracts the Connection, Statement, and ResultSet objects from the application.*

from specific parts of the implementation. It also enables the programmer to select the proper driver for the required application.

The `Connection.getConnection` method accepts a URL that enables the JDBC object to use different drivers depending on the situation, isolates applets from connection-related information, and gives the application a means by which to specify the specific database to which it should connect. The URL takes the form of `jdbc:<subproto-col>:<subname>`. The subprotocol is the kind of connectivity to the database, along the lines of ODBC, which shall be discussed in a moment. The subname depends on the subprotocol but usually allows you to configure the database that the application will look at.

DATABASE STATEMENT OBJECT

A `Statement` envelops a query written in the Server Query Language and enables the JDBC object to compose a series of steps to look up information in a database. Using a `Connection`, the `Statement` can be forwarded to the database and obtain a `ResultSet`.

RESULTSET ACCESS CONTROL

A `ResultSet` is a container for a series of rows and columns acquired from a `Statement` call. Using the `ResultSet`'s iterator routines, the

JDBC object can step through each row in the result set. Individual column fields can be retrieved using the get methods within the `Result-Set`. Columns may be specified by their field name or by their index.

JDBC AND ODBC

In many ways, Open Database Connectivity (ODBC) was a precursor to all that JDBC is intended to accomplish. It adequately abstracts the boring tedium of databases, and the proprietary APIs to those databases, from the application programmer. Furthermore, it gives a standard interface to many different kinds of databases so that you only have to create one source file to access them. Recognizing the relative acceptance of ODBC technology, JDBC offers a JDBC-to-ODBC driver that can be had for free from various Web sites.

 Because of copyright restrictions, these drivers will not be supplied on the CD-ROM, but you may visit the JDBC page on the JavaSoft Website at java.sun.com/jdbc and get the latest information and pointers to them.

With this special bridge, JDBC applications can talk to the same database access engine as non-Java applications. Furthermore, integrating JDBC into your existing business process can be done fairly easily because the bridge ensures that no additional work is required to enable Java Database Connectivity.

Setting up a Bean for JDBC

Because this is not necessarily a JDBC book, you won't hear a lengthy discussion on the details inherent in using JDBC effectively and properly. Scores of database-specific Java books are on the market today, and another book, *Advanced Java Networking* (also from Prentice Hall), explores JDBC to some extent. You are urged to select one of these books to guide you through the incantations required when using JDBC. *Java-Beans Developer's Resource* will, however, show you how to go about using an external mechanism to handle your persistent storage.

Setting up JDBC

In order to be able to use JDBC, you must first establish the connection and obtain a driver for our database. This is done in a fairly straightforward manner, and database gurus may find this to be an almost trivial task. Once you have the correct `DriverManager` for your database, you can obtain `Connection`, `Statement`, and `PreparedStatement` objects:

```
public class StoreInDatabase
{
    Connection dbConnection;

    StoreInDatabase()
    {
        // create the URL representation of our Database
        String url = "jdbc:odbc:NameOfDatabase";

        // load the database driver
        Class.forName("sun.jdbc.odbc.JdbcOdbcDriver");

        // make the connection to the database
        dbConnection = DriverManager.getConnection(
            url, "username" "password");
    }
}
```

The table that will be stored in the database is called *BeanTable* and looks something like the screen capture from Microsoft Access 97 shown in Figure 6.5.

BeanName	SerializedBean
GooberBean	hdh283hdjhd89139hd":929j9129eje:hdsjdafo

Figure 6.5: *Database table for your Bean storage.*

Invoking persistence with JDBC

In order for your database object to handle storing other Beans, you will need to create the `storeBean` method that accepts one Bean as a parameter. The first thing you need to do is take the Bean you want to make persistent and convert it into a string representation. This is not much different than the serialization mechanism, except this time instead of writing to a file stream, you will be writing directly into a string (as shown in Figure 6.6) and the code that follows.

The `StringStream` object that is used for these examples does not actually exist. You will need to construct a `StringStream` that uses the default `StringWriter` and `StringReader` objects provided in the Java Developer's Kit 1.1.

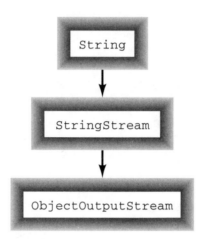

Figure 6.6: *Storing a serialized representation into a string.*

```
public class StoreInDatabase
{
    Connection dbConnection;

    StoreInDatabase()
    {
        // create the URL representation of our Database
        String url = "jdbc:odbc:NameOfDatabase";

        // load the database driver
        Class.forName("sun.jdbc.odbc.JdbcOdbcDriver");

        // make the connection to the database
        dbConnection = DriverManager.getConnection(
            url, "username" "password");
    }

    public void storeBean(
        Object obj
    )
    {
        // the string we will store into
        String stringRep = new String();
```

```
        // the output stream we will store into
        StringStream stringStream =
            new StringStream(stringRep);

        // the object output stream based on the string stream
        ObjectOutputStream outStream =
            new ObjectOutputStream(stringStream);

        // write the Bean to the object stream
        obj.writeObject(outStream);
    }
}
```

Once you have the string for the Bean, you can invoke on our database as you normally would. You will want to give the object a unique name in your table.

```
public void storeBean(
        Object obj
    )
    {
        // the string we will store into
        String stringRep = new String();

        // the output stream we will store into
        StringStream stringStream =
            new StringStream(stringRep);

        // the object output stream based on the string stream
        ObjectOutputStream outStream =
            new ObjectOutputStream(stringStream);

        // write the Bean to the object stream
        obj.writeObject(outStream);

        // get a prepared statement
        PreparedStatement pstate =
            dbConnection.prepareStatement(
                "INSERT INTO NameOfDatabase" +
                "VALUES (?, ?)");

        // set the parameters for the statement
        pstate.setString(1, obj.getName());
        pstate.setString(2, stringRep);

        // execute the statement
        pstate.executeUpdate();
    }
```

Restoring a Saved State from JDBC

Now that you know what your table looks like and how your Bean will be stored in it, restoring the Bean to a full-fledged working object first entails obtaining the Bean from the database via a SELECT call. Now place this code in another method named restoreBean.

```
...ommitted for brevity...
    public Object restoreBean(
        String beanName
    )
    {
        // create the statement
        Statement statement =
            dbConnection.createStatement();

        // get the result
        ResultSet result = statement.executeQuery(
            "ClintonQuery");

        // walk through the result for the information
        String stringRep = null;
        while(result.next())
        {
            stringRep = result.getString(1);
        }
    }
```

Once the serialized string representation for the Bean is obtained, you can deserialize it using normal deserialization steps as discussed earlier in this chapter. First, obtain the ObjectOutputStream and go from there:

```
    public Object restoreBean(
        String beanName
    )
    {
        // create the statement
        Statement statement =
            dbConnection.createStatement();

        // get the result
        ResultSet result = statement.executeQuery(
            "ClintonQuery");

        // walk through the result for the information
        String stringRep = null;
        while(result.next())
        {
```

```
        stringRep = result.getString(1);
    }

    // get a string stream for the string representation
    StringStream stringStream = new StringStream
(stringRep);

    // get an object input stream
    ObjectInputStream objectIn =
        new ObjectInputStream(stringStream);

    // get the object and return it
    return objectIn.readObject();
}
```

The storage of Beans within databases can be vastly more complex if you so desire. What you have seen is the simplest possible case with one table, one Bean, and one possible storage schema. Many applications that intend to store a large number of Beans will do so in a much more elegant and efficient manner. However, for purposes of explanation, discussion of these more difficult methodologies has been limited.

The next section takes you to the realm in which Beans must be stored on disk. While persistence is still possible, the purpose of Bean packaging is to give the end-user a simple file to pass around and reuse. After all, some Beans may be so complex that they contain hundreds and hundreds of Java classes. By using the packaging mechanism, you can create one file that gets passed around from user to user.

Packaging the Button

As Java applications become more and more complex, a simple means of transmitting those applications across the Internet is required. Because of performance problems associated with HTTP Servers, a single transaction for all Java objects, images, sounds, and other support files is the best and most efficient means to transmit Java data across a network. As a result, early browsers supported the *ZIP* file for packaging all Java files into one giant file. With Beans and the latest JDK, the *ZIP* file becomes standardized for Java in the form of a *JAR*. Besides being cute (after all, you are going to put your Beans in a Jar), the JAR file enhances the Java Internet experience by limiting time spent waiting for objects to load.

Packaging as a Standard

The JavaBeans architecture does not specify under any circumstances that any one way is the preferred and accepted means to package Beans and distribute them. Rather, it simply says that the Java Archive is the preferred delivery mechanism for Beans. Indeed, a GUI builder may well load a JAR and save it in either a *project* format while the Bean project is unfinished, or it could very easily export the JAR in another format. Nevertheless, the Java Archive will be the accepted means for browsers to download Java applets, and Beans applets should follow that standard as well.

JAR File Format

The problem with ZIP files is that they are not platform-independent. As Apple Macintosh users are well aware, ZIP files are not really supported on the Mac. Rather, they use Self Extracting Archive (SEA) files for compression and packaging. Because of the lack of platform independence, Java, the platform-independent language, requires something greater than ZIP for cross-platform packaging.

WHAT IS A JAR?

Enter the Java Archive, or JAR, file. JAR files enable you to package classes, images, sounds, and other binary files, in a cross-platform manner.

JAR files are backward-compatible with previous applet formats, and are an open standard that is publicly available for comment and scrutiny.

USING A JAR

Actually incorporating a JAR into your HTML code is fairly easy. In fact, the latest JDK includes support for JAR files, as well as command line utilities (written in Java, by the way) to package, unpackage, compress, and decompress Java Archives. The following HTML code snippet illustrates how a JAR file is used within the `applet` tag:

```
<applet code="MyApplet.class" archives="jars/myapplet.jar"
 width=600 height=300>
blah
</applet>
```

As always, the `code` tag is present, but it is modified by the `archives` tag. You can very easily specify multiple archives if you so desire. Note that the `class` file represented by the `code` tag must be present in one of the archives specified in the `archives` tag.

The command-line `jar` utility is included as part of the JDK. You can use this utility to create your own JARs, which you can later specify on your `applet` tag. The `jar` command is a simple, easy to use utility that makes creating archives very easy. In fact, if you are already familiar with Unix's `tar` command or the ubiquitous Windows `zip` command, then you are pretty much familiar with the JAR format.

Simply typing the command `jar` at your system prompt will yield the following statement:

```
%prompt% jar
Usage: jar {ctx}[vfm0M] [jar-file] [manifest-file] files ...
Options:
  -c  create new archive
  -t  list table of contents for archive
  -x  extract named (or all) files from archive
  -v  generate verbose output on standard error
  -f  specify archive file name
  -m  include manifest information from specified manifest file
  -0  store only; use no ZIP compression
  -M  Do not create a manifest file for the entries

If any file is a directory then it is processed recursively.
Example: to archive two class files into an archive called
classes.jar:
  jar cvf classes.jar Foo.class Bar.class
Note: use the '0' option to create a jar file that can be put in
your CLASSPATH
```

Just like its Unix counterpart, the jar program will let you compress a bunch of objects using the c command line option. If you want to see the compression status as it happens, you can modify the command line argument with the v option (for verbose). You will also need to specify the name of the archive that you would like to create by using the f tag, followed by a file name. Finally, you will need to specify the files that you would like to archive:

```
%prompt% jar cvf MyNewJarFile.jar *.class
```

If your files are arranged in a hierarchical directory structure, with sub-directories, the hierarchical structure will be maintained and the files and directories will be stored recursively. This is particularly useful for Java packages, which are created as nested directories.

Manifest Files

On the Cruise Ship Lollipop, the captain has a list of people who are on board the vessel at any given time. This is called the Ship's Manifest. A manifest in Java is, quite simply, a list of classes that are in an archive. Manifests are totally optional for non-signed, non-secure archives of Java objects. However, a manifest is required if you wish to introduce any kind of security or encryption into your archive. Adding these attributes to a class will be talked about in a moment, but in this section you will look only at the manifest file and its makeup.

MANIFEST VERSIONS

The first line in the manifest should be the version of the particular archive. It should be specified using the `Manifest-Version` tag, followed by a colon (:) and the version number (in standard `x.x` decimal version notation. No bonus points for revving an operating system to the number 95 to make it seem useful):

```
Manifest-Version: 1.6
```

MANIFEST CONTENTS

Typically, a manifest will contain only those classes that are to be signed in some manner. You can go ahead and create an unsigned version of the manifest for your `RainbowButton` from the earlier chapters. The format of the manifest for one Java class is as follows:

```
Manifest-Version: x.x
Name: <directory path>/<Java class>
Hash-Algorithms: <hash-algorithm> <hash-algorithm> ...
<hash-algorithm>: (base 64 representation of the hash)
```

The various hash algorithms will be discussed in a moment, but for now, keep in mind that the whole purpose of the Java Archive is to create a central mechanism for keeping track of all your files, be they Java classes or multimedia sound files. With that in mind, you can easily add images and sounds to the manifest in the same manner as you did the Java class.

ADDING A BEAN TO A MANIFEST

When you create a JAR file that contains a slew of Java classes, potentially every one of those Java classes can be a Bean in its own right, particularly if you view the recommended design patterns as not only a Bean paradigm, but as a Java syntactic guideline as well. When a Java object begins to look into a JAR file, it will load every Java class contained therein. For those classes that could very easily be Beans, a Beans container will load each of them and treat them as full-fledged Beans.

For extremely simple cases, this is exactly what you desire. However, in many instances a Bean will have several support objects that you would prefer not be exposed to the builder or end user. For these cases, an entry should be made in the manifest file for every class that should be considered a Bean. By following the attribute tag that we outlined earlier, you can state which Java objects in a JAR file are Beans by specifying them appropriately in the `Manifest` description using the `Java-Bean` attribute:

```
Manifest-Version: x.x
Name: <directory path>/<Java class>
Java-Bean: true
Hash-Algorithms: <hash-algorithm> <hash-algorithm> ...
<hash-algorithm>: (base 64 representation of the hash)
```

SPECIFYING PROPERTIES IN A MANIFEST

It is also quite acceptable to specify the values of certain properties contained within the Bean inside the manifest file. In so doing, you can create generic Bean objects that are customized only within the manifest itself. For example, if you were to create an entry for a car Bean that you would like to have an automatic transmission, you would list the property `Automatic-Transmission` as true:

```
Manifest-Version: x.x
Name: BMW/BMW_Z3.class
Java-Bean: true
Automatic-Transmission: true
```

Adding Security to the JAR

The biggest problem with Internet security is that any kind of preventative measure that can possibly be thrown up can immediately be broken. No matter what you, as developers, try and do to prevent our applications from being compromised and our systems from being invaded by pernicious programs, there will always be a 14-year old hacker lurking in the dark alleys of the Web laughing at our efforts. Therefore, when you talk about security and JavaBeans, you are really talking about technology that is antiquated almost at the very instant of its conception. Nevertheless, you will charge on and attempt to at least clarify some terminology and provide an example using Java's built-in technology.

This is by no means a thorough text on Internet security or even Java security. Keep that in mind as you move along.

SECURITY AND JAVABEANS

The first thing to realize about Bean security is that JavaBeans is nothing more than Java code to begin with. Therefore, Beans that are composed into an applet will follow the same strict Java sandbox that prevents a downloaded applet from modifying the local machine (see Figure 6.7). By the same token, Beans that are put together to form a Java application will not, like all Java applications, be restricted by a sandbox or any security policy for that matter.

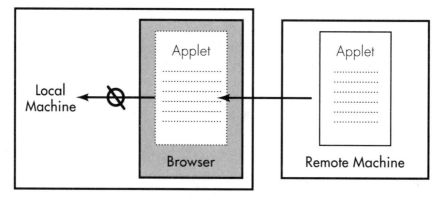

Figure 6.7: *The applet sandbox and security.*

Users of Java and Internet applications will have to deal with the same problems that they've always had. In the computer world of yesterday, you bought applications from various vendors, be they shareware authors or your local Egghead Software store. You understood that when you downloaded a shareware application you were at the mercy of the author. You had no way of telling if the shareware program was malicious and contained a virus or a script that sent sensitive information to another machine.

Consequently, many users chose the easy, and more expensive, option of purchasing shrink-wrapped software from Egghead or any number of other software stores. A certain degree of trust was maintained between the user and the vendor. After all, if Microsoft Word contained a virus it would damage Microsoft's reputation.

Well, the same quandary exists today. If you download software from the Internet, you are incurring a certain level of risk in that the source of the software may be *untrusted*. Microsoft's statement that "Web surfers will only visit sites they trust" was more of a misunderstanding of the what the Internet is all about than a meaningful technology pronouncement. The fact is that there are no boundaries on the Internet, and as an example that copyright lawyers will love to point out, the distinctions between the official Star Trek Web site and any number of fan-created Web pages is often blurred. The graphics look the same, the text sounds mightily official, and the content is often borrowed from official sources.

Copyright issues aside, the fact is that users can be ferreted off to another official-looking web site without any knowledge whatsoever. Expecting a user to distinguish from an official Web site that can be *trusted*, and a malicious Web site that looks the same is asking for too much. What's needed is an automatic mechanism for determining who is trusted and who is not, one that allows the user to determine beforehand that they will trust information only from, say, CNN's Web site and not a competing news organization's.

CERTIFICATES AND AUTHORITIES

A *certificate* is, quite simply, a chunk of code that says "you can trust me." Certificates are issued by entities called *Certificate Authorities*, that are entrusted with the task of giving out certificates for various organizations, companies, and people. As an example, let's say that the Heath Corporation wishes to supply screen savers of Dancing Fish and you, the user, want to download them. The Heath Corporation has been issued a certificate from a Certificate Authority and publicly displays that certificate on its site. You download the certificate and add it to your *Identity Database*. You are now ready to accept any downloads of files containing the Heath Corporation's certificate.

The certificate comes in two parts, called *keys*. A *public key* is the part of the certificate that you can obtain. A *private key* is used by the company to sign their code with a digital signature. Code locked by a private key can only be unlocked and used by the corresponding public key. In theory, the Heath Corporation's private key will never be given out and they will protect it with their lives. Just because the Heath Corporation's public key is available on their Web site doesn't mean that other folks can spoof their signature. This is called public-private encryption and authentication. The private key is kept close to the vest to lock a program and to authenticate its existence, and only the public key may unlock it.

CREATING A CERTIFICATE AND IDENTITY

Java provides a great command-line utility called `javakey` to allow you to build in security in your applications and JAR files. The `javakey` util-

Some people transmit their public key along with their e-mail messages. This is so that you can use a public key to unlock a message and make sure it came from the proper source. This is what is known as *authentication*, because you are able to authenticate the sender.

However, another form of security is also possible. This ensures that even if your e-mail message is stolen en route, only the intended recipient can view it. In order to accomplish this, you would sign and then encrypt your message using both your private key and the recipient's public key. On the other end, the intended recipient can unlock the message by first applying your public key, just as in authentication. But in order to read the result, the recipient must also apply his or her private key to the message. Then, and only then, will the recipient be able to read the message.

ity can be used to create identities, generate keys (certificates), and lock and unlock archives. It has a very simple command-line interface and is intended for use by novice security programmers. Future versions of the javakey utility may include a user interface of some kind. The output to the javakey utility is as follows:

```
%prompt% javakey
javakey
        l       list of the identities in the database.
        c       create a new identity.
        r       remove an identity from the database.
        i       import a public key, a key pair, etc.
        g       generate a key pair, a certificate, etc.
        d       display a certificate.

for more information, see documentation.
```

In order to create an identity, you simply invoke the utility with the -cs option and create an identity called ClarkKent:

```
%prompt% javakey -cs ClarkKent true
```

Now, you need to generate the public and private keys for Clark-Kent. You will need to specify the public key file for the identity as well as the private key file. Use the -gk option on the command line. The number 512 represents the number of bytes in the encryption scheme:

```
%prompt% javakey -gk "ClarkKent" DSA 512 KentPublic Kent Private
```

Once completed, you will need to generate the certificate based on the public and private keys. Here, refer to the X.509 International Standards Organization (ISO) framework. In X.509, the RSA (*Rivest, Shamir, and Adleman*, the creators of RSA) algorithm is recommended, though not required. Because of copyright restrictions (RSA is a proprietary algorithm), JDK includes support only for the Digital Signature Algorithm (DSA, an algorithm in the public domain). Future versions of the JDK will include support for RSA.

A certificate contains a small chunk of information in addition to the public key as shown in Figure 6.8. The version is nothing more than the current revision of the certificate. The version number is maintained and administered by the entity that owns the certificate. The serial number is bestowed upon the certificate by the Certificate Authority. The algorithm, issuer, and period of validity are set by the certificate's owner. The owner will then embed its public key into the certificate. Finally, the Certificate Authority will sign the entire certificate, assuring you that it contains the *Good Certificate Authority's Seal of Approval*.

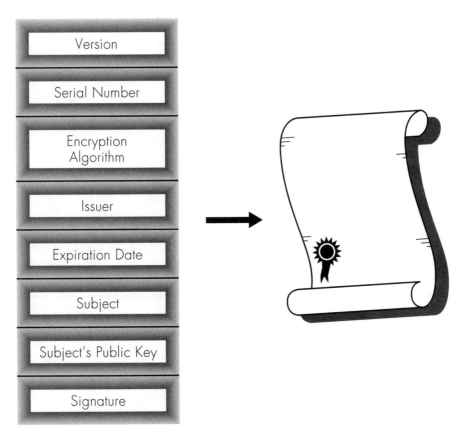

Figure 6.8: Contents of a certificate.

Generating a certificate first requires that all the information that is contained in a certificate is first placed into a *certificate directive* file. The certificate directive file is nothing more than a simple text file that contains all the elements in the certificate. A sample certificate directive file for the ClarkKent certificate follows (it is stored and referred to later under the filename `ClarkKent.cert_dir`):

```
# the certificate version and serial number
issuer.cert=1
serial.number=1001

# the algorithm is determined from the command line

# the id of the signer
issuer.name=ClarkKent

# expiration dates
start.date=10 Aug 1997
end.date=1 Dec 1997

# the id of the subject
subject.name=clark_applet

# the components of the X500 name for the subject
subject.real.name=Kal El
subject.org.unit=Krypton
subject.org=Justice League
subject.country=US

out.file=clark.x509
```

Most of the time, a certificate will be created and issued to you by a recognized certificate authority. If you were to post this certificate on a Web page along with an applet signed by yourself, people would have to be crazy to download the applet and certificate. After all, you are most probably not a recognized certificate authority.

You will then need to use the `javakey` program to generate the certificate based on the directive file:

```
%prompt% javakey -gc ClarkKent.cert_dir
```

You should then create the JAR file as you normally would and as outlined earlier. Subsequent examples will refer to the JAR file as the filename *ClarkKent.jar*.

Now you need to create the *signature directive* file. The signature directive, like its certificate directive cousin, allows you to place all the parameters for the signature into one file. The `javakey` will then use those parameters to generate a secure signature which you can later use. Here is a sample signature directive file for our ClarkKent example. It is stored under *ClarkKent.sig*:

```
# Which signer to use. This must be in the system's database.
signer=ClarkKent

# Cert number to use for this signer. This determines which
# certificate will be included in the PKCS7 block. This is
# mandatory and is 1 based.
cert=1

# Cert chain depth of a chain of certificate to include. This is
# currently not supported.
chain=0

# The name to give to the signature file and associated
# signature block.  This must be 8 characters or less.
signature.file=CK.sig
```

Once you have the signature directive file, you will need to create the signature and apply it to the JAR file using the `javakey` program:

```
%prompt% javakey -gs ClarkKent.sig ClarkKent.jar
```

ADDING A TRUSTED IDENTITY

In order to download applets from other places, you may want to set up a local identity database. In it, you can place the identities of the locations from which you will allow a download, as well as their corresponding certificates. When a JAR is downloaded from a remote location, the browser or applet container will consult the identity database and attempt to match the certificate in the database with the certificate contained within the download. If they match, the container will allow the program to continue. If they do not, the authentication is rejected and the container should not let the applet execute.

Keeping Track of Identities and Certificates

Maintaining a local identity database can be a difficult and time-consuming process. Typically, the local database will be handled by a system administrator. One of the problems with the whole security issue is that in our new networked world, there are many, many locations where you, the computer owner, have to be your own system administrator. The fact is that certificate management and user-driven control over security is difficult, and potentially dangerous. If you don't know what you are doing, you could very easily allow pernicious programs to penetrate your system.

As the Internet becomes more and more mainstream, certificate and security management will become a very important area in which usability experts can greatly improve the current state of things. As always, Microsoft will provide a solution delivered from the end-user's perspective, complete with pretty interfaces and well-studied user interactions. Other companies such as VeriSign will provide much of the internal plumbing for such usable applications.

Packaging a Serialized State

Now that you've gone about creating a serialization file for our class, you can store it in the manifest and JAR as well. Putting it in the JAR is as simple as compressing it along with the rest of the files in the archive. It is up to your application, of course, to deserialize the object at runtime. Simply placing a serialization file in your archive will not automatically mean that the object will get reset to its persistent state. Often, GUI builders, like those that will be discussed in the next chapter, will automatically search for and load any existing serialized states when it comes time to assemble an application using your Bean. Other times, the application itself may have to be developed so that the serialized state is loaded every time.

Summary

Putting together a Bean is a somewhat straightforward process. Luckily, the JAR specification is equally simple. Java Archives will be the mechanism that will be used within the industry to supply and pass around Beans. In so doing, JavaBeans has a simple and elegant packaging utility. The JAR files will then be used by various GUI builders that will go about assembling applications. As we will discuss in the next section, a GUI builder will take a bunch of existing JARs and allow you to put them together into an application or applet. There are several GUI builders on the market today, but we feel Symantec's Visual Café will be the most robust Java development environment.

PART THREE

Advanced Beans

This chapter focuses almost entirely on the truly cool things you can do with Beans. The biggest advantage to using JavaBeans is the wealth of GUI-based development tools that are available with which to develop and publish them to the world. Simple and intuitive, these tools can be used to build systems of Beans without even once seeing a line of source code. From here on out, you will use a GUI builder only. You also take a look at the networking capabilities of the JavaBeans environment. Starting with OLE and OpenDoc, you'll see how Beans interact with other component models. Then you'll take a look at a simple introduction to Java RMI (Remote Method Invocation) and show you how to use RMI to interact with Beans across a network or on different machines.

CHAPTER
7
GUI Builders

Using Existing Beans

Pulling Beans Together

Exporting Beans

The Visual GUI Builder is the preferred way to assemble JavaBeans components into an application. So far, you have seen the details of the Beans APIs and the source code that uses them, but not the single most important aspect of JavaBeans programming. After all, Beans without builder support is nothing more than a superfluous class library for Java. This chapter introduces Penumbra Software's Super Mojo builder, and Symantec's Visual Café Pro environment. This chapter is intended to be a simple introduction into the world of GUI builders. It is not an endorsement of either product, rather it is an example of how one GUI builder works and how the others will, more than likely, function. Your job is to try to evaluate the many GUI builders available and make a decision on your own.

This chapter is purely speculative. It provides a taste for what GUI builders are all about and why they are so important to the future of JavaBeans. Symantec's Visual Café Pro and Penumbra's Super Mojo were chosen because they are the most aesthetically pleasing and feature-rich GUI builders on the market. In addition, Super Mojo is written using 100 percent pure Java code. It alone represents some of the great potential that Java has as a full-fledged development language. Please also be aware that the screen grabs in this chapter are from an early Beta release of Super Mojo and a non-Beans compliant version of Café and may not represent the actual screens in the shipping editions of the products.

Café is a very stable product and the clear industry leader. Super Mojo is written in Java, and is intriguing in its own right. Both Symantec's Visual Café and Penumbra Software's Super Mojo are full-featured JavaBeans GUI builders. They allow the easy re-use of JavaBeans components in a completely graphical environment. If you so desire, you can build an entire JavaBeans application without once seeing a line of source code. In essence, Café and Super Mojo fulfill the promise of giving non-programmers the ability to program. To obtain Visual Café, contact Symantec at www.café.symantec.com. To obtain Super Mojo, contact Penumbra Software at www.penumbrasoftware.com

The CD supplied with this book includes an early beta release of Super Mojo. To obtain the full-featured version, please contact Penumbra Software through their Web page.

Loading a Bean

The first thing a GUI builder must do is actually load a Bean and display it graphically. Using introspection, as discussed in Chapter 5, *Bean Introspection*, the builder will search for any support classes, including information objects, property editors, property sheets, and customizer widgets. Typically, the Bean will be loaded into the machine and the machine will start up any property editors, property sheets, and customizers that are needed. If there are no customizers, then the GUI builder will simply load the Bean and get it ready for incorporation into the larger applet or application that you are composing.

Locating and Loading a JAR File

A simple file dialog box will appear asking you to select the JAR file that you wish to load. Once you select the JAR file, a customizer may appear if the Bean supports it. If not, you will be given the opportunity to place the graphical representation of the Bean on the composition area. In this example, you will be adding two Beans, a simple button Bean and an equally simple text field Bean. In Figure 7.1, you can see how the Beans are placed on the composition area.

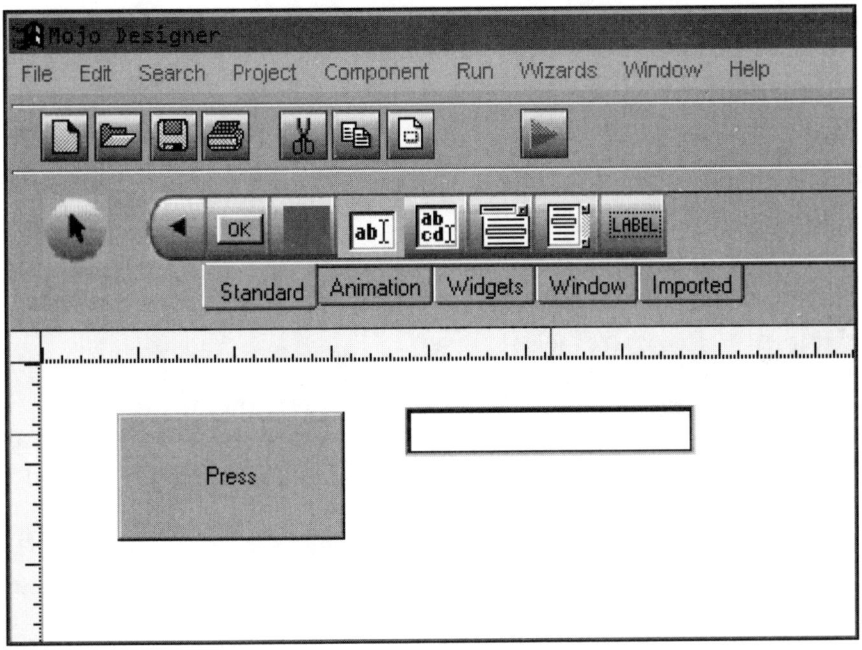

Figure 7.1:   *Beans on the composition area.*

Examining the Property Sheet

By selecting one of the Beans, you can modify its properties by clicking and typing in the property sheet shown in Figure 7.2. As discussed in Chapter 4, *Bean Properties*, a property sheet is a simple table of all the properties contained in a Bean and their respective values.

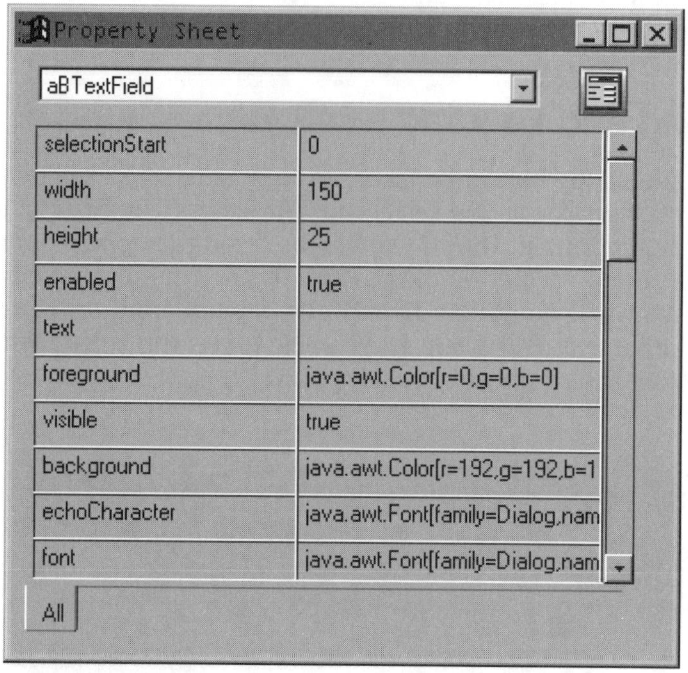

Figure 7.2: *Bean property sheets.*

Editing a Property

A property can be edited by selecting the property on the property sheet. In Figure 7.3, selecting the *background color* property will automatically invoke the color property editor. As you can see, this is a very rudimentary color editor that allows only the 16 basic Java colors.

Admittedly, the default color editor is about as boring as a sitcom on TV. If you wanted to incorporate a more complex and visually active color editor, you could create one similar to Figure 7.4. All you would need to do is to declare the editor as a Java object called `ColorPropertyEditor`.

As you saw in Chapter 5, *Bean Introspection*, when you load the Bean into the GUI builder, the builder looks into your Bean. When it looks into your Bean, the builder will discover the existence of a property whose type is `Color`. It will then automatically look for a Java object named `ColorPropertyEditor`. What it will find is a Java object containing the fancy color wheel. It will then use that color wheel object whenever a property of type `Color` is edited.

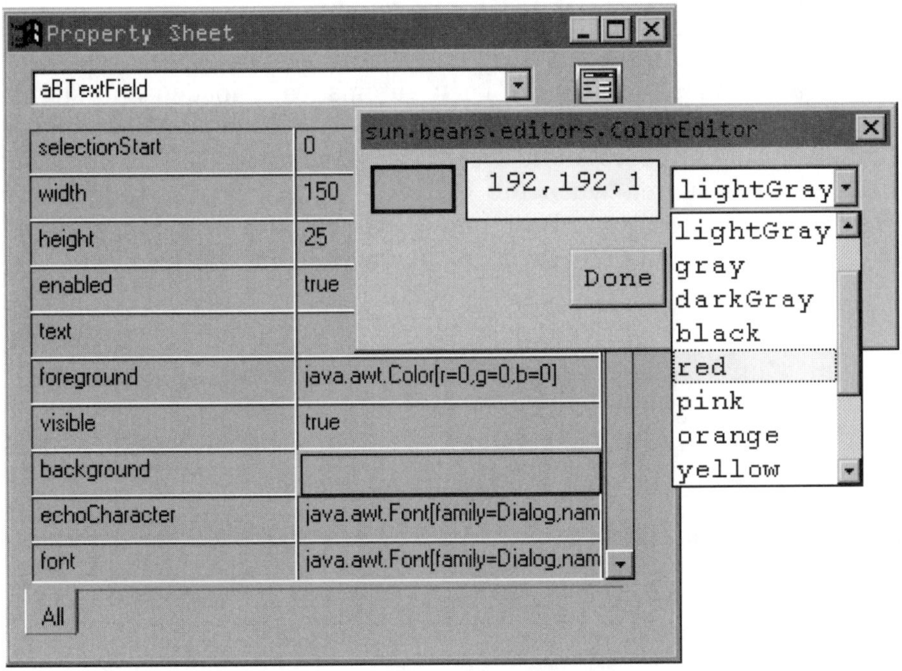

Figure 7.3: Default Color property editor.

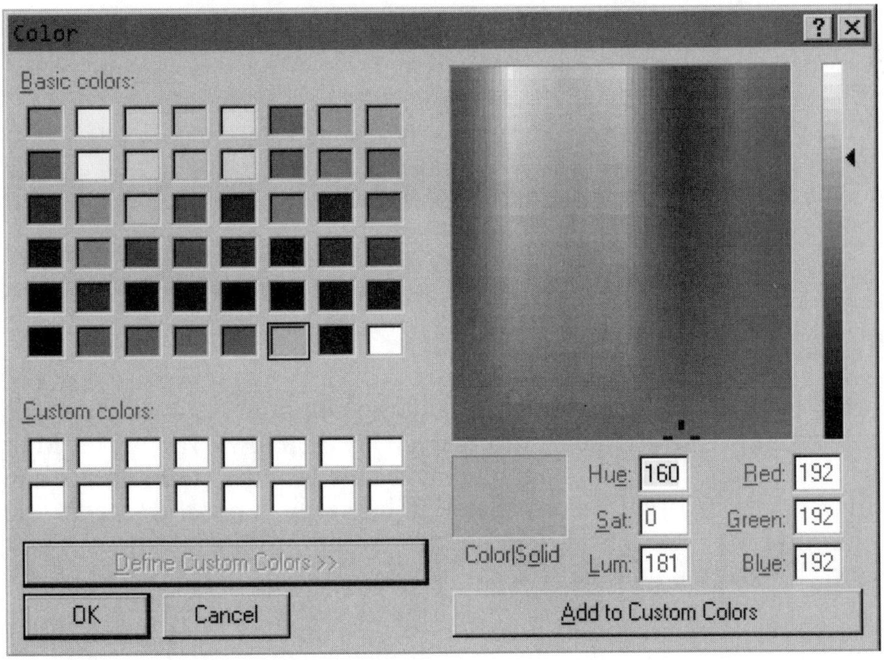

Figure 7.4: User-created ColorPropertyEditor object.

Following a Customizer

If you had chosen to create a `ButtonCustomizer` object for your `Button` Bean, then it would have been automatically loaded and started once the JAR was loaded. Because this example Bean is extraordinarily simple, it was not necessary to create a customizer for it. Therefore, the Bean was not started when the JAR was loaded. From within Super Mojo, the customizer for a Bean may be started by selecting the customizer button on the property sheet, as shown in Figure 7.5.

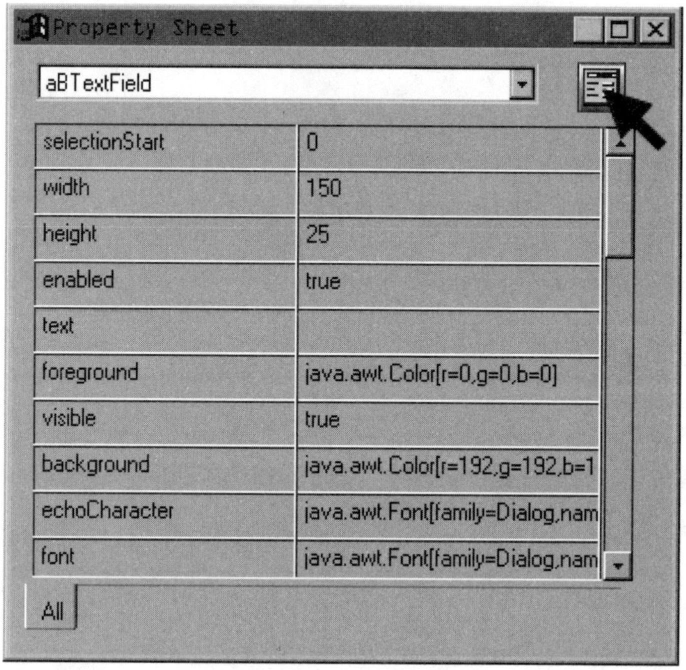

Figure 7.5: *Loading a customizer Wizard.*

Packaging the Bean

Super Mojo makes it very easy to take the components on the designer window and convert them into a Bean in their own right. The Make Bean menu selection will help you make sure that the entire design window is saved in a JAR file as a Bean. If, however, you just wanted to run the contents of the design window as an application or applet, simply select the Run menu item.

Now that you've loaded and configured a couple of Beans, you will need to go about attaching them and declaring *interactions* between the two. Super Mojo is successful is in the rapid application development stage. It is not, however, a GUI builder in the sense that you will be able to load a bunch of Beans into a composer and connect them.

Much confusion has arisen over this topic and the differences between the two tool models. Super Mojo is a rapid application development tool that allows you to construct a visual environment out of Java and Java-Beans components. On the other hand, some people may want a subtly different tool, one that simply loads existing Beans, helps you customize them, and lets you connect them. Symantec's Visual Café product is a rare exception in that it allows both models. In the following discussion, you will see how Visual Café's interaction model can assist you in assembling an application out of Beans.

Creating a Bean Application

Once you have loaded a couple of Beans into the GUI builder, you can bring them together using what Visual Café terms *interactions*. An interaction is, quite simply, an event that can be fired from one Bean to another. So, using the interaction paradigm, you can have Beans fire events to one another.

Other GUI builders may call the connections between Beans something other than *interactions*. Remember, this chapter focuses on GUI builders in general, with Symantec Visual Café and Penumbra's Super Mojo used only as examples.

Selecting the Source

You will create an interaction by which a press of your button will rename the button's caption to whatever is currently in the text field. This can be done in mere seconds without once typing a line of source code. You will first need to select the button Bean and head to the Object menu and select Add Interaction from the dropdown list shown in Figure 7.6.

Following the Interaction Wizard

Choosing the interaction menu selection will start the Interaction Wizard from within Symantec Visual Café. You will then need to follow the Wizard step-by-step and create an interaction that will allow the `Button` Bean to read the value of the `TextField` Bean and set its own label.

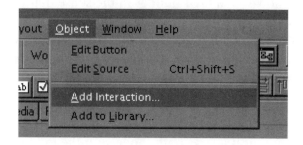

Figure 7.6: *Adding an interaction.*

SELECTING THE TARGET

When the Wizard starts up, you are asked to select the event on which the interaction will be performed. In this case, you will want this interaction to happen when the button is clicked and you are presented with the image in Figure 7.7.

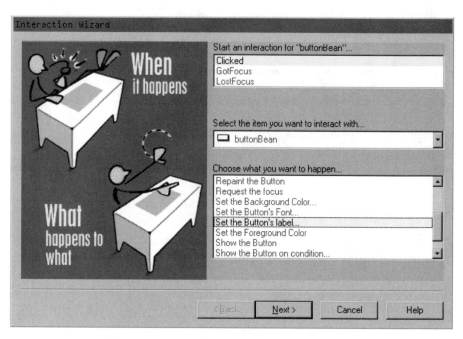

Figure 7.7: *The interaction Wizard.*

Next, you will need to select the target for the interaction itself. The target will be the location at which the action will be directed. In this case, the target is again the button since the button's label is the thing that is going to get changed.

When you go to the next page of the Wizard, you will be asked to determine the value of the label field that is going to get set when the interaction is triggered. As has been mentioned before, you will want the button's label to be set with the value of whatever is currently in the text field Bean. The Interaction Wizard allows you to specify the source of the value (in this case the text field) and the means by which the value is obtained from the source. With a text field, you have the option of selecting a value corresponding to the data in the entire text field or just the data that is highlighted. You will want to select all of the data, so choose that option (Figure 7.8).

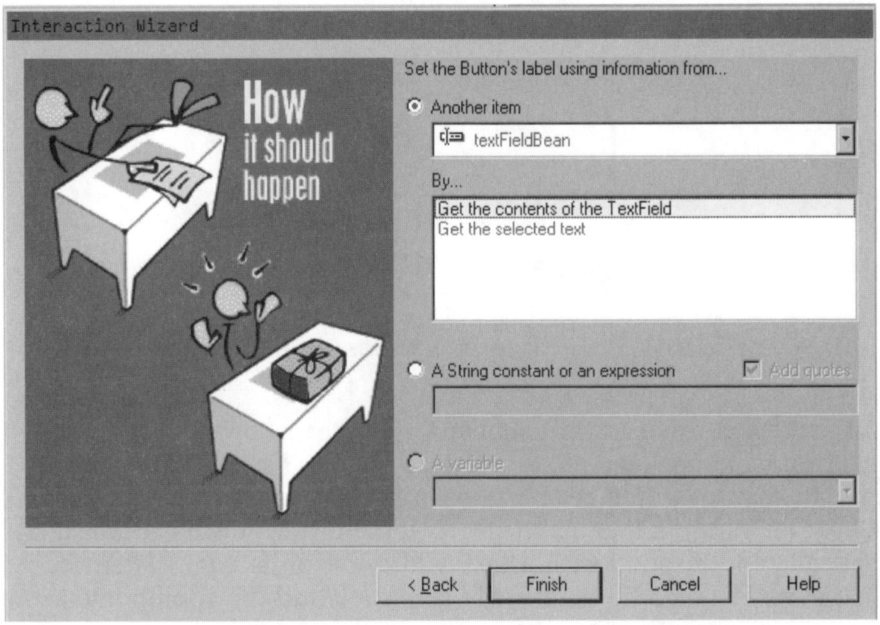

Figure 7.8: *Completing the interaction.*

Pressing Finish will enable the interaction and generate any source code that is required under the covers. Remember, your goal is to let non-programmers program, and the interaction wizard makes it highly intuitive and simple.

Testing the Interaction

Once you compile your application and generate the Java class files for the source code underneath the GUI, you will be able to run your application. When you do, you can enter a value in the text field and press the button. You should see the button's caption change to the value contained in the text field.

Interactions and Events

What this example has done is somewhat akin to the event model that was discussed in Chapter 1, *Advanced Java*, and Chapter 3, *Bean Events*. In order to make interactions fire events rather than direct method invocations, you will need to make a few modifications. Currently, the interactions in this simple example are handled as shown in Figure 7.9. The button handles a *click* event and queries the text field for its value.

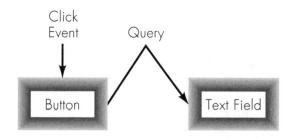

Figure 7.9: *Interaction-based event model.*

In an event-driven model similar to JavaBeans' own event model, the text field would be required to register itself as a listener of the button. In turn, the button would have to register itself as a listener of the text field. Whenever a button fires a button event, the text field will get called automatically and respond with a text field event of its own. When the text field event is fired, the button will get called and the appropriate action can take place; in this case the button would modify its label as shown in Figure 7.10.

In order to add a delegation-based event interaction system to your Beans, your GUI builder must be capable of recognizing events within a Bean. When you select the button in your GUI builder, you will be able to add listeners to it. So, you can drag and drop the text field, a button listener, onto your button and it will be registered with the button. In so doing, the button will store the text field as one of its listeners, and every time a button event is triggered by the user, it will fire the event to its list of listeners.

As discussed in Chapter 3, the builder may choose to construct an adaptor to interpose itself between the two Beans. So, in this case, Café may choose to place an adaptor in between the button and the text field. For more information on adaptors, see Chapter 3.

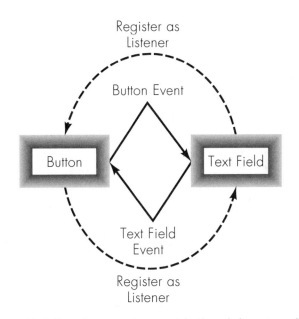

Figure 7.10: *Interactions with the delegation-based event model.*

When the text field receives the event, it can in turn fire a text field event back to its list of text field listeners. In order to complete the circle, you will have had to drag and drop the button Bean onto the text field Bean, signaling to the text field that the button wants to be a listener for text field events.

Once you've finished linking the source and targets of both kinds of events, you can watch as your *button press* triggers a *button event*, which will cause the text field to get its label and send it as a *text field event* to all of its *text field listeners*. This will, in turn, cause the button's *text field event* handler to change the value of the *button's label* as shown in Figure 7.10.

Interactions enable applications to communicate with one another through the Java event model. Once you have put together a Bean application, you will need to save it along with its interactions, events, and current state. This is done through serialization, of course, but Café also will let you store the current state of the *project* in its own project format. The Save features of any GUI builder should be robust and flexible, and Café has both characteristics down pat.

Saving a Bean

Symantec's Visual Café Pro also allows you to store your Bean or Bean project by simply invoking the Save operation in the menu bar. If the project is a full-fledged applet or application, be it composed of several Beans or not, then Visual Café will save the Bean as it would a normal applet or application and constituent source code.

If, however, the project is just a Bean, then Visual Café will give you the option of storing the project in a JAR file, as source code, or as something referred to as a *Café Component*. A Café Component is a specialized Bean that is optimized for the Café environment. Its use depends on the existence of Visual Café, so, in theory, it is not write once, run everywhere.

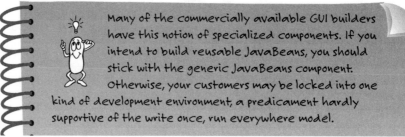

Many of the commercially available GUI builders have this notion of specialized components. If you intend to build reusable JavaBeans, you should stick with the generic JavaBeans component. Otherwise, your customers may be locked into one kind of development environment, a predicament hardly supportive of the write once, run everywhere model.

GUI builders are the single most important aspect of JavaBeans development. You have seen a taste of what GUI builders are all about. As Beans matures and becomes more of a standard for Java computing, several GUI builders, complete with a full set of features, will be available. For now, however, you have seen at least what they are intended to do.

Other GUI Builders

Without a GUI builder, JavaBeans is nothing but a glorified class library. Because of its tools, Beans is capable of fulfilling its promise. To that end, several vendors have produced JavaBeans-enabled tools. This chapter focused on Super Mojo and Café because of their unique characteristics. This space is reserved for some others worth mentioning.

In addition to Symantec, Microsoft has its own line of excellent tools. Microsoft's latest Visual J++ application (version 1.1) supports not only the JavaBeans specification, but ActiveX as well. So, using similar Java code, you can generate both a JavaBean as well as an ActiveX control. If, however, you are like most Java zealots and only wish to reuse an ActiveX control within your Java applications, Visual J++ will assist you in converting your ActiveX control to Java code. Microsoft's Visual J++

Web page (www.microsoft.com.visualj) contains a wealth of sample code as well as a trial version.

Borland has the great distinction of being part of Oracle Corporation's Java initiative. Borland will supply most of the development tools for Oracle products, Java included. Borland's JBuilder is just "a tool" that supports a wide variety of back-end database access schemes, including a suite of JDBC Beans. Borland may be contacted at `www.borland.com/ jbuilder`

Summary

If all of your Beans are architected with the idea that they will at some time be used within a GUI builder, then you will be following the intent of JavaBeans. Remember JavaSoft's original definition of a Java Bean that was discussed in Chapter 2, *Component Models*: "A Java Bean is a reusable software component that can be visually manipulated within a builder tool."

In keeping with this philosophy, the GUI builder enables your Beans to be used and constructed within a graphical environment. Your ultimate goal should be to let non-programmers program. However, it is important not to confuse the issues associated with GUI builders with the GUI properties of a Bean. While they do indeed affect one another, they are distinctly different topics. The next chapter looks into how and when GUI properties of a Bean are used and invoked. With GUI merging, your Beans can be truly plug and play within disparate containers. But, with GUI visibility, your Beans can have some control over whether or not they are displayed at all.

Buying an Espresso Machine

There are those who would tell you that the only truly great espresso machine is one of restaurant-quality, with pistons to handle the force required to build a good cup of espresso. In fact, they are correct, but that's no reason why you shouldn't investigate a simpler machine.

When looking for an espresso machine, the biggest determiner of which product you buy will, of course, be price. For the simplest possible machine, you should look at a stovetop espresso maker. It won't really generate espresso since the force required to tamp the ground coffee beans and subsequently shoot water through them doesn't exist. But for simple steamed coffee, it works.

A steam press machine can often be found at your local department or appliance store. These are the cool looking machines you should buy if you want decent espresso, or just want to impress your friends. Obviously, the geek credo always applies: The more gadgets and doodads that stick out of it, the better.

The pump style machine will give you the minimum pressure required to tamp and shoot the beans, but at a significantly greater price. For an even greater cash outlay, you can purchase a piston-powered machine just like the barista (coffee bartender) at Starbucks.

CHAPTER 8

Bean GUI Issues

- GUI Merging
- Generating GUI properties

Without a graphical representation of some kind, a JavaBean is nothing more than a glorified class library. Because Beans can have a Graphical User Interface (GUI) representation, they can be used within a GUI builder. The notion that software engineering can be accomplished by those who are totally unfamiliar with programming as a professional occupation, thus can become a reality. This chapter covers some of the basics of JavaBean GUI issues. Sometimes, Beans may be able to modify how they are represented within their containers. This concept is called *GUI merging* and is covered in the next section.

GUI Merging

GUI merging allows JavaBean objects to change how they are represented within their containers. I'll discuss some of the intricacies of GUI merging in a moment, but let's first talk about why such a tool is necessary. GUI merging allows you to place Beans in a wide variety of containers. As you will see in Chapter 9, *Bean Integration*, those containers could exist in another component model altogether, such as ActiveX. In the Java Beans world, those containers could be anything from a simple menu bar, to a complex pop-up menu system. You want a Bean to be able to be graphically displayed in any of those environments. Most importantly, the Bean should know nothing about which environment it is in. It should simply tell its parent container, "Display me please," and the parent should just do it.

What is GUI Merging?

GUI merging is the idea that a component can have a limited control over how it is represented in a graphical environment. As mentioned earlier, components that create their own GUI framework would be ideal, but that framework should be able to be manipulated, managed, and displayed by its container. For example, when you put an engine in a car, you can't actually see it from the dashboard. On a Chevrolet, you get a cute little MPH gauge with dials, on a Ford Taurus you get a digital gauge, and on a BMW you get an MPH gauge and a tachometer as well. The engine could very well be the same in all three cars, but the way it is represented to the user (in this case the driver) is different because the container, the make and model of the car, differs in all three cases.

In much the same way, you want your Beans to provide a standard list of inputs and outputs, as discussed in Chapter 3, *Bean Events*, and Chapter 4, *Bean Properties*. Your beans should be able to create a GUI, and to percolate that GUI up to its container. When the container gets a request to display the GUI, it can do so as it pleases.

 It is important to realize that GUI merging is only alluded to in the Bean specification. It is not implemented at all in the `java.beans` package. Unfortunately, JavaSoft has not found the time to include GUI merging support in the current version of the BDK. GUI merging is an important technology, if only because Windows and Visual Basic developers have been able to take advantage of it for some time. Therefore, I will provide my own GUI merging capability and describe it to you here. Keep in mind that the solution shown here will not work if you want to use your Bean in any other component architecture.

Setting up GUI Merging Within a Bean

In order to facilitate GUI merging in your Beans, two objects have been created for your use. The standard Java event model will send requests for GUI changes to containers. The container can then receive the event and handle it independently of the Bean's operation. If the container sees fit to not display the Bean, your Bean will not be affected.

GUI EVENTS

The `GUIEvent` object that has been created allows you to encapsulate a Java `Object` within an event object. When this event is fired to a listener, as you will see in a moment, it will be parsed and handled appropriately. This object simply allows you to place an entire GUI framework inside the context of an event:

```
public class GUIEvent extends EventObject
{
    // private GUI properties
    private Object guiObject;

    GUIEvent(
        Object source
    )
    {
        // call the parent constructor
        super(source);
    }

    // accessor for the guiObject
    public Object getGUIObject()
    {
        return guiObject;
    }

    // mutator for the guiObject
    public void setGUIObject(
        Object guiObject
    )
    {
        this.guiObject = guiObject;
    }
}
```

As you can see, the `guiObject` property holds your Bean's GUI framework so that it can be fired to a `GUIListener` object.

GUI LISTENERS

A `GUIListener` is an interface that allows you to fire `GUIEvent` objects to facilitate GUI merging. When a listener receives a `GUIEvent`, it must then go about handling it as you will see in a moment. For now, examine the interface and notice that two methods have been created. The first method allows you to add GUIs to a container. The second lets you remove these GUIs:

```
public interface GUIListener extends EventListener
{
    public void addGUIObject(
        GUIEvent evt);

    public void removeGUIObject(
        GUIEvent evt);
}
```

HANDLING GUI EVENTS

If you were to implement the `GUIListener` interface, you would need to create both of the methods just described. Inside the add method, you would need to do whatever it takes to add a GUI object to your user interface. Inside the remove method, you would have the liberty of removing the GUI object from your user interface. Therefore, you might want to set up your own mechanism for tracking GUI objects. This should be done independently. In the example that follows, you will see how `GUIEvents` should be handled.

Using GUI Merging

Suppose you had a bunch of `CarBeans` and a container with a `MenuBar`. Somehow when you create a `CarBean`, you want to place it on the `MenuBar` so that you can later get information on it. The `CarBean` will be built to fire `GUIEvents` when it deems necessary. The `Showroom` container will support the `GUIListener` interface and receive `GUIEvents`.

THE SHOWROOM

Our `Showroom` is a simple Java application that instantiates a `Frame`. According the Java Abstract Window Toolkit (AWT) API reference, you will need to attach the `MenuBar` object to the `Frame`. You can add elements to a `MenuBar` object by invoking the `add` method and passing `MenuItem` objects to it. The `MenuBar` will then display the `MenuItem` object on its bar. As you might expect, menu bars in Java can be nested with even more menus, which can, in turn, have even more menus of their own. However, don't attempt to explore those intricacies of the AWT here.

Start by creating the simple initial GUI for the Showroom object:

```
public class Showroom extends Frame
                    implements GUIListener, ActionListener
{
    // the Menu bar in question
    MenuBar menuBar;

    Showroom()
    {
        // set the GUI
        super("Bean Showroom");
        setLayout(null);
        resize(310, 450);

        // create the menu bar
        menuBar = new MenuBar();
        setMenuBar(menuBar);
    }

    // GUIListener methods
    public void addGUIObject(
        GUIEvent evt
    )
    {
    }

    public void removeGUIObject(
        GUIEvent evt
    )
    {
    }

    // action listener method
    public void actionPerformed(
        ActionEvent evt
    )
    {
    }

    public static void main(
        String args[]
    )
    {
        Showroom showroom = new Showroom();
        showroom.show();
    }
}
```

Now go ahead and add a simple file menu to the `MenuBar`. The following code snippet demonstrates how `MenuItems` are added to a `MenuBar`:

```
public class Showroom extends Frame
                       implements GUIListener, ActionListener
{
    // the Menu bar in question
    MenuBar menuBar;

    Showroom()
    {
        // set the GUI
        super("Bean Showroom");
        setLayout(null);
        resize(310, 450);

        // create the menu bar
        menuBar = new MenuBar();
        setMenuBar(menuBar);

        // create a couple of stupid menus
        Menu fileMenu = new Menu("File");
        fileMenu.add("Open...");
        fileMenu.add("Save...");
        fileMenu.add("Save As...");
        fileMenu.add("Exit...");

        // add the menus to the menu bar
        menuBar.add(fileMenu);
    }

    // GUIListener methods
    public void addGUIObject(
        GUIEvent evt
    )
    {
    }

    public void removeGUIObject(
        GUIEvent evt
    )
    {
    }

    // action listener method
    public void actionPerformed(
        ActionEvent evt
    )
    {
    }
```

```
    public static void main(
    String args[]
    )
    {
        Showroom showroom = new Showroom();
        showroom.show();
    }
}
```

THE CAR

The `CarBean` is a nothing-special Bean with a couple of internal properties. Since Chapters 3 and 4 cover the intricacies of events and properties
sufficiently, there is no need to go into detail about how they are created.
Because this Bean supports `GUIListener` objects, you will need to
implement the `addGUIListener` and `removeGUIListener` methods
as well.

You will also need to implement the `GUIEvent` firing mechanism. In
this Bean's case, you want the `GUIEvent` to be fired whenever the Bean
is added to a container. Thanks to Java's wonderful peer notification system, whenever a `Component` is added to a container, the `addNotify`
method is invoked. Therefore, create a `GUIEvent` firing stuff within the
`addNotify` method of the `CarBean` as shown:

```
    public void addNotify()
    {
        // do what we would have done anyway
        super.addNotify();

        // first create the menu
        Menu menu = new Menu(this.name);

        // now create items for it
        MenuItem item = new MenuItem("Price...");
        item.setActionCommand("price-" + this.name);
        item.addActionListener(this);
        menu.add(item);

        item = new MenuItem("Details...");
        item.setActionCommand("details-" + this.name);
        item.addActionListener(this);
        menu.add(item);

        item = new MenuItem("0-60...");
        item.setActionCommand("zero-" + this.name);
        item.addActionListener(this);
        menu.add(item);

        item = new MenuItem("Drive It!");
```

```
        item.setActionCommand("drive-" + this.name);
        item.addActionListener(this);
        menu.add(item);

        // now create the GUI event
        GUIEvent guiEvent = new GUIEvent(this);
        guiEvent.setGUIObject(menu);

        for(int x = 0; x < guiListeners.size(); x++)
        {
            GUIListener listener =
                (GUIListener) guiListeners.elementAt(x);

            listener.addGUIObject(guiEvent);
        }
    }
}
```

Notice how the `ActionListener` is set to `this` in the `addNotify` method. What `this` means is that even though the GUI will be owned and displayed by the container, any events that are fired by the GUI will end up right back at the instance of the `CarBean` from which it was created as shown in Figure 8.1.

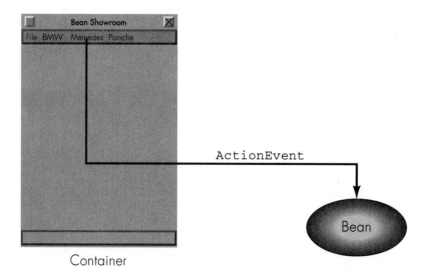

Figure 8.1: *GUI ActionEvents are fired back to the Bean, not the container.*

In order to support this kind of `ActionListener` functionality, you will need to implement the `actionPerformed` method and handle the menu event appropriately:

```
// action listener methods
public void actionPerformed(
    ActionEvent evt
)
{
    if(evt.getActionCommand().startsWith("price"))
    {
    }
    else if(evt.getActionCommand().startsWith("details"))
    {
    }
    else if(evt.getActionCommand().startsWith("zero"))
    {
    }
    else if(evt.getActionCommand().startsWith("drive"))
    {
    }
}

public void addNotify()
{
    // do what we would have done anyway
    super.addNotify();

    // first create the menu
    Menu menu = new Menu(this.name);

    // now create items for it
    MenuItem item = new MenuItem("Price...");
    item.setActionCommand("price-" + this.name);
    item.addActionListener(this);
    menu.add(item);

    item = new MenuItem("Details...");
    item.setActionCommand("details-" + this.name);
    item.addActionListener(this);
    menu.add(item);

    item = new MenuItem("0-60...");
    item.setActionCommand("zero-" + this.name);
    item.addActionListener(this);
    menu.add(item);

    item = new MenuItem("Drive It!");
    item.setActionCommand("drive-" + this.name);
    item.addActionListener(this);
    menu.add(item);

    // now create the GUI event
    GUIEvent guiEvent = new GUIEvent(this);
    guiEvent.setGUIObject(menu);
```

```
        for(int x = 0; x < guiListeners.size(); x++)
        {
            GUIListener listener =
                (GUIListener) guiListeners.elementAt(x);

            listener.addGUIObject(guiEvent);
        }
    }
}
```

IMPLEMENTING THE ADD ROUTINES

Now you need to modify your `Showroom` object to include three instances of the `CarBean` object. You will need to set your properties and add the `Showroom` container as the `GUIListener`. Just to be snooty, create instances for a BMW, a Porsche, and a Mercedes, since all three have introduced some pretty cool two-seater convertibles in the last year:

```
public class Showroom extends Frame
                        implements GUIListener, ActionListener
{
    // the Menu bar in question
    MenuBar menuBar;

    // car beans
    CarBean bmwBean;
    CarBean porscheBean;
    CarBean mercedesBean;

    Showroom()
    {
        // set the GUI
        super("Bean Showroom");
        setLayout(null);
        resize(310, 450);

        // create the menu bar
        menuBar = new MenuBar();
        setMenuBar(menuBar);

        // create a couple of stupid menus
        Menu fileMenu = new Menu("File");
        fileMenu.add("Open...");
        fileMenu.add("Save...");
        fileMenu.add("Save As...");
        fileMenu.add("Exit...");

        // add the menus to the menu bar
        menuBar.add(fileMenu);
```

```
    // create the cars
    bmwBean = new CarBean();
    bmwBean.setName("BMW");
    bmwBean.setZeroTime("6.5");
    bmwBean.addGUIListener(this);
    add(bmwBean);

    mercedesBean = new CarBean();
    mercedesBean.setName("Mercedes");
    mercedesBean.setZeroTime("5.5");
    mercedesBean.addGUIListener(this);
    add(mercedesBean);

    porscheBean = new CarBean();
    porscheBean.setName("Porsche");
    porscheBean.setZeroTime("7.5");
    porscheBean.addGUIListener(this);
    add(porscheBean);
}

// GUIListener methods
public void addGUIObject(
    GUIEvent evt
)
{
}

public void removeGUIObject(
    GUIEvent evt
)
{
}

// action listener method
public void actionPerformed(
    ActionEvent evt
)
{
}

public static void main(
String args[]
)
{
    Showroom showroom = new Showroom();
    showroom.show();
}
}
```

Now implement the add and remove routines. Since you are using a
MenuBar, and since the MenuBar requires the addition of only Menu-

Item objects, you need to first check for the proper type of GUI object from within the add method. Using the Java instanceof operator, check for MenuItem. If the type is correct, go ahead and add the object to your MenuBar:

```java
public class Showroom extends Frame
                        implements GUIListener, ActionListener
{
    // the Menu bar in question
    MenuBar menuBar;

    // car beans
    CarBean bmwBean;
    CarBean porscheBean;
    CarBean mercedesBean;

    Showroom()
    {
        // set the GUI
        super("Bean Showroom");
        setLayout(null);
        resize(310, 450);

        // create the menu bar
        menuBar = new MenuBar();
        setMenuBar(menuBar);

        // create a couple of stupid menus
        Menu fileMenu = new Menu("File");
        fileMenu.add("Open...");
        fileMenu.add("Save...");
        fileMenu.add("Save As...");
        fileMenu.add("Exit...");

        // add the menus to the menu bar
        menuBar.add(fileMenu);

        // create the cars
        bmwBean = new CarBean();
        bmwBean.setName("BMW");
        bmwBean.setZeroTime("6.5");
        bmwBean.addGUIListener(this);
        add(bmwBean);

        mercedesBean = new CarBean();
        mercedesBean.setName("Mercedes");
        mercedesBean.setZeroTime("5.5");
        mercedesBean.addGUIListener(this);
        add(mercedesBean);

        porscheBean = new CarBean();
```

```
        porscheBean.setName("Porsche");
        porscheBean.setZeroTime("7.5");
        porscheBean.addGUIListener(this);
        add(porscheBean);
    }

    // GUIListener methods
    public void addGUIObject(
        GUIEvent evt
    )
    {

        if(evt.getGUIObject() instanceof Menu)
        {
            Menu menu = (Menu) evt.getGUIObject();
            menuBar.add(menu);
        }
        else
        {
            … error checking …
        }
    }

    public void removeGUIObject(
        GUIEvent evt
    )
    {

        if(evt.getGUIObject() instanceof Menu)
        {
            menuBar.remove((Menu) evt.getGUIObject());
        }
        else
        {
            … error checking …
        }
    }

    // action listener method
    public void actionPerformed(
        ActionEvent evt
    )
    {
    }

    public static void main(
String args[]
    )
    {
        Showroom showroom = new Showroom();
        showroom.show();
    }
}
```

Beyond GUI merging lies the question of how Beans interact with the windowing system in which they are placed. After all, if a Bean component is placed within a container, it should support the same window manager constructs that the container is required to support. In addition, a Bean can have several GUI-related properties that define when and how it is visible to others. This concept is discussed in the next section.

Visibility

JavaBeans also supports the idea that, like their ActiveX counterparts, Beans can be run as both client objects, with full GUI support, as well as server objects, without a GUI representation. The JavaBeans `Visibility` interface can help you set up your Beans for both client and server use by letting you set the property of a Bean that determines whether or not its GUI interface will be visible.

The Visibility Interface

The `Visibility` interface should be implemented by any Bean that wishes to give users a chance to tell it not to use a graphical user interface. Whereas GUI merging gives a Bean control over *how* it is displayed, using the methods described in the `Visibility` interface, your Bean can get control over *when* it is displayed.

The `dontUseGui` and `okToUseGui` methods should be called by outside containers and Beans to hide a graphical interface. With an invocation on `dontUseGui`, your Bean should immediately cease and desist from using its graphical representation and should switch to an alternative representation, if available, or suppress output altogether. The `dontUseGui` command may be reversed by the `okToUseGui` command which does the opposite.

 The `dontUseGui` method accepts no parameters and has no return values. It should be declared within any Bean that implements the `Visibility` interface. Upon invocation, some kind of internal mechanism within the Bean should be toggled to prevent the use of any graphical elements:

```
public void dontUseGui()
```

The `okToUseGui` should toggle the results of the `dontUseGui` method. Upon invocation, the same internal mechanism that prevents the use of a GUI should be changed to allow the use of a GUI:

```
public void okToUseGui()
```

■

The `avoidingGUI` method lets an external Bean or container find out whether or not a call to `dontUseGui` has been made on a Bean. If it has, the `avoidingGui` method will return True. If the Bean is currently using a GUI and is allowed to do so, the `avoidingGui` method returns False.

 The `avoidingGui` method returns True if the internal mechanism that was set upon invocation of `dontUseGui` registers that a GUI is not currently being used by the Bean. It should return False if the Bean is allowed to use a GUI:

```
public boolean avoidingGui()
```

■

You can allow your Bean to have some say over whether or not an external Bean or container will make a call to `dontUseGui`. If your Bean absolutely, positively requires a graphical interface, than the `needsGui` method should return True. However, external containers and Beans may choose to ignore the function. It is probably good style to build Beans that may be used on the server end to function without a GUI.

 The `needsGui` method should be declared and implemented by any object implementing the `Visibility` interface. If the Bean cannot function without a graphical interface, the method should return True. If the Bean is able to proceed with computation or other activities without a graphical interface, the method should return False:

```
public boolean needsGui()
```

■

Using the Visibility Interface

The `Visibility` interface should be implemented by any Bean that wants some control over how other Beans react to its GUI properties. The important thing to remember when implementing its methods is that careful consideration should be taken, both at the design time of the overall Bean and at the time the `Visibility` interface is implemented, to ensure that the `needsGui` method returns the appropriate value. If a Bean can be designed to function without a GUI, then the `needsGui` method (and the Bean as a whole) should be structured appropriately. The other three methods of the `Visibility` interface should be designed around the needs of the GUI property.

Summary

Many of the GUI properties of Beans can be controlled using the techniques found in this chapter. After all, without the GUI properties discussed in this chapter, Java Beans is nothing more than a class library. Using the contents of this chapter, you can make sure that your Bean has some say in how it is represented graphically. This will become more important as you will see in the next chapter. ActiveX is a highly prevalent component model in its own right. Indeed, in its previous incarnation as OLE Controls, ActiveX could be considered the world's first and most successful component architecture. In order for the GUI properties and other Bean to become truly useful, you must learn how to integrate properly with ActiveX.

Espresso Drinks

Where would we be without an espresso? The world would not have that quick shot of caffeine, without which it would not be able to function. Thousands of workers charged with making little teeny cups and saucers would be unemployed. The coffee snob behind the counter of your neighborhood espresso bar would have to get a real job. And, your brother, the goatee-wearing former beatnik, would find himself sound asleep at the wheel of life.

Truth be told, espresso is one of the greatest drinks ever made. By simply pressing a little bit of extremely finely ground coffee beans, running very hot water through the grindings at an even greater force, and catching the result at the other end, you can have an elegantly tasteful beverage in about 20 seconds. What a caffeine kick!

By adding the espresso to your favorite Dilbert mug and pouring in a mixture of half steamed milk and half steamed milk foam, you will have the traditional Italian breakfast drink, cappuccino. If you were to adjust the mixture so that it was three-fourths steamed milk and one-fourth steamed milk foam, you would have a latte (the additional milk reduces the acidity of the drink, producing a different flavor). Now, if you were to add some delicious Ghirardelli chocolate syrup to the espresso, add only steamed milk, and garnish with some Fat-Free Cool Whip, you would have the most wonderful drink of all: Café Mocha! Add a flavor shot, and you can easily have a delicious Raspberry-Banana mocha (and one heck of a sugar rush)!

Don't just stand there, impress your friends with this new-found knowledge. In 30 days or less, you too can be a coffee snob!

CHAPTER
9
Bean Integration

- ActiveX Technology
- ActiveX and Beans
- Netscape's Beans Effort
- LiveConnect and Beans

Without some kind of connectivity capability that allows Beans to talk to and be embedded within other component models, the entire notion of a reusable component model would be lost. After all, you should be able to take the hard work and effort you invest into Bean development and use them anywhere. If Java is truly write once, run everywhere, then the same should hold true for JavaBeans. Using a Bean component referred to as the *ActiveX Bridge*, you can build JavaBeans that can be enclosed within ActiveX and OLE containers.

In so doing, your Bean can function within popular programs such as Microsoft Word, Visual Basic, and others. This chapter seeks to show you why such a technology is required, and how you would go about developing a *Bean for all seasons*.

ActiveX Primer

So you've heard all the hype, and the Microsoft Marketing Machine has invaded your desktop with promises of activating your Web page. Did you know that you can build servers using ActiveX controls? Microsoft's own Internet Information Server will let you extend the core capability of an HTTP server with mere ActiveX controls. The question is not exactly "what is ActiveX?" because the answer is that ActiveX is nothing more than what JavaBeans is: a reusable component architecture. No, the question is "why ActiveX?" and, perhaps more to the point, "from whence ActiveX?" To understand what ActiveX is and why you would want to use it, you must understand where it came from and what its roots are.

History of ActiveX

ActiveX is really nothing new. It has been around and sitting on your desktop since the very early days of Microsoft Windows. Sure, it has evolved considerably since then, but at its core the technology remains the same. ActiveX is built on top of the OLE/COM/DCOM framework. The next few sections discuss these three alphabet soup technologies and how they work together to form ActiveX.

OBJECT LINKING AND EMBEDDING

Today when you purchase Microsoft Word from your local software retailer, you are in fact getting a bunch of programs all on the same CD-ROM. The Microsoft Word that you see and love is a collection of mini Object Linking and Embedding (OLE) components that talk to one another and are displayed graphically on your screen. This is quite possibly the most profound example of component technology you will find in existence today. Whatever your position on Microsoft, whether you take the dogmatic opposition to Lord Gates and his Merry Band or look at Bill Gates as *The Man Who Changed Computing Forever*, you must agree that Microsoft Word, no matter how clunky, obese, or powerful you regard it to be, is a wonderful component model in and of itself.

OLE is the framework that is used to build all of those disparate components. The Font Toolbar is an OLE object, the Spell Checker is an OLE object, and the Office Assistant is an OLE object. Each of these parts is farmed out to individual development teams working simultaneously to get their portion included in the final build of the product. In so doing, component design at its best takes places. The development team in charge of the Office Assistant knows nothing about the development team in charge of the various Toolbars. When the product is ready to be assembled, it's sort of like taking a bunch of Lego Bricks and making a city. Each component slips into the overall framework and everything works. This is precisely what is trying to be accomplished with JavaBeans and component models in general.

COMPONENT OBJECT MODEL

If OLE objects are the *parts* that are used to put applications together, the Component Object Model (COM) is the *glue*. It is the underlying communication mechanism that allows OLE clients and servers to talk to one another. Microsoft Word OLE components use COM to send messages to one another. The Font Toolbar will send a COM message to the OLE Editor Server. The Editor will then respond accordingly.

COM is a Microsoft proprietary technology, and that is the crux of the opposition to it. No matter how many standards bodies Microsoft sells it to, it currently exists only on the Microsoft platform. You may ask yourself why other operating systems do not include support for COM, and the answer is both technical (it is difficult to port COM) and philosophical (most companies loathe and fear Microsoft). Nevertheless, the fact is that Microsoft and COM are intertwined and married to one another, for good or for bad. If you program in COM, you are locked into Microsoft Windows, for better or for worse.

DISTRIBUTED COM

No matter how gee-whiz neat COM is to propeller heads, it is quite a limiting distributed object technology. Chapter 10, *Bean Networking,* discusses some of the networking alternatives to COM in the Common Object Request Broker Architecture (CORBA) and Remote Method Invocation (RMI). Because COM is sometimes considered inferior to these other technologies, Microsoft introduced Distributed COM, or DCOM (pronounced *dee-COM*). DCOM focuses primarily on the networking protocols between COM and OLE objects on disparate machines.

DCOM is based on the industry-standard Distributed Computing Environment (DCE) specification. DCE, together with Remote Procedure Call (RPC), provide COM objects a means to invoke on one another across a network. DCOM incorporates the best of COM for intra-machine communication, but adds layers of support for safe and secure communication for inter-machine communication. Because of its makeup, DCOM is ideally suited for seamless and hidden (from the user) messaging across the Internet.

BRINGING IT ALL TOGETHER

Often, OLE, COM, or DCOM objects and technologies are mentioned under one moniker, be it OLE or COM. Because the three are so tightly woven together and practically synonymous among developers, they are rarely (except in very geeky conversations) talked about as separate entities. Microsoft itself has contributed to this confusion by taking the three technologies and putting them under one umbrella.

ActiveX is the combination of OLE, COM, and DCOM. When Microsoft finally smelled the coffee (pun intended) and saw the beauty (and income potential) of the Internet, they began to stretch COM, DCOM, and OLE to the Internet and a distributed heterogeneous environment. When they were done, ActiveX was born and the component wars were on.

Building a Control

Generally, ActiveX controls are built using a Microsoft tool such as Visual C++ or Visual Basic. However, Microsoft's Visual J++ 1.1 provides a simple ActiveX Control Wizard that will allow you take a Java object and convert it into a COM object, essentially making it an ActiveX control (see Figure 9.1).

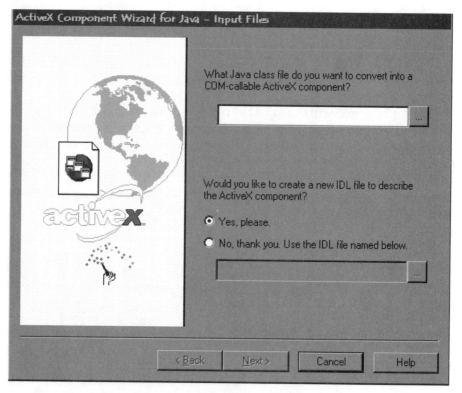

Figure 9.1: The ActiveX Wizard in Microsoft Visual J++.

Using a Control

Once the Wizard is applied to a Java class file, a COM object is registered and available for other objects to invoke on it. Of course, in order for other objects to invoke on the COM server you created from a Java class file, they must also be ActiveX objects. For all intents and purposes, this means that all objects that wish to invoke on an ActiveX control must speak the COM protocols.

A control that is embedded within a web page can have full reign over a client's machine once it is downloaded. In so doing, an ActiveX control in a web page can potentially do much more than a similar Java applet. Java applets are restricted by their sandbox security model and are prevented from accessing the client's local resources, including disk space and network connections. ActiveX controls that are downloaded have no such restriction and are therefore somewhat more robust.

ActiveX and Security

So, you've seen how useful ActiveX can be. It breaks the Java sandbox model and allows true interactive Internet content. For some cases, it can really make a difference in whether a Web site is *active* or just plain dull. For all of its security problems, ActiveX is still a halfway decent technology. But, there's the rub. By its very nature, the Internet requires a secure transmission connection. It's absolutely essential. You simply cannot have users unwittingly downloading binaries to their machine.

WHY ACTIVEX IS FLAWED

Back before the Internet became popular and Bulletin Board Systems (BBS) were all the rage, the number one rule of networking was to always be careful when downloading. You never knew where those programs had ended up. For many years, people downloaded applications and ended up with viruses strewn across their hard disk. Such were the perils of computing, and all of us geeks knew it then and know it now.

For the mainstream computer user, not the gee-whiz propeller head, downloading is something that is rarely, if ever, done. Instead, ActiveX gives us what is essentially *push technology*; a means by which the server decides when and what to put on your machine. For these novice computer users, an ActiveX control that brings a virus to their system is more than an annoyance, it's almost catastrophic. ActiveX controls are a dangerous technology if security is not managed very carefully.

AUTHENTICODE

To counteract the perception that ActiveX controls are insecure, the massive marketing machine at Microsoft rolled into full gear to bring us Authenticode, a technology originally from VeriSign. Some aspects of authentication and certificate-based security were discussed in Chapter 6, *Bean Persistence and Packaging,* and Microsoft is making full use of the technology. While it is most certainly not ripe now, perhaps the famous

Microsoft usability engineers will make certificates and authentication a household word, bringing true ease-of-use for security constructs.

For the time being, the ease-of-use is simply not there. A user must still administer his or her own certificates and security restrictions. Authenticode wraps itself around an ActiveX control in much the same way that a certificate is wrapped around a Java Bean (in fact, Authenticode is nothing but an umbrella for various kinds of certificates and encryption schemes). You, the user, will need to set up an Authenticode access list on your local machine. When your browser attempts to download an ActiveX control, it will match certificates and authenticate the control. In theory, if the control is not from a recognized source (i.e., a trusted source), then it is not downloaded. If the control's certificate matches a certificate in your access list, then it is downloaded and run just as it normally would.

Microsoft hopes that users will be willing to go to content sites, download a certificate, add it to the access list, and therefore allow controls from that content site to be downloaded at will. You wouldn't, for example, go to *Satan's House of ActiveX Controls* and expect for the controls there to be harmless. On the contrary, a control site run by the *Prince of Evil* would almost certainly contain pernicious ActiveX controls to begin with. However, if you went to the Microsoft site, you could be assured that the certificate you download from there would be kind, generous, and willing to part with about three billion dollars of Bill Gates' personal wealth. This is where Microsoft's statement that Web surfers "will only visit sites that they trust" comes from.

Authenticode is fine and dandy as far as the Microsoft marketing machine is concerned. However, as you saw in Chapter 6, all computer security can be broken. There is no foolproof way to prevent anyone from creating an ActiveX control that can be malicious. The only way to prevent such an attack is to turn off ActiveX controls altogether, an edict that would be truly ironic if it were to come from Microsoft itself.

ActiveX controls are a truly wonderful technology. However, they suffer from two fatal flaws. First, they are insecure. They lack a means to prevent malicious controls from being downloaded. This is extremely bad, but Authenticode can minimize the damage if it is implemented properly and managed by the end-user. ActiveX controls are also Windows binaries, meaning that they are not platform-independent. That's fine for the 85 percent of the computer world that runs some version of the Microsoft operating system. And Microsoft itself will tell you that they could care less about those that do not use Windows. As far as they are concerned, it's your loss. That's why Beans are so important to the Java revolution. Thanks to the Java sandbox, Beans, because they are nothing but Java classes, are platform-independent and, when used within an applet, are totally secure.

Building an ActiveX Bean

If ActiveX is a good technology, JavaBeans is an exceptional technology. It's clear to Java experts that JavaBeans is the way to go. It's platform-independent, inherently secure, and just plain easy to write. As seen in Chapter 7, *GUI Builders*, there are an abundance of tools on the market with which to build Beans. What if you wanted to take your Beans and live in that other world of ActiveX as well? Using the Beans to ActiveX Bridge, you can accomplish just such a feat. In fact, the steps necessary to convert your Bean into an ActiveX control are so simple, that you just may wonder what the big deal is to begin with.

How the Bridge Works

Because OLE requires all components to be placed in its TypeLib registry, the ActiveX Bridge first converts the existing Bean into an OLE control by executing a packaging application. Figure 9.2 shows that the packaging application assembles all the necessary information for the TypeLib file including all of the components properties, events, and methods, by washing the Bean contained in a JAR file through a source generator. The source generator creates Java stub files for the Bean that allow the OLE interaction to take place.

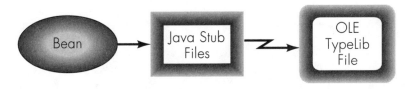

Figure 9.2: *How the Beans to ActiveX Bridge works.*

Once all of the TypeLib information is put together, the packager places the control in the TypeLib registry by compiling all of the generated stub files. It then deletes any source files that it might have created, but allows the .class files to remain in the original JAR file. In so doing, the JAR file may be exported to other systems without the need for repackaging. It will be both an OLE control and a regular JavaBean.

Converting a Bean to a Control

As just outlined, the conversion process is actually quite simple thanks to the GUI-based packaging tool. The packaging tool does all the work for you, provided that you supply it with a JAR file containing your Bean.

This section outlines how to use the packaging tool to convert an existing Bean into an ActiveX control. The next section will go into detail about how to use the control once it is converted.

The screen grabs are for the standard ActiveX packager defaults. There is a bug with the packager that prevents you from loading your own Beans into it unless the Bean is placed within the hierarchy of a Java package. Therefore, the screen grabs are subject to change since the packager was still in beta at the time this book was written.

USING THE PACKAGER

The packager is a Java application that will take all of the Beans in your JAR file and turn them into ActiveX controls. The first thing you need to do is start the application from the MSDOS window:

```
%prompt% java sun.beans.ole.packager
```

Now you will need to specify the JAR file from which you would like to load your Beans as shown in Figure 9.3. The JAR file need not be in your CLASSPATH, but it should be accessible from within the application.

```
: Ole Bean Packager                                    _ □ X

        ActiveX Packager For Beans - Version Beta-1

                        Step 1 of 5

    In this step, you have to specify the jar file which contains the Bean


  c:\bdk\jars\buttons.jar

                                                      Browse

                    <Back    Next>
              - Copyright Sun Microsystems - 1997 -
```

Figure 9.3: *Selecting the JAR file from the packager.*

SELECTING THE BEAN

Once you load the JAR file that you are interested in converting, you must select from within it the Bean that should be converted (see Figure

9.4). The packager is limited to one Bean conversion per cycle, so if there are multiple Beans in the JAR file that you would like to convert, you will need to run the packager again for each Bean. After you select the Bean, you can move on to the next step.

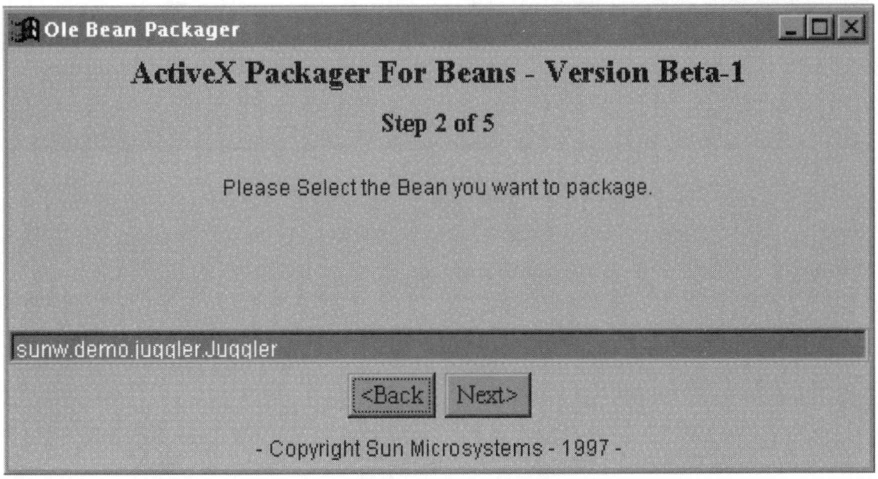

Figure 9.4: *Selecting the Bean to convert.*

GIVING THE BEAN AN ACTIVEX NAME

Naming the Bean is a totally arbitrary step. You may want to keep the same name, or you may want to rename the control to something that will allow you to discern it from other, native controls. In any event, the name you choose will have no effect on the resulting control. Simply select the name in the packaging tool and move on to the next step shown in Figure 9.5.

SPECIFYING THE TARGET DIRECTORY

The target directory is where the packager tool will place the resulting Java stubs and so forth. Your completed ActiveX control will be placed here and registered with the TypeLib registry as located in that directory. So, think carefully about where you want the target directory to be located and specify that location in the packager as shown in Figure 9.6. If you want to move the control to another location later on, you will need to re-register the control with the registry (not exactly an easy task as seasoned OLE programmers will note).

GENERATING THE CONTROL

Once you've specified all of this information, you will need to specify how you would like events to be mapped from Beans to ActiveX (see Figure 9.7). Chapter 3, *Bean Events*, discussed how Beans events are noth-

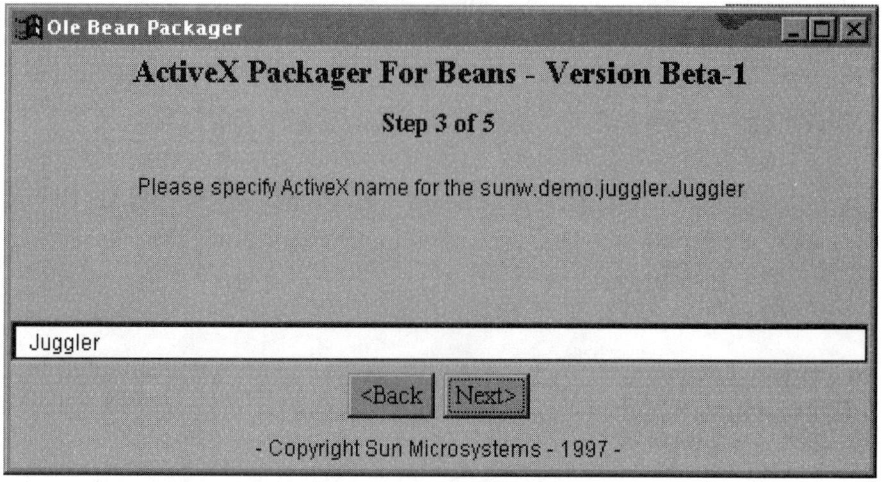

Figure 9.5: *I've kept the same name.*

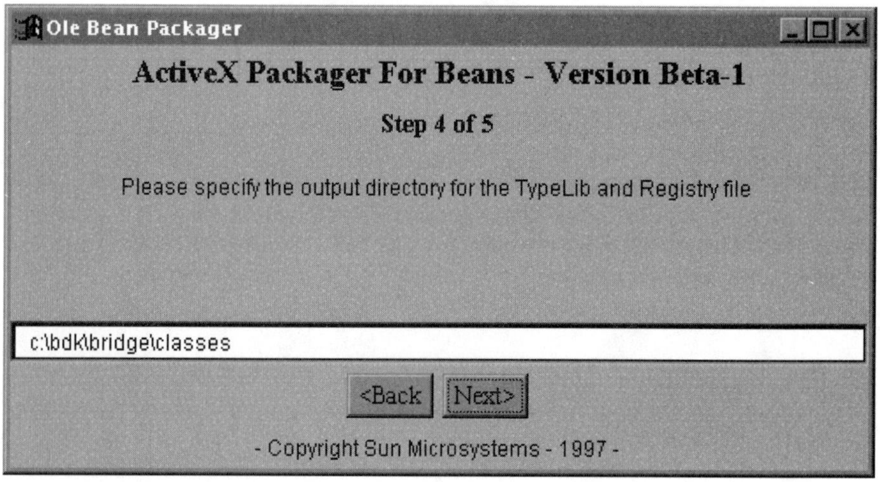

Figure 9.6: *The target directory has been selected.*

ing more than Java events. In ActiveX, events are handled quite differently as I will discuss in a moment. In short, if you choose to uncrack the event, you will revert to ActiveX events. If you choose to crack the event, you will be able to map JavaBeans events directly to ActiveX and be able to use the event information to which you are accustomed in Beans from within ActiveX containers.

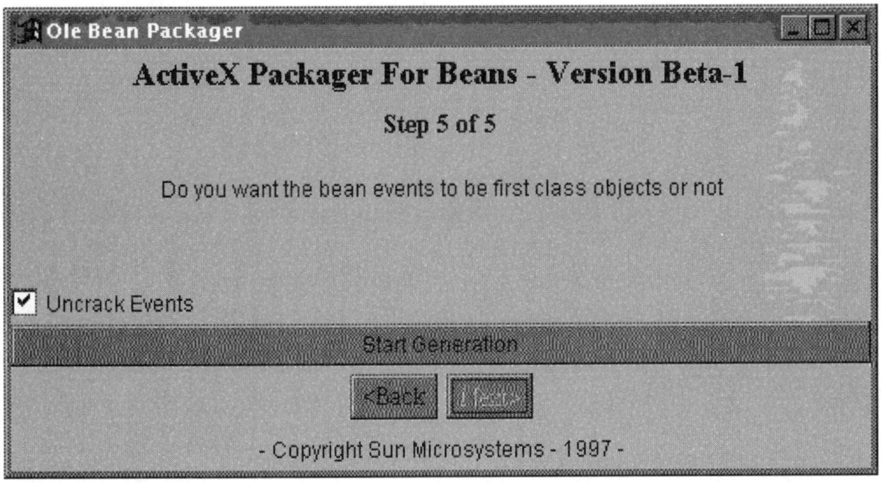

Figure 9.7: *Choosing the style of events for your new control.*

Issues with Converting

There are several issues associated with moving from JavaBeans to ActiveX. Some of these are rather mundane, while others will force you to rethink your entire Beans architecture. This section will attempt to outline most of these issues. However, as with every conversion process, there are some instances in which conversion will simply not be likely. If, however, you follow these architectural guidelines, you will be able to convert most of your Beans to ActiveX controls.

EVENTS

Because ActiveX containers may only communicate with one source interface at a time, all of the Beans event source interfaces will be merged into one unique interface. This interface will act as the source interface for your ActiveX Bean and allow other ActiveX controls to talk to it. There is, however, a problem with this. If you have several source interfaces that have the same name, you will need to change them.

As an example, let's look again at the following `ButtonListener` interface that was designed back in Chapter 3. It contains one method called `fireButtonEvent`. If you had another interface being used by this Bean and it had the same `fireButtonEvent` method, then the event conversion would fail:

```
import java.util.event.EventListener;
public class ButtonListener extends EventListener
{
    public void fireButtonEvent(
        ButtonEvent buttonEvent);
}
```

Another important issue concerning the conversion from AWT events to ActiveX events is the makeup of the event that is transmitted to the listener. As you can see in the previous code snippet, the `fireButton-Event` method receives a `ButtonEvent` object that inherits from the generic `EventObject`. This is the normal and expected way of doing things in the AWT.

However, in ActiveX, OLE events are delivered with a bunch of extra variables that describe the event. Using the packaging tool, however, you can specify in which manner you would like your ActiveX Bean to receive events. If you choose to crack the event in step 5 (depicted in Figure 9.7), you will receive the following event signature for the `fireButtonEvent` method:

```
Private Sub RainbowButton_fireButtonEvent(
    ByVal modifiers as Long,
    ByVal buttonCommand as String,
    ByVal ID as Long,
    ByVal source as Object)
...
End Sub
```

If you choose to uncrack the event, you will receive the following event signature:.

```
Private Sub RainbowButton_fireButtonEvent(
    ByVal ButtonEvent as Object
)
...
End Sub
```

As you can see, the first option is the preferred OLE method. The event is split into a bunch of extra variables and you can determine the characteristics of the event from these variables. However, in using the uncracked method, you will receive an OLE `Object` that you will need to know how to parse.

PROPERTIES

All properties are accessible from within ActiveX controls in the same manner as they are within Beans. The bridge will automatically invoke the proper accessors and mutators for the property. If the property is *bound*, the `bindable` flag is set in the OLE property's description. If it is *constrained*, the `requestedit` flag is set. Any `PropertyChange-Events` are forwarded via the OLE `IpropertyNotifySink` interface. `PropertyVetoExceptions` are also supported, just as in Beans.

Native Java types are converted to OLE types as outlined in Table 9.1.

Table 9.1: *Java to OLE-type mappings.*

Java Type	OLE Type
boolean	VT_BOOL
char	VT_UI1
double	VT_R4
float	VT_R2
int	VT_I4
byte	VT_I2
short	VT_I2
long	VT_I4 (truncated)
java.lang.String	VT_BSTR
java.awt.Color	VT_COLOR
java.awt.Font	VT_FONT
Arrays (1 dimension)	VT_ARRAY | type
Else	VT_DISPATCH

INTROSPECTION

Introspection is not supported by ActiveX. As a result, Introspection is only useful during the time in which packaging is done. For the time being, all Beans that rely heavily on introspection should make alternative architectural decisions.

PERSISTENCE

ActiveX containers will serialize your ActiveX Bean as long as the Bean supports persistence either via the serialization mechanism or some other kind of external mechanism (such as JDBC). For more information on serialization, check out Chapter 6. Only the IPersistStorage, IPersistStreamInt, and IPropertyBag interfaces are currently supported. Furthermore, all serialization must be done in one thread. ActiveX does not support multi-threaded serialization.

METHODS

All methods that would normally be available to other Beans will be exposed by ActiveX for other controls to invoke. However, ActiveX does not support overloadable methods. In such cases where there are identical methods with different parameter lists, the method with the most parameters will be used. If your Bean is to be used within an ActiveX control, be sure to design your methods appropriately.

All arguments and return values are automatically marshalled by the bridge into the data types mentioned in Table 9.1. All exceptions thrown by the method will be packaged into the OLE `EXCEPINFO` object and returned to the calling container.

CUSTOMIZERS

Any customizer that you create will be used within the ActiveX container just as it would within a Bean container. If you are using Visual Basic or some other ActiveX GUI Builder, the customizer will be used when the ActiveX Bean is selected on the palette. The next section discusses the use of ActiveX Beans within Visual Basic.

PACKAGING

The ActiveX Bridge currently expects all Beans to be placed within JAR files. This means that any Bean that you would like to convert must be loaded from within a Java Archive. For more information on Java Archives and packaging Beans in general, take a look at Chapter 6.

Using the Bean Control in an ActiveX Container

Once you have converted your ActiveX control, it is time to use it from within Visual Basic 5.0 to create an application. Of course, if you are using an earlier version of Visual Basic, the control will still work, but the menus and instructions are slightly different. This application involves no more steps than creating a normal ActiveX control would. Because the packaging tool already stored your ActiveX Bean into the OLE registry, you should be able to automatically load it from within Visual Basic. From there, connecting the Beans to other OLE controls is very simple.

LOADING THE ACTIVEX BEAN

After starting Visual Basic, you should go to the Projects menu and select Components. Search for and select the Juggler Bean Control from the list shown in Figure 9.8. Once it is selected, you will notice that it can be found on the Visual Basic palette. As you can see, the packager automatically appends the words *Bean Control* to the name you specified in step 3 (Figure 9.5). Here, you will select the Juggler Bean and Explicit Button Bean that were installed when the ActiveX Packager was installed.

CONNECTING THE ACTIVEX BEAN TO AN OLE CONTROL

Once the Juggler is loaded onto the palette (see Figure 9.9), you should be able to select it and plop it down on the form.

If you click an instance of the Juggler Bean on the Visual Basic form, the properties panel on the right of the screen will change to reflect the properties of the Bean. Now, select another control from the palette, and plop it down on the form as shown in Figure 9.10.

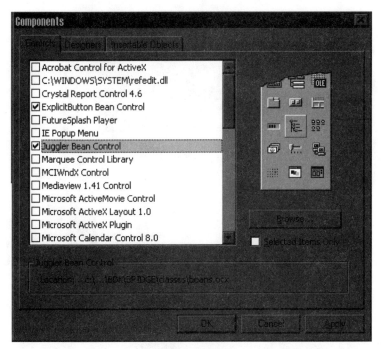

Figure 9.8:   *Selecting an ActiveX control to add to Visual Basic.*

Figure 9.9:   *JavaBeans components as ActiveX
Controls within Visual Basic.*

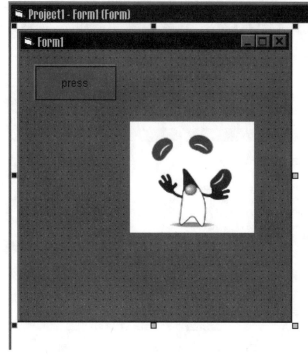

Figure 9.10: *JavaBeans/ActiveX Controls on Visual Basic Forms.*

RUNNING THE APPLICATION

In order to modify the button so that it stops the Juggler when it is pressed, you will need to add a line of Visual Basic code to your application. To do so, double-click on the `ExplicitButton` that you dropped onto the form. That should bring up the code editor window shown in Figure 9.11. You will need to add the line of code that reads `Juggler1.stop`.

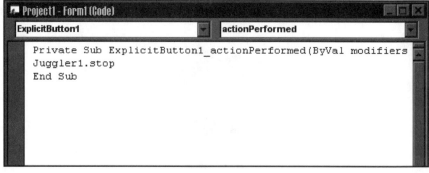

Figure 9.11: *Modifying the code in the control to stop the Juggler.*

Once you have added the code, select Run from the Project window, press the button, and watch your Juggler stop in mid-stream!

So, as you can see, making a Bean into an ActiveX control is actually quite simple. There's not that much work involved to begin with because the packaging tool does most of the work for you. Netscape Communications Corporation is working on their own bridge for Beans to be able to talk to LiveConnect components. Furthermore, Netscape's JavaScript language will be able to talk to a Bean and relay information to it from both other Beans as well as other disparate sources. The next section discusses, in depth, this portion of the JavaBeans integration technology.

JavaScripting a Bean

Netscape Communications, the thorn in the side of Microsoft, can no longer be considered just another Internet startup. With its full embrace of bleeding edge technologies such as CORBA, Java, and more; Netscape is a scrappy, innovative little Silly Valley company that seems to know what it is doing. When it was but an infant, Netscape bloomed by taking advantage of a phenomenon that was just beginning to take root: the Internet. Now, Netscape has introduced, and plans on making common-place Internet technologies ranging from ubiquitous Java to esoteric CORBA. In so doing, the Internet Revolution that it took such great advantage of at the onset can once again propel the company against industry titan Microsoft.

A key component of Netscape's strategy is JavaScript, an interpreted language that exists on the client side within your Web page. This section outlines the key features of JavaScript and how it can be integrated with JavaBeans.

What is Javascript?

When Java was first unveiled, and Marc Andreesen wisely embraced it, Netscape had a little language of its own already in the works. To capitalize on the unstoppable Java wave, Andreesen and Netscape renamed their language JavaScript and yet another alternative to Microsoft proprietary technology was born.

HELLO, WORLD, JAVASCRIPT STYLE

JavaScript is a simple, interpreted scripting language that shares its roots with Visual Basic Script, Tool Control Language (TCL), and the shell scripting languages so inherent on Unix platforms such C-shell, Bourne-shell, and Perl. If you are a Windows/DOS user, your most intimate experience with scripting technologies is probably the batch file mechanism.

JavaScript programs are executed by the browser in a manner very much unlike their Java cousins. JavaScript scripts are washed through an interpreter just like Java, but unlike Java, those programs remain in standard English format. JavaScript programs have no bytecode like Java; rather they are written directly into the HTML using the <SCRIPT> tags. In the example that follows, you can see a simple Hello, World program using JavaScript. Everything within the <SCRIPT> tag is considered code for the language specified in the LANGUAGE parameter:

```
<HTML>
<BODY>
    <SCRIPT LANGUAGE="JavaScript">
        document.write("Howdy, pardner!")
    </SCRIPT>
</BODY>
</HTML>
```

Notice how the syntax looks eerily similar to Java. This is not by accident. JavaScript programmers more than likely fall into one of two camps. First, there are those who are not interested in programming, and want a simple quick and dirty solution for client side Web programming. And then there are Java programmers, who do want a means to get Java applets to communicate more effectively on a Web page.

FUNCTIONS AND JAVASCRIPT

Now, suppose instead of directly writing your hello message onto the browser, you wanted to have the browser to be able to call a JavaScript function in much the same manner as a Java object would invoke a method on another Java object. In order to create a function, you must declare it in the HTML as a function:

```
<HTML>
<HEAD>
    <SCRIPT LANGUAGE="JavaScript">
        function HelloWorld()
        {
            this.document.write("Howdy, Pardner!")
        }
    </SCRIPT>
</HEAD>
</HTML>
```

This time the script was placed within the <HEAD> tag in the HTML. This is considered good JavaScript style, but is not entirely necessary. Whenever you wish to declare functions for later use, place them within the <HEAD> tag. Later on, you can call those functions from within the <BODY> tag.

In order for the browser to actually call this function, you need to create another JavaScript region in which you will invoke the `HelloWorld` method. In the example that follows, there a bunch of text in the HTML, followed by a script that calls the `HelloWorld` function, followed by more text:

```
<HTML>
<HEAD>
    <SCRIPT LANGUAGE="JavaScript">
        function HelloWorld()
        {
            this.document.write("Howdy, Pardner!")
        }
    </SCRIPT>
</HEAD>
<BODY>
    <H1>Hail to the Redskins!  Hail Victory!</H1>
    <SCRIPT LANGUAGE="JavaScript">
        HelloWorld()
    </SCRIPT>
    <H1>Braves on the Warpath!  Fight for ol' DC!</H1>
</BODY>
</HTML>
```

PASSING PARAMETERS

Sometimes, you will need to pass parameters to your function and your function will need to act appropriately upon them. In JavaScript, parameters are passed by value, not by reference. This is because JavaScript has no pointers. The following example passes in a name to the `HelloWorld` method. The `HelloWorld` method will then act upon the name being passed:

```
<HTML>
<HEAD>
    <SCRIPT LANGUAGE="JavaScript">
        function HelloWorld( name)
        {
            this.document.write("Howdy, " + name + "!")
        }
    </SCRIPT>
</HEAD>
<BODY>
    <H1>Hail to the Redskins!  Hail Victory!</H1>
    <SCRIPT LANGUAGE="JavaScript">
        HelloWorld("Jenny")
    </SCRIPT>
    <H1>Braves on the Warpath!  Fight for ol' DC!</H1>
</BODY>
</HTML>
```

Notice how function parameters do not have types associated with them. JavaScript functions should be written intelligently in order to handle the parameters, so that the values stored within them are used by the appropriate types.

JAVASCRIPT OBJECTS

A JavaScript object is declared using the same `function` keyword that was used earlier. This is highly unusual, and programmers of high-level languages such as Java and C++ will more than likely experience a few convulsions over this. But, fear not, JavaScript's object mechanism actually works. Objects are created by using the `new` keyword on the name of the function and passing in the appropriate values.

In the next example, you are going to create a `HelloPerson` object that accepts two parameters; the name of the person and their age. You will then modify the `HelloWorld` object to accept a `HelloPerson` object and print out the appropriate message:

```
<HTML>
<HEAD>
    <SCRIPT LANGUAGE="JavaScript">
        function HelloWorld(helloPerson)
        {
            this.document.write(
                "Howdy, " + helloPerson.name +
                helloPerson.age + "!")
        }

        function HelloPerson(name, age)
        {
            this.name = name;
            this.age = age;
        }
    </SCRIPT>
</HEAD>
<BODY>
    <H1>Hail to the Redskins!  Hail Victory!</H1>
    <SCRIPT LANGUAGE="JavaScript">
        helloPerson = new HelloPerson("Joe Gibbs", 50);
        HelloWorld( helloPerson);
    </SCRIPT>
    <H1>Braves on the Warpath!  Fight for ol' DC!</H1>
</BODY>
</HTML>
```

JAVASCRIPT TALKING TO JAVA

Now, what you need to be able to do is to take a Java class and embed it in the same HTML file in which the JavaScript code resides. In so doing, you can have your Java applet call a JavaScript function, and have your

JavaScript function call a function within the Java applet. You can then take it one step further and have two separate Java applets on the same page that communicate with one another using JavaScript. One applet can call a JavaScript function that will in turn call a method on the other applet.

Building an Applet   The following code is a simple `HelloWorld` object in Java. It contains one method that returns a `String`, `get-Hello`:

```
public class HelloWorld extends Applet
{
    public void init()
    {
        System.out.println(
            getHello("Ralph the wonder llama", 1));
    }

    public String getHello(
        String name,
        int age
    )
    {
        return "Howdy " + name + " " + age + "!";
    }
}
```

Accessing an Applet from JavaScript   Now, take your `Hel-loWorld` object and embed it within the HTML. You will then modify the previous `HelloWorld` function to use this Java object. Notice how straightforward and simple this kind of communication mechanism is. All you need to do is specify a `NAME` in the `APPLET` tag, and access it using `document.NAME`:

```
<HTML>
<HEAD>
</HEAD>
<BODY>
    <H1>Hail to the Redskins!  Hail Victory!</H1>
    <APPLET CODE="HelloWorld.class" NAME="helloWorld"
            WIDTH=100 HEIGHT=100>
    </APPLET>
    <SCRIPT LANGUAGE="JavaScript">
        document.write(document.helloWorld.getHello("igor",
3));
    </SCRIPT>
<H1>Braves on the Warpath!  Fight for ol' DC!</H1>
</BODY>
</HTML>
```

JAVA TALKING TO JAVASCRIPT

Going the other way around is a bit more complicated and requires access to Netscape's Open Network Environment (ONE) classes for Java. But, since this is basically a Netscape endeavor, and not a Java endeavor, asking for a non-proprietary solution is probably asking for too much. After all, it is in Netscape's best interest to get you to use ONE rather than another object model. The ONE objects and associated documentation may be obtained by contacting Netscape on their developer's Web Site:

```
http://developer.netscape.com/
```

Getting a Handle on JavaScript   When you obtain Netscape's Live-Connect Software Developer's Kit, you will have access to the `netscape` package. You should then use the `JSObject` object to get a handle on the JavaScript interpreter on the browser window in which the applet is running (see Figure 9.12).

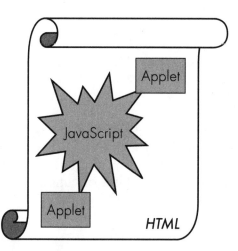

Figure 9.12:   *Accessing JavaScript from within Java.*

In order to do this from within your Java code, simply import the `netscape` package and create an instance of the `JSObject` object:.

```
import netscape.javascript.*;

public class ElleFant extends Applet
{
    public void init()
    {
        JSObject javascriptObject = JSObject.getWindow(this);
    }
}
```

Calling a JavaScript Function Now that you have the JavaScript window, you can then go about invoking on a JavaScript function. Suppose you had the following HTML code for a JavaScript function called `getPeanut`. Note that the applet has been included in the applet tag:.

```
<HTML>
<HEAD>
    <SCRIPT LANGUAGE="JavaScript">
        function getPeanut()
        {
            this.document.write(
        }
    </SCRIPT>
</HEAD>
<BODY>
    <APPLET code=ElleFant.class …>
    </APPLET>
</BODY>
</HTML>
```

The `ElleFant` object can invoke on the JavaScript function `get-Peanut` by simply using the `eval` method in the `JSObject` object. The `eval` method has a very simple syntax that includes the expression that you would like to have executed by the JavaScript interpreter.

 The `eval` method in the `JSObject` object accepts one parameter, a `String` expression. The expression will be parsed by the JavaScript interpreter and should take the form of:

```
JSObject.getWindow().eval("myFunction\(\)");
```

Notice how the `eval` method uses the backslash (\) character to indicate the presence of parentheses within the expression. The API of the `eval` method is as follows:

```
public void eval(

    String expression)
```

■

In order to invoke the `getPeanut` method, specify `"getPeanut()"` as the expression for the `eval` method:

```
import netscape.javascript.*;

public class ElleFant extends Applet
{
    public void init()
```

```
        {
            JSObject javascriptObject = JSObject.getWindow(this);
            javascriptObject.eval("getPeanut\(\)");
        }
    }
```

Alternatively, your applications may use the `call` method in the `JSObject` object. The call method allows you to send parameters. In this case, parameters are not being passed to the JavaScript function, but this method will be demonstrated in a moment.

The `call` method of the `JSObject` object accepts two parameters. The first parameter is the string name of the function, and the second parameter is an array of Java `Object`s that are to be passed as parameters to the Java-Script function:.

```
public void call(

    String functionName,

    Object arguments[])
```

■

JavaScript and Beans

Now that you have all the tools necessary to include the scripting glue for our disparate JavaBeans, you can have the Beans talk to one another on the same page. It is important to note that what you are doing is actually having applets that happen to be composed of Beans talk to one another. As discussed in Chapter 2, *Component Models*, JavaBeans are nothing more than Java objects. What you choose to do with those objects is of no consequence to the Beans. So, if you were to take a bunch of Beans and put them together to form an applet, then you can proceed on to the next section.

Hooking Beans Together with JavaScript

As you have seen, in order to provide the scripting glue between two or more Beans, you need to have access to JavaScript as well as Netscape's ONE. Without both of these two components, you will not be able to use JavaScript to bring your Beans together. Furthermore, you are not actually connecting Beans, but applets built out of Beans.

Handling Event Mechanisms

The first thing that you need to do is to build a JavaScript function that mimics the event listener that your Beans are using. This JavaScript function, which would be called `fireButtonEvent` for the `RainbowBut-`

ton example, will accept one parameter, the `javaEvent`. When the applet uses Netscape ONE to fire an event to the JavaScript interpreter, the function that is called will then relay the event to the other applet on the page. In so doing, the applet receiving the event need not register itself with the firing applet. Here, in the `AppletOne` object, a `Button-Event` will be fired to the JavaScript interpreter. In order to fire events, you will need to use the `call` method rather than the `eval` method of `JSObject`:

```
import netscape.javascript.*;

public class AppletOne extends Applet
{
    public void init()
    {
        ButtonEvent buttonEvent = new ButtonEvent();
        Object objArray[] = new Object[1];
        ObjArray[0] = buttonEvent;

        JSObject javascriptObject = JSObject.getWindow(this);
        javascriptObject.call("fireButtonEvent", objArray);
    }
}
```

The JavaScript code for this event handling routine is listed here. As mentioned, it takes one parameter, the `javaEvent`, and promptly fires it to the other applet on the page:

```
<HTML>
<HEAD>
    <SCRIPT LANGUAGE="JavaScript">
        function fireButtonEvent(
            javaEvent
        )
        {
            document.AppletTwo.fireButtonEvent(javaEvent);
        }
    </SCRIPT>
</HEAD>
<BODY>
    <APPLET code=AppletOne.class name="AppletOne">
    </APPLET>
    <APPLET code=AppletTwo.class name="AppletTwo">
    </APPLET>
</BODY>
</HTML>
```

As you can see, `AppletTwo` must have the same `fireButtonEvent` implemented in order to receive this event. Both `AppletOne` and `AppletTwo` are also listed in this HTML code. Later on, when a Bean wishes to receive the event, it must have registered itself with the main applet class.

INTROSPECTION, PERSISTENCE, AND MORE

While function calls can be relayed from applet to applet on the same page, JavaScript is also able to use the full suite of introspection and persistence mechanisms contained within Beans. As long as the applet that controls the Bean allows it, JavaScript functions can be created that invoke the JavaBeans introspection mechanism that was discussed earlier. In so doing, the JavaScript function can get a handle on which functions exist within the Bean. However, the JavaScript function will be unable to cast the `Class`, `Method`, `Field`, etc., objects to JavaScript objects and invoke or use them as can be done within Java. After all, JavaScript is simply a scripting language. An elegant and pretty useful scripting language, but a mere scripting language nonetheless.

Remember, JavaScript is indeed cool, but it is not the answer to all your programming needs. To accomplish the truly powerful tasks that your programs make possible, you still need Java or a similar language.

Summary

JavaBeans integration with other object models and networking technologies is the central determining factor in whether or not JavaBeans will be adopted by the general computing populace. With the combination of GUI builders and other technologies, JavaBeans is a fine alternative to ActiveX and Visual Basic. But, with the addition of a strong component integration model, JavaBeans becomes the defacto standard for component technology. After all, if Java-Beans can accept legacy ActiveX controls and also have the ability to create ActiveX controls with little additional effort, there is no reason to use ActiveX. By the same token, if JavaBeans plays well with JavaScript and the event and property interaction mechanisms within Beans can be used within JavaScript, then JavaBeans can become closely tied with the browser and more complex applications may be built. As you will see in the next chapter, component integration is the first step in this seamless interaction between Java-Beans, Java, and legacy systems. A strong networking model is also necessary to propel Beans into the mainstream.

CHAPTER

10

Bean Networking

- **B**eans and CORBA
- **B**eans and RMI
- **N**etworked Beans

This chapter covers the introductory material necessary to enable your applications to use the basic Java networking capabilities provided for in Java Interface Definition Language (IDL) and Java Remote Method Invocation (RMI). Much of the technological basis for the networking constructs discussed here can be found in *Advanced Java Networking*, another book from Prentice Hall (from which I graciously borrowed excerpts). *JavaBeans Developer's Resource* only covers the basics of setting up a client/server system and how Java, and therefore JavaBeans, can talk to these servers in much the same way as Beans can talk to ActiveX objects. The approach of this chapter is to first describe rudimentary Java clients and servers, thus giving you a taste for the technology itself. The last portion of this chapter concentrates on Beans-specific networking capabilities.

Firing CORBA Events

Common Object Request Broker Architecture (CORBA) is a complex distributed object specification. A distributed object is just like a local object except that it resides in another process. CORBA is not for the faint of heart, and should be attempted only by seasoned object programmers. The basic tutorial that follows does not do this powerful communication mechanism justice, rather it is meant to provide what you need to know to get started.

What is CORBA?

CORBA is a standard developed by the Object Management Group (OMG), the world's largest computer consortium. It is not a product; it is not a vision; it is not vapor ware. Many companies have chosen to implement CORBA, most notably Iona Technologies and SunSoft.

Like all academic projects, CORBA has become a kitchen sink standard. Everything you could possibly want is covered in the specification, if not actually implemented by the various CORBA vendors. Much of what CORBA has to offer is intended to be hidden from the programmer. The programmer APIs are not defined; rather each vendor is charged with creating its own API. SunSoft NEO, for example, implements its own Object Development Framework to facilitate interaction between programmers and the Object Request Broker (ORB).

CORBA-STYLE COMMUNICATION

Let's say your Aunt Fran calls you from South Dakota. When she dials your number, the phone eventually rings on your side. You pick up the phone, have a conversation, hang up the phone, and terminate the connection. Your Aunt Fran is the requester, or client, and you are the called party, or server. Aunt Fran doesn't care where your phone is in your house. She doesn't care if it's a cordless phone. She doesn't care if it's a conventional phone or a cell phone. All she knows is that she dials a number, you answer, you talk, and you hang up. In other words, Aunt Fran does not care how the call is implemented; she only cares that the call goes through.

If Aunt Fran were to dial using the socket paradigm, she would have to dial the number, specify which phone to ring, specify who should answer the phone, and it would be a shot in the dark. If the call doesn't go through, she won't be told why. She'll probably wait and wait for a phone to ring even though it never will.

Remember also that CORBA does not specify how something will be implemented. Aunt Fran should be just as happy using a satellite phone as she would be using a regular phone. Java is the only language you can use to create a networked object with most of the alternatives in this book. While Java may be the greatest thing since the fork-split English muffin, many large-scale distributed systems are still written in C++, C, or heaven forbid, COBOL. CORBA enables you to use those legacy systems without having to rewrite everything in Java.

THE CORBA VISION

As an example, let's say your beanbag has a beautiful interface. You can employ a few operations on it, you can fluff it, and you can sit on it. Do you care what goes on underneath? If someone were to come by one day and replace your cloth beanbag with a vinyl beanbag would you still know how to use it? Yes, because the interface didn't change, only the implementation did.

The beauty of CORBA is that you can create a whole bunch of interfaces that are implemented in a variety of ways. If you want to talk to an object, you have the interface; in essence a contract that states what you will give the object and what you will get from the object in return. Because of that, objects are interchangeable as long as they share the same interfaces.

For the Internet, this means that an object can be deployed and then people can be told what they must do in order to use it. Later on, if an enhancement to the object is discovered, you can merely swap the old inferior object with the new enhanced one, and no one will ever know or care. One of the ways the people at Sun do this is with their support feedback tool. Customers can submit problem reports for products using a Java interface that communicates over the Internet with an object. From time to time the object is either fixed or upgraded, but the customers never know. To them, the interface remains the same. Figure 10.1 shows a graphical representation of how object implementations are different from their interfaces.

In geek terms, this is referred to as *three-tier client-server computing.* The first tier is the client, whether it is a Java applet or a Windows 95 OLE client, and it communicates with the second tier. The second tier is the object you implement in CORBA using the IDL. Finally, the third tier is your data source, perhaps a database or other implement. Information is passed through the three tiers with the idea that changes may be made to any tier, and no effect will be seen on any of the other tiers. Figure 10.2 shows how the data is kept from the client by using object servers as the middlemen.

COMMUNICATION WITH CORBA

Similarly, when you request information from a CORBA object, you don't care how it is implemented, you only care that your request goes through and that the object responds. CORBA, the ORB specifically,

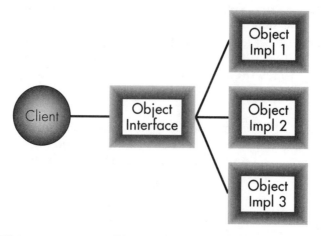

Figure 10.1: *Clients only care about interfaces, not implementations.*

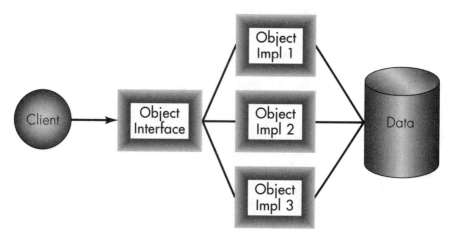

Figure 10.2: *The three tier client server architecture.*

ensures that your request gets there, and if it doesn't, you will find out. Moreover, the ORB will start up a server if one isn't already running.

Unlike TCP/IP and sockets, CORBA ensures reliability of communication. If a request does not go through, you will know about it. If a server isn't there, it starts up, and you are told if there is a problem. Every possible communication contingency is covered in the specification.

But this kind of reliability comes with a price. CORBA lends a ton of functionality to devise object schemes that work. However, it also places a heavy burden on the programmer with all of the overhead required in a call. In short, CORBA programming is far from easy, but as a tradeoff you receive significant gifts for your effort.

Just as Java objects are defined as collections of operations on some state, CORBA objects are similarly defined. Unlike Java, CORBA enables you to define your interface definition separately from your implementation. As you can see in Figure 10.3, splitting the interface from the implementation enables you to create multiple objects from the same interface, each handling the method signatures differently. In the end, however, the greatest advantage to the split is that your interfaces are likely to remain static, while your implementations will change dramatically over time.

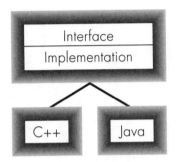

Figure 10.3: *Programming language becomes irrelevant when you define the interface separately from the implementation.*

Software architects spend considerable time and energy creating objects and their interfaces, leaving the implementation up to their staff. The interface implementers code their objects in the ORB of their choice. Once the objects are finished and registered with the system, they are ready to be invoked. One of the few advantages to C++ over Java is this kind of separation between implementation and interface. CORBA allows you to have the same kind of functionality.

A client that invokes on an object knows only the interface definition. The implementation of the object is of no concern to the requester, who cares only that the object request gets to the server and that a response is sent back. Theoretically, client programmers and server programmers don't need to know any of the details of each other's implementations.

The interfaces are defined using the IDL. This enables the programmer to know what methods can be invoked on an object. A typical CORBA object life cycle requires the most time in developing the interfaces. Once you are satisfied with the interface, you move on to the implementation.

In the business world today, a great push toward Java is taking place. Because of its tremendous advantages over C++, many organizations are planning an eventual move to Java programming with the idea that several of the language's drawbacks will be addressed appropriately in subsequent revisions. If these organizations had taken a CORBA-like approach to their original software design, then the migration would hardly be an issue. Because each CORBA object has an interface that is published and well known, changing its implementation does not involve changing the implementations of any other object that talks to it. As you can see in Figure 10.4, objects in CORBA talk to interfaces, while objects not written using CORBA talk directly to one another.

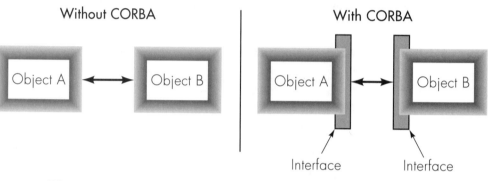

Figure 10.4: *Objects talk to interfaces, not to implementations.*

CORBA objects can be written in any language for which *language mapping* is specified. Therefore, the implementation can vary between objects, but the client should not care. The language mapping is defined by the OMG, and the various vendors then choose to implement the mapping. NEO, for example, does not implement the Smalltalk mapping, but has created its own Java mapping.

DIFFERENT VENDORS, DIFFERENT ORBs

What if you create a client that accesses your chosen ORB and another object comes along, written in another ORB, and you would like to talk to it? In the early days of CORBA, you would have to rewrite your client; no small task considering that clients are where the pretty stuff is located. You'd have to redo all of your pretty graphics and recompile your client for the new ORB. For that reason, ORB consumers often remained a one-ORB shop. If their servers were created in Orbix, their clients generally were as well.

In the new CORBA world, all objects and clients speak to one another using the Internet Inter-ORB Protocol, or IIOP. IIOP (usually pronounced *eye-op*) ensures that your client will be able to talk to a server written for an entirely different ORB. Note how this takes advantage of the client abstraction spoken of earlier. Now, your clients need not know what ORB the server was written in and can simply talk to it.

Furthermore, the ORB is the only fully native portion of the entire CORBA system. The ORB is specific to the platform on which it runs.

Orbix, Iona Technologies' entry into the CORBA market, runs on just about every platform imaginable because they have made the effort to port Orbix to every platform imaginable. SunSoft's NEO, on the other hand, runs exclusively on Solaris, but does so better than any other CORBA option.

 Because Orbix's ORB was written with quick portability in mind, it tends to offer less power than NEO's does and also has significant problems with scalability. Again, this is a tradeoff issue, and one that must be evaluated on a case-by-case basis. With the universal acceptance of IIOP, there is no reason why your CORBA objects need to be written in one ORB only.

ADVANTAGES OF CORBA

CORBA is an example of *distributed object* programming. If you were to create two objects, say a `Character` object and a `String` object, you would be splitting up functionality across different objects. Your `String` object would instantiate several `Character` objects, and all would be happy in your plain vanilla object-oriented world. This process is shown in Figure 10.5.

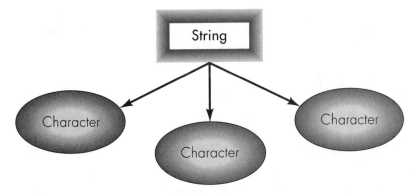

Figure 10.5: *Objects are composed of other objects.*

If, however, you were to take things one step further and have your `String` object instantiate its `Character` objects on a different machine, you would be entering the distributed object world and all the insanity that revolves around it (see Figure 10.6). When instantiating objects across multiple machines, certain precautions and measures must be taken to ensure the proper routing of messages. If you were to use CORBA as your basis for creating these objects, all of those situations would be addressed already.

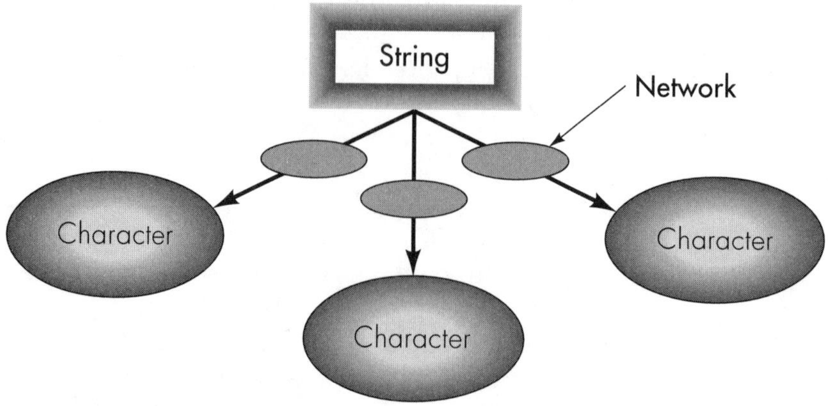

Figure 10.6: *Objects can be distributed across multiple networks.*

CORBA gives you the tools needed to distribute your objects across multiple machines running on perhaps several different networks. You need only to instantiate your object before using it just as you normally would use a local object.

As mentioned already, CORBA makes a big distinction between interface and implementation. The interface is the list of methods through which you will communicate; the implementation is how those methods are created. Let's say I was talking to a marketeer. We would both be speaking English (the interface), but I would have to talk slowly, explaining everything in a clear and concise manner (the implementation).

COMMON OBJECT SERVICES

If you have ever programmed in C++, chances are you used a class library of some sort. The famous Rogue-Wave class libraries give you a great number of classes and objects that you can reuse in your code, ranging from the sublime `String` classes to the vastly more complex `HashTables`.

Likewise, part of the CORBA specification deals with a set of distributed class libraries known as the Common Object Services. The Common Object Services refer to specific types of objects that are beneficial to programmers in a distributed environment, including transaction objects, event service objects, relationship objects, and even life cycle objects.

Perhaps the most useful of all the Common Object Services is the Naming Service. The Naming Service provides you with a directory-like system for storing and organizing your objects so that other programmers can access and invoke them. In Figure 10.7, the string Object One is mapped to the physical object 1, but Object Two is mapped to the physical object 3. In so doing, an object is not obtained by a physical object reference, but by an easy-to-understand string.

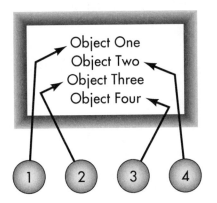

Figure 10.7: *With the Object Naming Service, every string is mapped to an object.*

The Naming Service allows you to also change maps on the fly. In fact, the Naming Service, and all Common Object Services for that matter, are nothing more than CORBA objects. Therefore, if you can get the interface to the Naming Service, you can create a client that modifies it yourself.

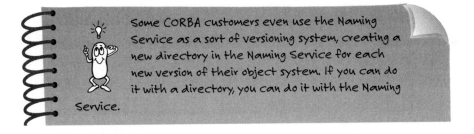

Some CORBA customers even use the Naming Service as a sort of versioning system, creating a new directory in the Naming Service for each new version of their object system. If you can do it with a directory, you can do it with the Naming Service.

OBJECT ADMINISTRATION

One of the biggest obstacles to distributed computing is the management of objects across multiple platforms and multiple networks. Though the CORBA specification does not specify an administration scheme, several vendors have created administration tools you can use to manage your entire system.

Tasks that run the gamut from server startup and shutdown all the way to machine-specific parameters are addressed in these tools. Often, the tools are written in the same CORBA implementation that they manage, and many even have Java interfaces. Most of the tools address the issue of object registration and invocation. When an object is registered, it is stored in a location called the *Interface Repository*. Accessing objects from the Interface Repository is often quite difficult, has great overhead, and requires a significant knowledge of the OS. The Naming Service addresses some of these concerns by creating a user-friendly front end to objects that are stored in the Interface Repository. In order to manipulate objects directly within the Interface Repository, you need object administration tools.

Because the object administration tools vary widely among CORBA vendors, they are not addressed in detail. The OMG, as a matter of fact, does not even specify the kinds of administration tools that are required to support an object system; that determination is left to the vendors. NEO includes a full suite of Java-based tools to manipulate your objects, and Orbix has similar tools available from the command line.

CLIENTS, SERVERS, OH MY!

Client programming in CORBA is significantly easier than creating a server. In the simplest sense, all you are doing is instantiating a class that just happens to be on a remote machine. This makes client programming in CORBA quite intuitive. When you instantiate a class in CORBA, you specify not only the name of the class, but the location as well. The location can be a specific machine or a specific server, but is usually determined by referencing the Naming Service.

The Naming Service contains a `find` method that enables you to retrieve an object by using a string name that you specify:

```
...
myFirstObject = NamingService.find("MyFirstObject");
myFirstObject.myFirstMethod();
...
```

Once an object is retrieved, invoking it is exactly the same as invoking a locally instantiated class. In fact, underneath the covers, a local class is instantiated. Let's say you get an object called `MyFirstCORBA` from the Naming Service and invoke `myFirstMethod` on it. In reality, the local copy of `MyFirstCORBA` maps this call to a method that invokes across the ORB to the remote object, as illustrated in Figure 10.8.

Writing a server is much more complicated and many vendors do not yet support full Java server capability. Later parts of this chapter, discuss full Java server capability and what it means for the future of C++ objects in CORBA. Needless to say, the ease-of-use aspects of Java help to minimize overhead and the learning curve of CORBA in general. Thus far, Java is not yet as capable of the performance numbers generated by identical C++ applications.

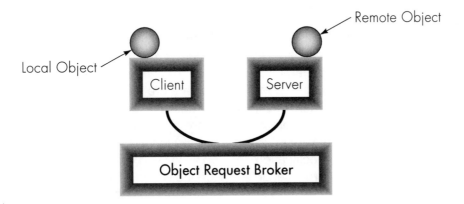

Local Object

Remote Object

Client

Server

Object Request Broker

Figure 10.8: *Objects invoke on remote objects via the Object Request Broker.*

WHAT CORBA MEANS FOR YOU

At first glance, CORBA seems like a gigantic 800 pound gorilla sitting on your desk. There's a lot of work involved in taming the wild beast, and once you have it under control there's a ton of work involved in keeping it under that control. CORBA can be very complicated, although much of its complication arises from distributed memory management, a problem obviated by Java's garbage collection. For JavaBeans, CORBA represents the ability to include components residing on different machines; in essence networked Beans.

For example, if you were creating a Bean to interface with a database of books in a library, the Bean component could reside on the server end. Later on, when you create a virtual card catalog and want to include the Bean in the library, you simply include it as you normally would. You can fire events to the library Bean and receive events from it as well. However, those events would be fired and received across a network, and would be *totally transparent to the user*. Distributed Beans are one of the single greatest uses for JavaBeans, allowing you to create a set of server-side Beans that can truly harness the power of the Internet.

Creating a CORBA Client

The first step to creating a CORBA client or server is to define the interface using the IDL. This book is not a comprehensive text on CORBA or Java IDL. For more information, consult Prentice Hall's *Advanced Java Networking*.

The completed IDL for the sample application server is shown here. It serves images to the `PictureArea` from the Rainbow Button Bean example used earlier. The `PictureArea` asks the server for an image corresponding to the current color on the button. To refresh your memory, here is the `PictureArea` code as it stands now:

There are several vendors from whom you can purchase a working CORBA product. Unfortunately, none of these vendors are truly interoperable. In this chapter, the examples are almost pseudo-code, and do not necessarily work line for line inside another CORBA product. The fact is that there are several CORBA products, and each of them has its serious deficiencies and advantages. If you regard this as slightly confusing, you are correct. This is, in fact, the single biggest problem with CORBA. Even though all of the vendors implement the same specification, they do so in such widely differing ways that none of them are truly capable of working with one another.

```
public class PictureArea extends Panel implements ButtonListener
{
    private Image currentImage;

    PictureArea()
    {
        super();
    }

    public void instantiate()
    {
    }

    public void fireButtonEvent(
        ButtonEvent buttonEvent
    )
    {
    }

    public Image getCurrentImage()
    {
        return currentImage;
    }
}
```

CREATING THE IDL

Now, you need to create the interface definition for the server. The server will implement this method later on and simply return a string corresponding to the name of the image. The method `getImageForColor` is implemented by any CORBA server you create:

```
interface PictureServer
{
    string getImageForColor(
        in long colorType);
}
```

Now modify the original `PictureArea` code so that it initializes the ORB in its `instantiate` method. This ensures that the ORB is only created and initialized when the Bean is being used outside a GUI builder. You don't want an ORB connection to be opened every time the `PictureArea` is loaded into a GUI builder. It would be a needless waste of network resources. When the `PictureArea` Bean is actually used and run from within a Bean application or applet, the CORBA portion of the Bean will be utilized. For now, there is no use for it:

```
public class PictureArea extends Panel implements ButtonListener
{
    private Image currentImage;

    PictureArea()
    {
        super();
    }

    public void instantiate()
    {
        // initialize the ORB
        CORBA corba = new CORBA();
    }

    public void fireButtonEvent(
        ButtonEvent buttonEvent
    )
    {
    }

    public Image getCurrentImage()
    {
        return currentImage;
    }
}
```

INVOKING ON A SERVER

Once the ORB is initialized and ready to go, ORB invocations can be made. Instead of simply loading an image every time you get a `Button-Event`, your `PictureArea` Bean now makes an invocation across the network and get a string corresponding to a filename for the image. You may then load the image and draw it on the screen. On the server end, any number of factors can determine what string is actually returned back to the client, but they are discussed in a moment. In order for the client to be able to talk to the `PictureServer`, it must first obtain a copy of the object, called an *object reference*, from the Naming Service. When you design our server in a moment, you will see that the `Pic-`

tureServer is stored in the Naming Service under the name PIC-
TURE-SERVER.

```java
public class PictureArea extends Panel implements ButtonListener
{
    private Image currentImage;
    private PictureServer pictureServer;

    PictureArea()
    {
        super();
    }

    public void instantiate()
    {
        // initialize the ORB
        CORBA corba = new CORBA();

        // get a remote object
        pictureServer = corba.NamingService.find(
            "PICTURE-SERVER");
    }

    public void fireButtonEvent(
        ButtonEvent buttonEvent
    )
    {
        // get an image filename from the picture server
        String imageName = pictureServer.getImageForColor(
            buttonEvent.getButtonColor());

        // load the image and do whatever it takes to display it
        currentImage = …something…
    }

    public Image getCurrentImage()
    {
        return currentImage;
    }
}
```

Creating a CORBA Server

Next, create the CORBA server code for the PictureServer. The
PictureServer will be created, compiled, and registered when you are
done. Registration ensures that your server can be located via the Naming Service. The truly wonderful thing about CORBA (and much of the
reason for all the support infrastructure in CORBA) is that this server is
automatically started when first invoked on. Because of this, you need
not set up the server initially. Simply registering it with the Naming Service will take care of any activation details for you.

The server should be a very simple Java application in its own right. In a moment you will see how to add the IDL machinery to it, but for now simply create the application and add the appropriate stuff to it. After applying the `idltojava` program supplied by most CORBA vendors to the IDL file you created earlier, you will end up with a list of six distinct files.

- `PictureServerRef`

- `PictureServerHolder`

- `PictureServerOperations`

- `PictureServerStub`

- `PictureServerServant`

- `PictureServerSkeleton`

These six files supply all of the internal machinery to your CORBA server. The code that you will add in a moment merely implements the IDL. The underlying framework for automatic activation and message routing is handled by the code contained in these generated files. To create a CORBA server, you need to extend the Servant object:

```
public class PictureServerImpl extends PictureServerServant
{
    PictureServerImpl()
    {
        super();
    }
}
```

IMPLEMENTING THE IDL

Now that the servant is setup for use by CORBA, you need to implement the methods specified in the IDL file. As you may recall, the only method that needs to be implemented by the `PictureServer` is the `getImageForColor` method that returns a string based on an integer that is passed in:

```
public class PictureServerImpl extends PictureServerServant
{
    PictureServerImpl()
    {
        super();
    }

    public String getImageForColor(
        long currentColor
```

```
    )
    {
        if(currentColor == Color.red)
            return "red.gif";
        else if(currentColor == Color.blue)
            return "blue.gif";
        else
            return "default.gif";
    }
}
```

PUTTING THE SERVANT INSIDE A SERVER

A server is very different from a servant, and the distinction is often lost on distributed object newbies. Imagine a thousand identical Sony televisions in the same room. There is absolutely nothing different between each of them. They all implement the same interface and do the same thing. In that sense, they are all *servants*. A servant is the basic implementation of an object. A *server*, on the other hand, is the physical container in which the servant resides. Each of the televisions in the room is a different server, and each of those server televisions uses an identical servant to accomplish its mission in life.

You need to create the server object for the servant to reside in. It is actually quite an easy process and involves first creating a `Picture-Server` class. You then need to initialize the ORB and obtain a servant instance. Finally, you need to use the servant instance to get an object reference for the servant:

```
public class PictureServer
{
    // private variables
    private CORBA corba;
    private PictureServerRef pictureServerRef;

    public static void main(
        String argv[]
    )
    {
        // link up with the ORB
        corba = new CORBA();

        // create the servant class
        PictureServerImpl pictureServerImpl =
            new PictureServerImpl();

        // create the an object reference for the servant
        pictureServerRef = PictureServerSkeleton.createRef(
            corba.getORB(), pictureServerImpl);
    }
}
```

Now, you need to insert code to have the `PictureServer` bind itself to a unique name in the Naming Service. Earlier, in the client example, you used the name PICTURE-SERVER and that is exactly what you need to do here:

```
public class PictureServer
{
    // private variables
    private CORBA corba;
    private PictureServerRef pictureServerRef;

    public static void main(
        String argv[]
    )
    {
        // link up with the ORB
        corba = new CORBA();

        // create the servant class
        PictureServerImpl pictureServerImpl =
            new PictureServerImpl();

        // create the an object reference for the servant
        pictureServerRef = PictureServerSkeleton.createRef(
            corba.getORB(), pictureServerImpl);

        // bind this server to the Naming Service
        corba.rebind("PICTURE-SERVER", pictureServerRef);
    }
}
```

REGISTERING THE ORB

Once the code is finished, the server must be registered with the ORB. Registration merely places the object and its interfaces inside the Interface Repository. The other ORBs in your system that wish to use the PictureServer object will first look in the interface repository for an object that it retrieves from the Naming Service. Remember, the Naming Service merely matches strings to objects. The physical object is always (though transparently in the example shown in this chapter) retrieved from the interface repository. Object registration varies greatly among the various ORB vendors.

While CORBA is certainly powerful and somewhat all-encompassing, there are not exactly throngs of people banging down the doors of the numerous CORBA vendors. There are a multitude of reasons for CORBA's lukewarm reception. Chief among them being that CORBA is not only difficult to program, but equally difficult to grasp. With the introduction of Java to the CORBA mess, the technology has actually become quite easier to use. However, Java brings with it its own distributed object technology called Remote Method Invocation (RMI). RMI is lightweight distributed objects. It's pure Java, so it's naturally easy. The next section explores RMI in some detail.

Talking to RMI Servers

Java RMI is often considered CORBA-lite, but in many ways it goes beyond that and offers a legitimate communication alternative to the vastly more complex CORBA philosophy. At the heart of RMI is the Java ethos of ease of use. As seen thus far with JavaBeans, Java API Engineers are rarely willing to complicate matters by making simple tasks overly complex. Rather, they seek to simplify things, often to such a point as to make the task seem almost trivial. At first glance, RMI seems like a trivial and non-noteworthy technology. But after further investigation, you will discover that the complexity of CORBA is gone, but much of its power and intention remains.

What is RMI?

RMI is similar to Java IDL in many ways. However, RMI enables you to create applications that communicate with one another without the costly overhead of CORBA. A remote method invocation is a form of the Remote Procedure Call (RPC) so common in C++. Instead of creating and instantiating an object on your local machine, you create it on another machine and communicate with that object as you would normally.

With the advantages of the Java language, you will be able to create distributed objects that communicate with one another. Unlike CORBA, your applications must be written in Java, but that may not be a bad thing in the end. It will be difficult to re-implement your legacy applications because they must be rewritten in Java. Yet, being able to write distributed applications without expending any real effort is highly attractive. If Java is your language of choice, then RMI may be your best communication alternative.

REMOTE METHODS

In the good old days of programming, all of the things you wanted to do resided in one program. If you needed a file, you simply opened it. If you needed to optimize your program, you either reduced functionality or sped it up. Lately, the notion of distributed programming has taken the industry by storm. Instead of opening a file, you open another application. Instead of reducing functionality, you farm out the work to another application and keep tabs on the process by communicating with it. Figure 10.9 illustrates the differences between local and remote object invocation.

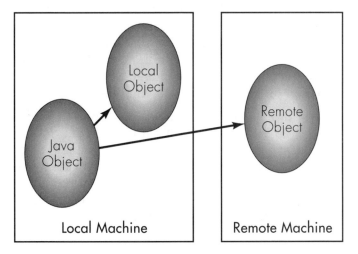

Figure 10.9: *Invocations on remote objects appear the same as invocations on local objects.*

Java RMI enables you to farm out work to other Java objects residing in other processes, or in other machines altogether. Not only can you execute steps in parallel using threads, but you can farm out work to other processes that will execute steps in parallel on a different machine!

How Does RMI Work?

When your client invokes your server, several layers of the RMI system come into play. The first, and most important to the programmer, is the *stub/skeleton* layer. The stubs are Java code that you fill in so that you can communicate with the other layers. For example, earlier you saw how the IDL to Java compiler generated a bunch of code that was later filled in and used as the framework for a distributed application.

Likewise, the Java RMI system automatically enables you to use several helper functions. By inheriting from the RMI classes, your class implements the stubs or skeletons. In geek parlance, stubs are reserved for client code that you fill in, and skeletons refer to server code.

Once the stubs and skeleton layers are completed, they pass through the other two layers in the RMI system. The first of these layers is the *remote reference* layer. The remote reference layer is responsible for determining the nature of the object. Does it reside on a single machine or across a network? Is the remote object the kind of object that will be instantiated and started automatically, or is it the kind of object that must be declared and initialized beforehand? The remote reference layer handles all of these situations, and many more, without your intervention.

Finally, the *transport* layer is similar to a translator that takes your RMI code, turns it into TCP/IP (or whatever communication mechanism is used), and lets it fly over the network to the other end. Because the RMI system supports *object serialization* (see Chapter 1, *Advanced Java*, and Chapter 6, *Bean Packaging and Persistence*), any objects passed as parameters to a remote method, no matter how complicated, are converted into simple streams of characters that are then easily re-converted into their original object representation.

As you can see in Figure 10.10, a client that invokes a remote server first talks to its stub code, which, in turn, sends the message to the remote reference layer, which then passes it through the transport mechanism to the other machine. The other machine takes what it gets through the transport layer, re-translates into the remote reference layer representation, which passes it on to the skeleton code where the request finally makes its appearance at the remote method.

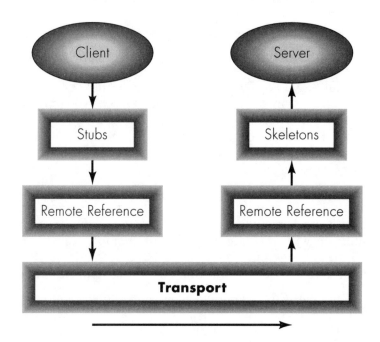

Figure 10.10: *Java RMI architecture.*

Stub/Skeleton Layer When your client begins to invoke a server on a remote machine, the API with which you, as programmer, are concerned is the stub/skeleton code. By inheriting from the appropriate RMI class, your object obtains several RMI methods that you are required to fill in.

When the invocation is actually made, the remote object could be a *replicated object*. A replicated object is an object that has several instances executing at the same time. For example, a given application may have several instances of the Java String class within its threads of execution. If the String class were a remote server object, a client that invokes it should not have to worry about its various instances. The stub and skeleton layer precludes this notion of replicated objects. When you write your application and code the necessary tools to talk to a remote object, you need not concern yourself with the implementations on the remote side.

The stub/skeleton layer also abstracts you from the various transport mechanisms in the other layers. In short, the stub and skeleton layers both make sure that your program is platform-independent. The system calls and routines are left for the other layers, and your code should not be tailored for one particular architecture.

Remote Reference Layer The reference layer serves two purposes. First, it handles the translation from the stub and skeleton layers into native transport calls on the hosting architecture. The early version of RMI was not as platform-independent as it purported to be. The problem lay in the Java Developer's Kit, and not in the RMI system itself. With the introduction of JDK 1.1, the RMI system now functions properly. The RMI system is truly platform-independent as it, and the Java language, were meant to be.

The reference layer is also in charge of carrying out remote reference protocols. These protocols may be point-to-point communication, i.e., local object to remote object invocations. Or, the reference protocol may refer to replicated objects. The RMI system ensures that when you invoke a remote object that happens to be replicated, all of the replicated instances will hear the same message. The replication strategy is customizable, but refer to the RMI System Architecture section of the RMI specification for further details.

There is a corresponding server side reference layer that accepts the client side instructions and re-translates them into programmer code. It ensures that the invocation is made reliably, and that the RMI system knows about any exceptions. Exceptions are thrown from this level for any problems in establishing connections, fulfilling invocation requests, or closing connections.

Basically, the reference layer is responsible for bridging the gap between programmer code and network communication. It is a go-between of data, taking what you want to do, and making sure it can be done using the network.

Transport Layer When the first miners found gold in California, they exclaimed, "Eureka!" Well, Eureka! This is where the action is. While you are not able to manipulate these routines yourself, it is important to understand how the transport is implemented. From here, you will understand the limitations of RMI and be able to make architectural decisions based on them.

The transport layer is responsible for setting up connections, maintaining them, alerting applications of problems, listening for connections, and shutting them down. The transport layer consists of four components: the objects, the space between local and remote address spaces, the physical socket, and the transport protocol. Figure 10.11 illustrates a simple transport model.

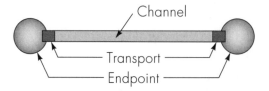

Figure 10.11: *The transport layer is responsible for all connection-related functions.*

The objects, or *endpoints*, are the beginning and end of an invocation. Between one object's transport endpoint to another object's transport endpoint resides the entire communication mechanism on which RMI is based. The *channel* between the address spaces is in charge of upholding the connection and monitoring for signs of trouble, say the loss of an object or maybe the loss of the physical connection itself. The socket *connection* is basically the same kind of socket seen in an earlier chapter. As mentioned before, sockets really are the basis for all communications in Java. Finally, the *transport protocol* is the language in which sockets talk to one another.

LOCAL VERSUS REMOTE OBJECTS

What are the semantic differences between local and remote objects? All along I have stressed that at the heart of the entire system is the notion that to the client programmer, everything looks exactly like normal, non-remote Java code. In fact, even Java IDL's client applications look no different than local Java code.

Java RMI is quite interesting from a semantic sense. Indeed, the very idea that instantiating an object that happens to be on another network is interesting in and of itself. To add to that the caveat that the remote object exhibits all of the properties of a local Java object adds a certain amount of usefulness to the whole matter.

What kinds of characteristics do Java objects exhibit? Well, most importantly, they are easy to implement. They are *garbage-collected*, meaning that once your program has no use for them, they are automatically de-referenced and their resources returned to the system. (A discussion of remote garbage collection is included in the next section.)

Java objects are, of course, platform-independent, as are Java RMI objects. When you make a remote method invocation in a non-Java language, chances are you must learn not only the nuances of the communication mechanism of your own machine, but that of the machine you are talking to as well. Imagine being a Solaris programmer who is trying to talk to a Windows 95 machine! It's hard enough to master Solaris interprocess communication without having to learn the esoteric Windows 95 communication layers as well!

Java RMI frees you from that morass, just as Java frees you from recompiling your code for multiple architectures. When you invoke a RMI method across different platforms, the RMI system adjusts its communication layers automatically; and because those layers are abstracted from you, the programmer, you never have to concern yourself with that confusing network code.

Garbage Collection   One of the biggest advantages to Java is that there are no pointers. There is no memory to de-allocate, and you never have to deal with memory storage schemes. Java's platform independence mantra wouldn't allow it anyway, but if you were to develop for multiple platforms, you would need to be concerned with the nuances of memory management for each architecture which, like mastering multiple transport layers, is a daunting task.

Java RMI is no exception to the rule. In fact, it contains a complicated garbage collection scheme based on Modula-3's Network Objects concept of object reference counters. RMI places an object reference counter into each object. Every time another object talks to the remote object, the object reference counter is incremented, and once the object no longer needs the remote object, the counter is decremented.

There are many protective layers around the garbage collection algorithm that prevent premature object de-allocation. Most of RMI's distributed garbage collection farms off the work to the local Java Virtual Machine's garbage collection algorithm. Thus, RMI does not reinvent the wheel, so to speak.

For example, when a local object begins a conversation with a remote object, it begin to talk through the RMI system's layers. As part of the remote reference layer, the local object creates a network object. On the other end, at the remote machine, the remote reference layer creates another network object that converses with the remote object. The remote Virtual Machine realizes that the remote object should not be de-allocated as long as the remote network object is referring to it (see Figure 10.12). Thus, the remote object is not blown away.

Back at the local machine, when it is no longer using the remote object, the remote reference layer removes all references to the local network object. Once the local Java Virtual Machine realizes that the local

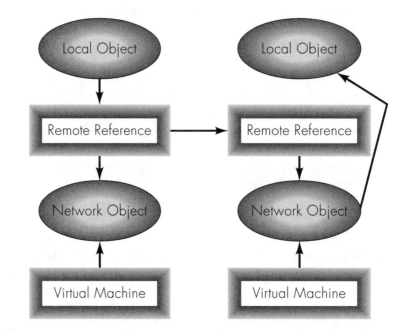

Figure 10.12: *The creation of network objects during object communication prevents Java's garbage collection from interrupting the conversation.*

network object is no longer used, it garbage collects it. As part of its `finalize` routine, the local network object sends a message to the remote network object through the reference layer that it should let go of its reference to the remote object. In so doing, the remote network object causes the remote Java Virtual Machine to garbage collect the remote object.

Security When you instantiate a local object from within a Java applet, security is not a concern. The applet security mechanism has already cleared your applet, and you are free to allocate and de-allocate your objects.

However, security is very much a concern for remote objects. When you try to instantiate a remote object, you must have permission to do so. The applet class loader that is in charge of getting every class your application requires may or may not be able to instantiate the remote object. As a result, RMI in applets is limited to invoking methods on classes that are already in existence. You are not allowed to create a remote object because the applet class loader will not let you.

APPLET VERSUS APPLICATION

Currently, RMI servers must be created as Java applications. Just as in Java IDL, servers cannot be embedded within a Web page. There are several reasons why, most notably that the applet security mechanisms prevent it; but for the time being, the RMI system does not support applet servers.

OVERVIEW OF RMI

Java's RMI system is a significantly easier and lighter weight approach to distributed objects than Java IDL. Contained completely within the Java language, RMI is an extension to the language itself, whereas Java IDL is a language-independent Java implementation. RMI is simple, fast, and effective for lightweight distributed systems. As your applications become more complex, Java IDL may be your best alternative.

Nevertheless, JavaBeans will still be able to fire events to remote RMI servers because the event firing mechanism in Java and in Beans is nothing more than a simple method call. As I have stressed, RMI's syntax does not change from invoking on a local method to a remote one. As a result, JavaBeans event firing using RMI is equally simple.

Creating an RMI Client

Before creating a RMI client and server, you need to know what the interface of the RMI server is going to be. If you choose to implement your `PictureArea` object as an RMI server, you will create a simple interface with a method that returns a string. The method will be invoked whenever the client wishes to receive the name of the object for the color. However, unlike the problem encountered with the CORBA client/server system, you need not marshal the data in the `Color` object between client and server. Since both are Java objects, both can understand what a `Color` object is.

CREATING THE INTERFACE

As in the CORBA example, the RMI interface has one method (`getImageForColor`) that accepts a `Color` object and returns a string corresponding to the name of the file containing the image for the color. The Bean is then responsible for retrieving and manipulating the image as it sees fit. In so doing, you maintain a modular structure in which the remote object has as little processing as possible to keep the network latency to a minimum:

```
public interface PictureServer
{
    public String getImageForColor(
        Color currentColor);
}
```

WRITING THE CLIENT

The client for the remote `PictureServer` is very straightforward and follows the RMI principles of obtaining an object from the RMI registry and then invoking on it. Here, you will retrieve the object from the Registry where it is stored under the unique string name `PictureAreaServer`. Note how all of your initialization is done in the constructor automatically whenever the `PictureArea` Bean is used. Because of this, you will then be able to use the `pictureServer` variable to invoke on the remote server:

```
public class PictureArea extends Panel implements ButtonListener
{
    private Image currentImage;
    private PictureServer pictureServer;

    PictureArea()
    {
        super();

        // initialize the remote object
        Remote remoteObject = Naming.find("PictureAreaServer");

        // narrow to an PictureServer
        if(remoteObject instanceof PictureServer)
            pictureServer = (PictureServer) remoteObject;
    }

    public void instantiate()
    {
    }

    public void fireButtonEvent(
        ButtonEvent buttonEvent
    )
    {
    }

    public Image getCurrentImage()
    {
        return currentImage;
    }
}
```

Once you get the object, you can invoke on it at will to retrieve the name of the image for the color that you specify. Once you get the name, you can handle any image processing that may be required:

```
public class PictureArea extends Panel implements ButtonListener
{
    private Image currentImage;
    private PictureServer pictureServer;

    PictureArea()
    {
        super();

        // initialize the remote object
        Remote remoteObject = Naming.find("PictureAreaServer");

        // narrow to an PictureServer
        if(remoteObject instanceof PictureServer)
            pictureServer = (PictureServer) remoteObject;
    }

    public void instantiate()
    {
    }

    public void fireButtonEvent(
        ButtonEvent buttonEvent
    )
    {
        // first get the color of the button now
        Color buttonColor = buttonEvent.getButtonColor();

        // now invoke on the remote server and get the image name
        String imageName =
            pictureServer.getImageForColor(buttonColor);

        // now do the image processing
        Image currentImage = mediaRepository.getImage(imageName);
    }

    public Image getCurrentImage()
    {
        return currentImage;
    }
}
```

Creating an RMI Server

By stressing that the RMI server should handle invocations quickly, one can resist the urge to have it handle all the image processing locally. Rather, the client process will own the responsibility for getting and displaying images. Simply implement the `PictureServer` interface and the corresponding `getImageForColor` method that is associated with it.

IMPLEMENTING THE SERVER

Creating an RMI server first involves implementing the method in the RMI interface that you wish to publish. Here, you want to make sure that this includes the getImageForColor method that has been specified in the PictureServer interface. As discussed, the getImageForColor method simply returns a string corresponding to the name of the file containing the image for the current color of the button:

```java
public class PictureServerImpl extends UnicastRemoteObject
                                implements PictureServer
{
    PictureServerImpl() throws RemoteException
    {
        // call the super class' constructor
        super();
    }

    public String getImageForColor(
        Color currentColor
    )
    {
        if(currentColor == Color.red)
            return "red.gif";
        else if(currentColor == Color.blue)
            return "blue.gif";
        else
            return "default.gif";
    }
}
```

BINDING TO THE REGISTRY

Now implement the main method for the PictureServerImpl server, and include the necessary code to bind to the RMI Registry:

```java
public class PictureServerImpl extends UnicastRemoteObject
                                implements PictureServer
{
    PictureServerImpl() throws RemoteException
    {
        // call the super class' constructor
        super();
    }

    public String getImageForColor(
        Color currentColor
    )
    {
        if(currentColor == Color.red)
            return "red.gif";
```

```
        else if(currentColor == Color.blue)
            return "blue.gif";
        else
            return "default.gif";
    }

    public void main(
        String args[]
    )
    {
        // create the local instance of the PictureServer
        PictureServerImpl svr = new PictureServerImpl();

        // out the local instance into the Naming server
        Naming.rebind("PictureAreaServer", svr);
    }
}
```

RMI and CORBA are what the industry terms open solutions. That is, both RMI and CORBA are in the public domain and easily accessible as public specifications and implementations. RMI however, is technically not an open solution since it is owned and produced by Sun Microsystems. Even though recent events have prodded Sun to submit Java to a standards body for review (and probably obfuscation as well), RMI is still more or less Sun proprietary. The Microsoft analog to RMI is the Common Object Model, or COM. COM was discussed in Chapter 9, *Bean Integration*, and showed you how to integrate your Beans with the ActiveX Internet model that Microsoft claims will change the world. I will now do the same for RMI and CORBA and show you how to integrate those two networking technologies with JavaBeans.

Issues for Networked Beans

Now that you have a basic understanding of the networking capabilities of RMI and CORBA, you can begin to tailor solutions for Beans. As stressed throughout this book, Beans are nothing but collections of Java classes. Each Bean is nothing more than a Java object, so the actual integration of network code into your Bean code is trivial. However, a few major architectural changes must be made to accommodate the latency of network invocations.

Networked Beans Architecture

The biggest issues at hand with Beans networking is the means with which events are fired. As discussed in Chapter 1 and Chapter 3 (*Bean Events*), in Java and in JavaBeans, events are fired using regular Java method calls. Since Java method invocations are always synchronous, your Beans are presented with quite a quandary. To fully understand this issue, take a brief look at the differences between asynchronous and synchronous communication.

ASYNCHRONOUS VERSUS SYNCHRONOUS

As mentioned before, Java methods are invoked synchronously. This means that when one object invokes on a method in another object, the calling object blocks until the called object is finished. The opposite, asynchronous messages, are somewhat different. Asynchronous invocation allows the calling object to make the invocation, then go about its business. The called object does whatever processing is required and return the call when it so pleases.

With *synchronous* communication you are given the satisfaction of knowing if a method succeeded or not. However, for that knowledge you will sacrifice performance because the calling object can only make one invocation at a time. With *asynchronous* communication you get performance because both the calling and called objects can execute while the waiting for one another, but you will lose the reliability that comes with knowing when an invocation succeeded.

WHAT THIS MEANS FOR BEANS

If you were to put together an application using several Beans, you would be fulfilling the promise of what JavaBeans is all about: building complex applications using reusable software modules. However, if you wanted to take your application and make it network aware, using any combination of sockets, RMI, CORBA, or COM, you would have somewhat of a problem.

Your entire application will be frozen whenever a network call is made. Obviously, you could use threads or even another form of communication to get around the problem, as shown in a moment. But for the time being, you need to understand why this is such a problem and why such lengths are required in order to correct it.

When you assemble an application using a bunch of Beans, and plug in a network Bean to get your application onto the network, you are trusting that each Bean will behave appropriately and that no one Bean will hog all the resources within the application. If your network Bean periodically makes invocations across the network, you need to know that the rest of your application will not be affected by one particular Bean's activity. If you were building an office suite that made network calls constantly, you would suddenly discover that your spreadsheet froze every time a calculation was being sent to the server. This would be annoying to say the least.

One way to circumvent the entire synchronous invocation issue is to use another form of communication. Sun has developed a networking technology called ICE-T that enables you to make asynchronous network invocations to back end C++ or Java servers. Your Beans may want to use ICE-T to handle their network traffic. ICE-T is, however, somewhat of a kluge to the pure Java solution. You want something that is contained within the language itself so that you are not beholden to third-parties for libraries to build your Beans.

The most logical answer is to effectively use threads in your design. The big problem with threads is that many people *over* use them. Thread-happy applications consume far more resources than you might imagine. Rather than promoting simultaneous execution of algorithms, they actually prevent it. However, spawning a thread to make a network invocation is quite an acceptable use of threads, as will be seen in the next two sections. In so doing, applications can very easily make use of network Beans, knowing that the Bean will not hog the application itself.

Firing Networked Events

Now that you have pretty much established that you are going to solve your quandary by using threads, you need to go about creating a threaded function in which your event-firing mechanism may reside. As you saw in Chapter 3, *Bean Events*, event firing takes place within a special function. In the `RainbowButton` example throughout this book, that method is called `fireButtonEvent`. If you were to redo the `fireButtonEvent` method to fire across a network, you would first need for the method to create a thread as shown in Figure 10.13.

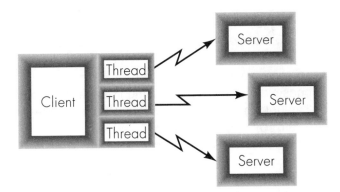

Figure 10.13: *Events fired across networks using threads.*

NETWORKED ADAPTERS

Certainly, one way to make a network invocation is to pop threads at the origin of the invocation itself. However, a clever alternative does exist, the process of which is shown in Figure 10.14. You could very easily create a special kind of network adapter whose entire job is to receive invocations from clients, pop a thread, allow the client to continue about its merry business, and keep the client from either knowing it is using a network or that threads are involved at all.

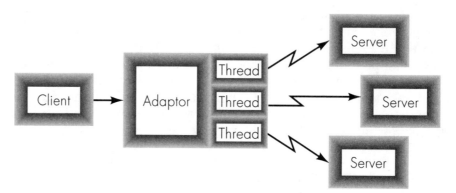

Figure 10.14: *Network invocation using threaded adapters.*

The advantage to using adapters is that clients can easily use network resources without knowing that they are. In the case in Figure 10.14, the client could simply be firing an event to a listener that happens to register with it. Unbeknown to it, the listener is clear across the network on another machine. No additional customization needs to occur on the client in order to make it work with the network.

 It just so happens that this kind of threaded adapter is what takes place in the normal JDK event calling mechanism. All events that are fired to components are first placed in the system's `EventQueue`. This special queue is responsible for efficiently passing the event on to the proper listener. You can get a handle on your system event queue by invoking the `getSystemEventQueue` method.

ENTERPRISE BEANS

Soon after the JavaBeans specification was frozen and the first release of the Beans Developer's Kit, JavaSoft unveiled their proposal for *Enterprise Beans*. According to their press releases and white papers, the intent is to tightly integrate CORBA and RMI support with Beans components by bundling a specialized CORBA/RMI Object Request Broker with every Bean. This arrangement would allow Beans to make network invocations using a high-level distributed object technology with great ease and little extra effort. In the meantime, Microsoft will more than likely find a way to seamlessly marry JavaBeans components with COM and ActiveX. This is one of the areas in which the two camps will find it very fruitful to be innovative. The Enterprise Beans segment of the Java-Beans technology is one worth watching very closely.

While the JavaBeans specification produced by Javasoft is non-deterministic on the state of Beans over a network, make no bones about it. The specification states in one section that it "regards CORBA as a key technology," but in a later section specifically states that "Beans were designed for interaction within one virtual machine." I believe, however, that networking and JavaBeans are very much intertwined. After all, if Java is the Internet language, and JavaBeans is the ultimate and most important API for Java, then certainly Beans must be totally network aware. I hope that this chapter has brought to mind some of these important networking issues. In the near future, you will see a more robust networking model for Beans, but for the time being spawning threads to overcome network latency is appropriate enough.

Summary

Networking your Beans together can make for truly astounding JavaBeans applications. Rather than being limited to widgets or graphical Beans for client-side programming, you can explore the full-depth and complication of server-side components. As Microsoft has proven with its server-side ActiveX technology, a viable server component architecture is absolutely essential for a component model to succeed in the Internet era. JavaBeans has not yet addressed many of these server-side issues, but as time goes on it will. For the time being, this short exploration into networking technologies and Bean interaction is adequate. As you will see in the next chapter, there are several organizations and companies investing heavily in Beans. As these companies are joined by the loyal legion of Java zealots from all corners of the industry, networking these components will become more and more important.

PART FOUR

Cool Beans

Part Four is an examination of how Beans are really being used. With a brief look at Beans-based applications coming around the pike followed by a discussion on licensing issues associated with Beans, Chapter 11 seeks to take the discussion about Beans to a more marketing-oriented level and will also briefly examine the future of Beans technology.

CHAPTER
11 Beans in the Real World

- **H**ow Beans are Being Used
- **S**elling Your Beans

Now that you've learned all about JavaBeans and why they are important, I'm going to take a few moments to examine what other organizations and people are doing with them. This chapter will focus on Beans in the Real World, a far cry from the myopic techno-geek world, where business is conducted on a daily basis. When reading this chapter, keep in mind how these organizations define a Bean in terms of its granularity. These Beans are much more than simple widgets for GUIs; rather they are complex modules of code that can be plugged and played at will. I'll wrap up the book with a brief examination of the Beans business model and how it fits in the Internet and the software business model espoused by the old-timers like Microsoft and IBM.

Using Beans

There are several companies that are architecting their entire Java solutions using Beans. First among these is, of course, Sun Microsystems. Sun's goal is to be the owner and shepherd of the JavaBeans revolution. Others have even loftier ambitions. IBM, for example, seeks to be the ultimate source for Enterprise Beans; Beans with great power and flexibility. Meanwhile, in Chapter 7, *GUI Builders*, you saw the impact that Symantec can have on the JavaBeans phenomenon, but they are not alone in the tools arena. One of the more exciting parts about the Java revolution is predicting what will happen. One safe prediction to make is that JavaBeans, and the attention it has received thus far, will propel Java beyond *just another language* and make it immediately useful for large-scale applications.

A Bean Warehouse

Sun regards the ownership and proliferation of Beans as one of its core competencies. They want to be *the* brokerage for all things related to JavaBeans. Their intention is to put together a warehouse for all vendors, be they Sun's own competitors or not, to place their Beans for immediate download and online sale. By selecting a Bean from `javabeans.sun.com`, you can be assured of obtaining both quality software from reputable sources as well as several Beans from midnight hackers.

Sun also has a distinct advantage in being the owner and progenitor of the Java language. After all, Sun determines what Java is and, to a lesser extent, how it is used. As a result, their entry into the component brokering business signals a new beginning for them. No longer just a hardware company, Sun looks to provide full Java hardware and software solutions.

Enterprise Beans

As JavaBeans neared its first customer ship date, a big announcement was unveiled. In cooperation with IBM and its Lotus software division, JavaSoft was ready to bring forth an era of Enterprise Beans. What exactly is an Enterprise Bean? Well, in Chapter 10, *Bean Networking*, you saw how a Bean can be used across a network. An Enterprise Bean is nothing more than a networked Bean with a lot of glop attached. Some of those extra features include a built-in ORB, a simple RMI server integration capability, and the notion of server-side Beans.

While JavaBeans is a fascinating architecture and a truly great way to program in Java, it falls short in the arena of networked applications. As you saw first-hand, building a network capability into a Java Bean involves a ton of work. However, with an Enterprise Bean specification freely available, you can easily integrate your networked applications directly into your Beans. Furthermore, there are still some less-than-enthusiastic Java programmers who feel that C or C++ may still be better options. For them, accessing C or C++ code from within a Java Bean can become dramatically easier with an Enterprise Bean.

IBM is charged with building the portion of the Enterprise Bean architecture that allows an ActiveX control to be converted into a Java Bean. Obviously, this is a major accomplishment. It should be noted that Microsoft itself is providing this capability along its full line of ActiveX-enabled tools. Nevertheless, the partnership between IBM and JavaSoft will yield significant results in the Enterprise Bean specification.

Bean Applications

The two biggest vendors of JavaBeans applications and reusable Java-Beans components will more than likely be Corel and Lotus. Corel is building an entire office suite composed entirely of JavaBeans components. They have built their entire series of spreadsheets, word processors, and databases with the idea that they can be broken apart and reused as part of Web page applets, Java applications, or other, more complex, applications. You can follow Corel's Java initiative by visiting their Web site (www.corel.com).

Lotus' SmartSuite product will be built entirely out of reusable Java-Beans components. Additional Beans will allow you to connect to Lotus Notes and Domino servers, giving you the ability to be truly network-aware and integrated with Lotus' other products. Lotus can be contacted at their Web site (www.lotus.com).

Now that you've seen the various initiatives for JavaBeans around the Java community, you can make decisions for your own architecture. Where do you want to take Java? Looking at the organizations that have been surveyed, you should have a better idea of where to focus your energies. After all, you don't want to spend time rebuilding a spreadsheet Bean when Corel will have one for you to use very shortly. But, an added concern that you should take into account is the entire realm of how to make money with Beans. As the great Tom Cruise once said, "Show me the money!"

Making Money

So, the big question is how are all these companies going to sell their Beans? The issue is slightly more thorny than you might believe. After all, in the traditional software world, you supplied your product to your customers by giving them a disk or CD which they could use to install the software on their machine. The idea that a person went to a store and *bought* a physical piece of software implied ownership of some kind. As long as that person was in possession of the physical medium on which the software was supplied, they owned it. In the component world, things are radically different.

Licensing and Ownership

When you supply a component to a developer, the developer will buy it from you and use it to assemble an application of his or her own. If Lotus were to supply all the Beans that make up its product as separate components that can be purchased and downloaded from a Web site, what is the incentive for Lotus itself to sell the completely integrated application? What is to stop a person from buying up all the various components, assembling them, adding a few new nuggets here and there, and shipping a product of his own? Will Lotus ever see any money from this re-sale? Does Lotus get to have its hands in this person's profits? These are but a few of the many, many questions surrounding the component revolution.

THE MICROSOFT WAY

Until now, the only example of true component technology in use has been Microsoft's Visual Basic controls. Visual Basic controls are highly prevalent everywhere today. Visit the ActiveX Web site on CNET (www.activex.com) and you can download one of several controls for use on your Web page or in your applications.

The Microsoft model for licensing these controls has always been to encourage control developers to charge for the use of their products by other developers. So, a company that makes a spreadsheet component could sell the component to a company that makes an office suite. But, the money stops there. The company that makes the office suite could then sell its product, without charging for the use of the control.

At least, that's the way it's supposed to work. What usually ends up happening is that the control developer charges a licensing fee for their control. The license specifically mentions how many products may be shipped with the control embedded inside them. If the office suite developer gets a license for 500 spreadsheet controls and wants to ship 7000 office suites, only 500 of those office suites may contain the control. If they wanted all of their products to ship with the correct control, they will need to obtain a license for more controls.

LICENSING

The big problem with all this licensing is that it's completely unenforceable (thus, the need for a *paper license*). A paper license is one that exists only on paper, with no locks within the software itself to prevent illegal or unauthorized use of the component. Theoretically, this works just fine. After all, in the olden days of software on diskette, the only thing that stopped people from copying disks was a paper license. Even though everyone knew that copying software was illegal, it still happened, and the software industry still churned along to the point that it is at now.

Another kind of license is a *software license*. A software license is a piece of code embedded within the software that prevents the software from executing anywhere that it is not permitted to execute. Some software licenses are *node-specific*, meaning that they allow the software to run on only one particular machine. This is very common on the UNIX world. Other times, the software license can be set up as a license server for an entire site. The *site license* specifically says that only five people may use the software at any given time. The license server keeps track of how many copies of the software are executing at any given time at the site.

Needless to say, these are all very complex and secure pieces of machinery. While the paper license is ineffective at policing how and when software is used, it is the easiest to implement. With the growing fungus of lawyers in this country, the threat of legal action is always a deterrent. On the other hand, if you absolutely positively require control over your software, then a software license is your only recourse. They can be complicated and difficult to administer, but they could solve your problem.

THE JAVA PROBLEM

But wait! There's one big problem with all of this: Java. For all its wondrous qualities as a language for the Internet and an alternative to the masochistic ways of the past, Java is completely worthless in the licensing world. Why? Well, let's say you build an applet and sell it to a customer. A customer places it on his/her Web page (like they are allowed to). People then come and play with it. The way browsers work today, if you visit a site with a Java applet, the applet class files are downloaded to your machine and executed locally as shown in Figure 11.1. Sure, the Java sandbox prevents any malicious code from harming your system, but that doesn't change the fact that the Java class is now sitting on your machine.

Now that the class file is sitting on someone else's machine, they can take the same applet class and reuse it elsewhere. This is a big problem if you are trying to protect your applet from being used illegally. Unfortunately, to fix this problem would require a vast alteration in how the lan-

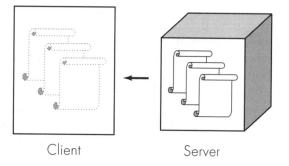

Client   Server

Figure 11.1: _Java applet classes are downloaded_
to your local machine.

guage operates, and would, quite frankly, ruin the language. Your only recourse in this case is a paper license that specifically says that the applet may not be used on a Web page without payment. Even then, good luck with enforcement.

The problem that then arises with components is slightly different, but very much related. If you sell the use of your Bean to a person that then uses it in an applet on their Web page, the Bean's class file is downloaded to any of the Web page's visitor's machine. The Bean is no longer in the exclusive possession of the person to whom you sold it. Once again, your only recourse is a paper license that should say that the Bean can only be integrated with another application upon payment to the author.

SOFTWARE LICENSES AND JAVA

In some cases, you may wish to embed a license within your Java code. In fact, several of the major license vendors today are building such a device. However, there are things you should know about these kinds of licenses. First, there should not be a problem with providing such a mechanism for a Java application. The issues of reverse engineering of code will be talked about in a moment, but for the most part a Java application with a license should function properly.

However, if you wanted to build a Java applet with a license, you will need to understand more than a few details about Java networking. For starters, you will need to make sure that the applet can get a license from a license server or at the very least be able to verify that it is running on a legal machine. To do this and still stay within the happy confines of the Java security model, the applet will need to make a socket (or other networking) connection back to the license server in order to verify itself. This will require some trickery on your end.

Another thing you should be aware of with applets and licenses is that the applet may suffer from some performance problems because of network latency. This might be unavoidable if you are intent on protecting your applet. Furthermore, the socket connection will actually be made from the machine to which the applet is downloaded (see Figure 11.2). If there is a firewall somewhere in between, all bets will be off. But, this is an overall Java issue, not just a licensing issue.

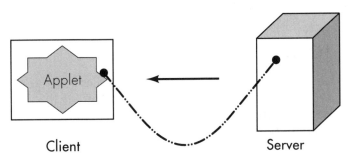

Figure 11.2: *Socket connections for licensing.*

PROTECTING YOUR CODE

Equally important to your business model decisions are the number of Java reverse engineering applications on the market today. Using one of these applications, you can take a Java class file and reverse engineer it back to its original Java code. There are, obviously, some fuzzy areas because such applications have never proved 100 percent capable of regenerating original code. Nevertheless, these applications do exist, and you should be aware of them.

> Remember, if you place your component in an applet, that component's class file is automatically downloaded to the client machine. From there, it can be reverse engineered, and your algorithms may be compromised.

I don't want to put the fear of God into you, but it's something you should be *aware* of. Don't get overly paranoid about your code being reverse engineered. After all, a very small percentage of the computing populace actually has the skills to do such a thing. As software developers in the olden days learned, sometimes these kind of evils are just meant to be lived with. You can try to conquer them, indeed there are some esoteric language constructs that these applications have trouble parsing (such as null arrays), but it may be an endeavor that is not worth the time spent on it.

The bottom line in all of this is that enforcing a specific kind of license scheme may prove difficult and not necessarily worth the time. These are, of course, tradeoffs that you will need to make on your own, but at least you are now aware of them. If you have further questions, consult a license vendor. Licensing technology for Java, like software and Internet technology in general, could very well make leaps and bounds between the time this book was written and the time it was published. Now that you taken a look at enforceability, or the lack thereof, take a moment to examine how some people plan on marketing and selling their Beans.

A Business Model for Components

At the heart of the problem of selling a component lies the dangerous truth about this brave, new world. Who is going to pay for the component? As discussed with Visual Basic, a viable business model for Beans developers is for the component architects to sell their Beans to the next level of developers. These developers pay a per-use fee or perhaps a general usage fee. They can then assemble a bunch of disparate components together and sell the finished product.

If you hearken back to the first example used in this book, the BMW Z3 Roadster, it might make a little more sense. BMW buys the tires, batteries, light bulbs, and simulated wood grain from outside vendors. BMW pays them a fee for their products. They then have an in-house manufacturing and engineering team build more components, and assemble those along with the third-party components to put together a car. Because BMW pays for high quality tires, and chooses really pretty wood and leather for the interior, the final price of the car is slightly higher than, say, a Mazda Miata. BMW passes the expense of the component on to you, the lucky consumer charged with financing the whole thing.

By the same token, if you, as a developer, purchase a component from Lotus rather than Jenny's House of Beans, your final product will be slightly higher in cost than had you gone the cheap route. But, your customers may value your choice of name brand components rather than an obscure brand. These are business decisions that those interested will be better suited to evaluate than the author of this book.

Summary

After reading this book, I hope that you are as excited and interested in Beans as I am. JavaBeans represents the most important API for Java. As shown, it is easy and flexible, and just like Java it can be a heck of a lot of fun. Whether you choose the geek route and develop with Makefiles and Emacs, or the elegant and simple route with a Java development environment, JavaBeans will make your Java life much easier. As you overcome the licensing issues and legalese associated with building and publishing Beans, you will find that a wonderful world of component technology awaits you. Once component interaction becomes more solidified with efforts from both the Sun and Microsoft camps, you will find that the disparate component models of OpenDoc, JavaBeans, and ActiveX can come together and give you the best of all worlds. This is a great time to be a software developer, and JavaBeans makes it easy.

Tiramisu

In much the same way that JavaBeans can be used to build applications, coffee and espresso in particular, can be used to make real food! Tiramisu is the greatest dessert that you will ever feast your eyes upon, a true chocolate and coffee lover's dream. Here is a basic Tiramisu recipe for your enjoyment. It was obtained from David Rosengarten's TV Food Network program, Taste.

Ingredients
EGGS, 8, with yolks and whites separated
SUGAR, 1/3 cup
MASCARPONE, 1 pound
HEAVY CREAM, 1 cup
EXPRESSO COFFEE, 2 cups cooled
BRANDY, 2/3 cup
LADY FINGERS, 30
BITTERSWEET CHOCOLATE, 2 ounces grated
COCOA POWDER, Dutch process, sifted, for garnish

Directions

Mix the sugar into the egg yolks, blending well.

Add a little Mascarpone at a time to the egg yolk mixture, and mix until smooth. Set aside.

In a separate bowl, beat the whipping cream until stiff peaks form. Set this aside as well.

In another bowl, beat the egg whites until stiff peaks form.

Fold the whipped cream into the egg yolk mixture, then fold in the beaten egg whites.

Spread about 1/3 of the cream mixture in a 4-6 quart glass baking dish or serving bowl.

Place expresso coffee in a large mixing bowl, and combine with the brandy.

Dip a lady finger into the expresso, lay it in baking dish on cream mixture.

Top with grated chocolate.

Continue in this manner, laying lady fingers side by side to cover the bottom.

Place another 1/3 of cream mixture on top of soaked lady fingers.

Cover this with another layer of expresso-soaked lady fingers.

Top with remaining cream mixture and grated chocolate.

Dust final layer with grated chocolate and cocoa powder.

Chill 2 hours to set.

APPENDIX A

Quick Start Guide

- Expert Developers
- Beginning Developers
- Additional Resources

This Appendix outlines the resources, both inside and outside this book, that a developer can use to get started with Beans development. Basically, developers are grouped into one of two categories; beginning Java developers or expert Java developers.

Expert Developers

Those people who have a firm understanding of object-oriented programming, Java, and networking technologies can be defined as expert developers. For that group, this book should be used slightly differently than it should for a general audience. Expert developers will appreciate the nuts

327

and bolts nature of Part Two, *Core Bean Technology* (Chapters 3 through 6). These are no-nonsense API outlines, usage guidelines, and tips. It may be advisable for expert developers to skip immediately to the chapters on networking and begin to shore up their Java networking skills. Chapter 11, *Beans in the Real World*, would be useful for possibly selling JavaBeans development projects to upper-management, people who may be skeptical about JavaBeans or Java in general.

Those developers interested in more JavaScript experience should consult the *JavaScript Developer's Resource*, also from Prentice Hall (see the *Additional Resources* section of this appendix). Expert developers will feel the need to skip the rudimentary aspects of Part One, *Introduction to Java and Components* (Chapters 1 and 2). Chapter 7, *GUI Builders*, may not be particularly useful to these advanced Java programmers since the choice of a Java development environment may already have been made. Chapter 9, *Bean Integration*, will be extremely useful in integrating your Java applications with other component models. The road map for expert developers looks like Figure A.1. Just follow the unshaded path.

Expert developers interested in developing Beans for public consumption should consult the *Additional Resources* section in this appendix for places to put their Beans.

Beginning Developers

Those programmers who are fairly new to Java, or component architectures, have different needs entirely. For these developers, a solid background and foundation is required before moving on to more complex tasks such as Introspection or JavaBeans integration with ActiveX. Beginner developers will need to read a few other reference books before tackling these advanced tasks:

- *Core Java*, Cay Horstmann and Gary Cornell, Prentice Hall Professional Technical Reference, © 1997

- *JavaScript Developer's Resource*, Kamran Husain and Jason Levitt, Prentice Hall Professional Technical Reference, © 1997

- *Just Java*, Peter van der Linden, Prentice Hall Professional Technical Reference, © 1997

Beginning developers will need to make sure that the basics of Java covered in Chapter 1, *Advanced Java*, are well understood before moving on. In addition, Chapter 2, *Component Models*, will provide the basis for a strong understanding of what components are and how they should be used. Once again, Chapters 3 through 6 are down and dirty

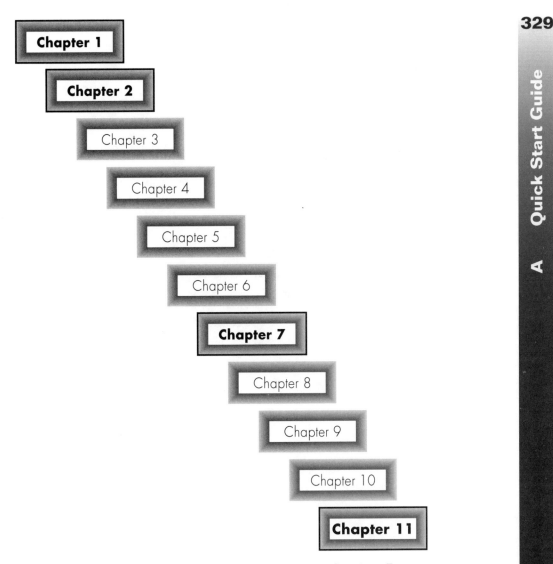

Figure A.1:   *Expert Developer road map for JavaBeans Developer's Resource.*

Java code. Get ready to get your hands dirty. Chapter 7, will be of great use since it is designed to cover JavaBeans development without having to write source code. Chapter 9, and Chapter 10, *Bean Networking*, will require a greater understanding of non-Java development including ActiveX, CORBA, and Netscape ONE. With that in mind, the road map for beginning developers looks like Figure A.2. Make sure you tackle Chapters 1, 2, and 7 first.

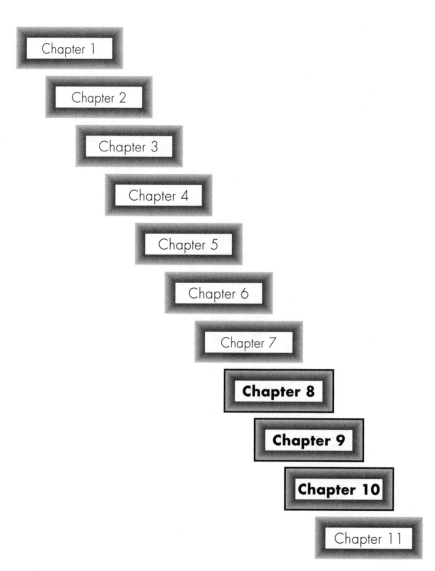

Figure A.2: *Beginning developer road map for JavaBeans Developer's Resource.*

Additional Resources

In addition, developers of all levels of familiarity with Java and components may benefit from a wide variety of online, print, and media resources from many sources.

Publications

Several books have been published on Java, but only a few of them warrant further discussion. The first three were previously mentioned and I've added a couple more technical reference-type books that are worthy additions to your Java library:

- *Core Java*, Cay Horstmann and Gary Cornell, Prentice Hall Professional Technical Reference, © 1997

- *JavaScript Developer's Resource*, Kamran Husain and Jason Levitt, Prentice Hall Professional Technical Reference, © 1997

- *Just Java*, Peter van der Linden, Prentice Hall Professional Technical Reference, © 1997

- *Advanced Java Networking*, Prashant Sridharan, Prentice Hall Professional Technical Reference, © 1997

- *Java in a Nutshell*, David Flanagan, O'Reilley & Associates, Inc., © 1996

Web Sites

There are more Web sites than you can count that are worth visiting. Here are a few key Java- and JavaScript-related ones:

- http://java.sun.com/: Java's home page. Brought to you by the wonderful people at Sun Microsystems, Inc. JavaSoft business unit.

- http://www.sun.com/: Home page of Sun Microsystems, Inc., the founder and progenitor of the Java language.

- http://www.microsoft.com/java: The Microsoft Corp. Java Web site.

- http://www.gamelan.com/: The ultimate Java Web site. Contains sample applets and source code.

- http://www.symantec.com/café/: Home page of the Symantec Java tools group.

- http://www.penumbrasoftware.com/: Home page of Penumbra Software

- http://www.microsoft.com/visualj/ Home page of Microsoft's Visual J++

- http://www.mediacity.com/~heath: Home page of the author of this book.

Newsgroups

Ah, Usenet. Where else can you get into a lively conversation about what is and is not canonical about Star Trek? Despite their overall contentious nature, there are a few newsgroups worth visiting. Please, don't start a flame war. Be a newsgroup lurker for a week or so and get to know the unique etiquette of each newsgroup before posting to the world famous *me too* discussion threads.

- comp.lang.java: Java newsgroup hierarchy. Every question you have about Java can be answered by this crew. The newsgroup just got reorganized into several subgroups, all of which are listed below. Consult each individual group's frequently asked questions (FAQ) list for its charter and accepted posting guidelines.

- comp.lang.java.advocacy

- comp.lang.java.announce

- comp.lang.java.beans

- comp.lang.java.databases

- comp.lang.java.gui

- comp.lang.java.help

- comp.lang.java.machine

- comp.lang.java.programmer

- comp.lang.java.security

- comp.lang.java.setup

- comp.lang.java.softwaretools

- comp.lang.java.tech

- comp.lang.javascript: JavaScript newsgroup. Every JavaScript question in the world can be asked here.

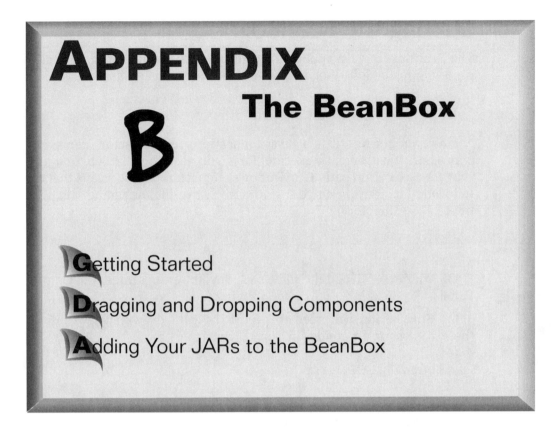

APPENDIX B

The BeanBox

- **G**etting Started

- **D**ragging and Dropping Components

- **A**dding Your JARs to the BeanBox

As part of the JavaBeans Developer's Kit included on the CD with this book, you will find a very simple little Java application called the Bean-Box. The BeanBox is the most rudimentary container you will find for playing with your Beans. The common misconception is that it is a full-fledged GUI Builder like those discussed in Chapter 7, *GUI Builders*. On the contrary! The BeanBox was designed as somewhat of a stop-gap while tools vendors put the finishing touches on their applications. For those of you that loathe tools, or do not own one yet, the BeanBox is a great way to try out your application.

Starting the BeanBox

The BeanBox is a Java application, therefore starting it *should* be as simple as typing the following incantation on the command line:

```
%prompt% java sun.beanbox.BeanBoxFrame
```

However, because it is a Java application, several factors come into play before it will actually execute. First, you need to make sure that Java is in your execution path. On Windows 95 machines, that means that the following line must be in your `autoexec.bat` file (assuming Java is in the `C:\JDK` directory):

```
SET PATH=<rest of your path here>;C:\JDK\BIN
```

On Windows NT, add the same path to your settings under the Control Panel.

On Solaris, you will need to export the path on which Java resides (here, it's assumed it resides in `/opt/java`):

```
set path=/opt/java/bin
```

Once Java is in your execution path, you need to alter your CLASS-PATH so that the Beans files are on it. If you look in the directory under which you installed JavaBeans, you will find a `beanbox` directory. Inside the `beanbox` directory is a classes directory. You need to set your CLASSPATH to include this classes directory:

```
SET CLASSPATH=C:\BEANS\BEANBOX\CLASSES
```

Now you will need to change to the directory (`beanbox`) in which the BeanBox resides, and type the magical incantation that will start the BeanBox in order to continue:

```
%prompt% java sun.beanbox.BeanBoxFrame
```

Using the BeanBox

Before proceeding, it is important to underscore that the BeanBox is not a production-quality GUI Builder. The BeanBox is a very simple, very buggy, basic device that you can use to test whether your Beans conform to the full JavaBeans specification. If the BeanBox is able to load your Bean, it is conformant. If it is unable to load your Bean, any number of things may be the cause. Your Bean may simply not conform to the Java-

Beans specification, or you might have encountered one of several bugs of the BeanBox.

BeanBox Contents

When the BeanBox finally starts up, you will see three panels. The first panel contains a list of all the Beans currently available for use by the BeanBox (see Figure B.1). You may load your own JARs dynamically, but trust me when I say that everything in your system must be perfectly set up and working. The BeanBox is not a production-quality device, and should not be treated as such. To add your own JARs, the best thing to do is to follow the advice in the next section.

Figure B.1: *The BeanBox palette of Beans.*

The second panel, shown in Figure B.2, is the main composition window in which you can drag, drop, and connect Beans.

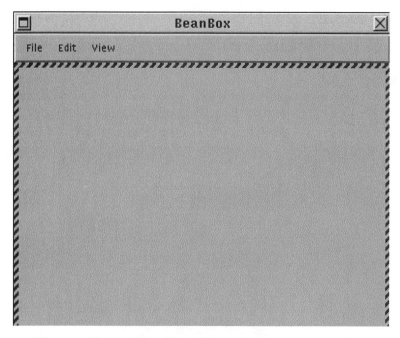

Figure B.2:   *The BeanBox composition window.*

The last panel is a simple property sheet that is loaded up when the Bean is selected (see Figure B.3). The property sheet contains a list of all properties and fires property change events to the instance of the Bean when a change is made inside one of them.

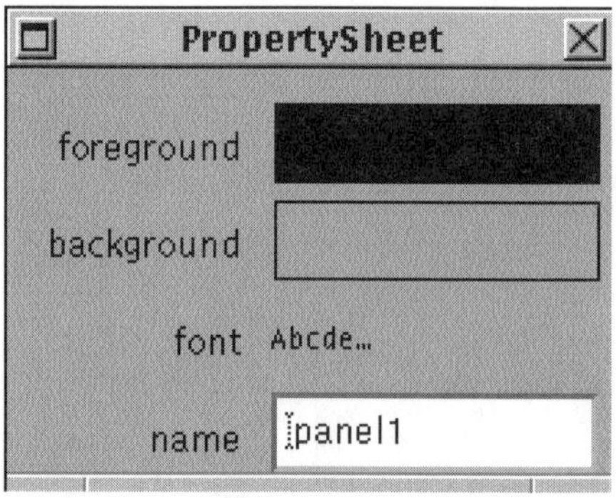

Figure B.3:   *The BeanBox property sheet.*

Loading a Bean

In order to load a Bean, simply select it from the palette window. When the BeanBox is through chugging along, it will dump the Bean into the composition window. From there, you can select the Bean and edit its properties in the property window. As an example, let's first select the `Juggler` Bean from the palette and place it in the composition window as shown in Figure B.4.

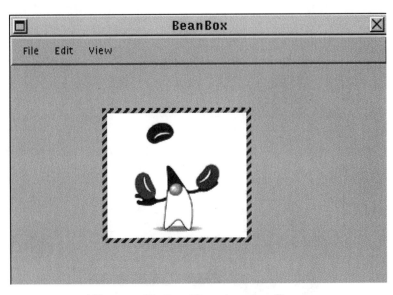

Figure B.4: *The Juggler Bean.*

You will see the property sheet window change as well. Edit the animation rate and watch Duke flip those Beans around!

Connecting Beans

Now what you want to do is to bring in another Bean and tie it to Duke. Go ahead and select the `OurButton` Bean from the palette. Select a location in the composition window and put it there (Figure B.5). You can also edit its properties if you so desire.

Now, while the `OurButton` Bean is selected, go to the `Edit` menu on the Composition window and select `Events`, followed by `action`, followed by `actionPerformed`. A rubber band will appear and follow your mouse around. Select the `Juggler` Bean and a dialog box shown in Figure B.6 will now appear.

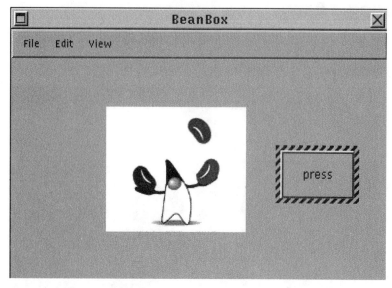

Figure B.5: *OurButton and Juggler cooperating in the composition window.*

Figure B.6: *Actions on the Juggler Bean.*

Select a method on the Juggler Bean that will get triggered by the press of the button. If you select stopJuggling, whenever the button is pressed the Juggler will stop.

The same techniques may be used for any of the other Beans in the BeanBox's palette. To add your own Beans to the palette, you will need to follow the instructions in the next section.

Adding Your Own JAR Files

You will also notice in Figure B.1 that the `RainbowButton`, `Sound-Machine`, `PictureArea`, and `BaseballPlayer` Beans (used throughout this book) have been added to the BeanBox's palette. Doing this is slightly tricky and requires an understanding of the CLASSPATH issues surrounding Java. To learn how to put together a JAR file, consult Chapter 6, *Bean Packaging and Persistence.*

Once you have a JAR file, simply place it in the JavaBeans Developer's Kit's `jars` directory. You will then automatically see it in the BeanBox's palette and be able to manipulate it as done throughout this book. Once again, be forewarned; the BeanBox is by no means a solid and dependable product.

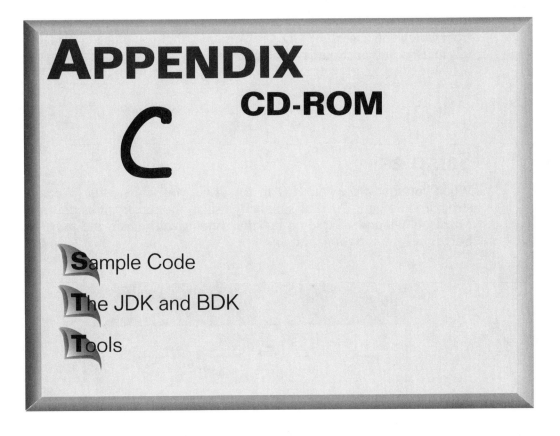

APPENDIX
C
CD-ROM

Sample Code

The JDK and BDK

Tools

The CD-ROM provided with this book includes several software packages that are particularly useful to JavaBeans developers. With tools and examples, you should be well on your way to becoming an expert JavaBeans developer.

Web Page

The CD-ROM includes a special Web page that covers most of the details in this appendix. It also includes hyperlinks and more descriptive information about each sample object or class. For better results, simply load the CD-ROM into your CD drive, and point your browser to the file located in the following directory, where CD ROOT is the base location from which you access the CD. On Windows, that could be a drive letter (as in D:) and on Solaris it would probably be a directory on your machine (like `/dev/cdrom`).

```
<CD ROOT>/www/html/index.html
```

Samples

When you first place your CD in the drive, you will see the directory structure in Figure C.1. For simplicity's sake, the screen grabs are from Microsoft Windows Explorer, but the content will remain the same on Solaris or from the command line.

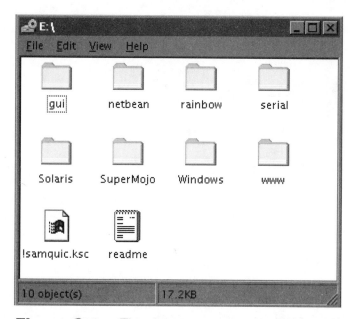

Figure C.1: *The directory structure of the CD as viewed from Windows 95.*

The `gui` directory contains some of the samples from Chapter 8, *Bean GUI Issues*. The `netbean` directory contains a first crack at some of the issues outlined in the section on Enterprise Beans in Chapter 10, *Bean Networking*. The `rainbow` directory houses all of the sample code associated with the `RainbowButton` Bean that is developed throughout the text. The `serial` directory has some simple Bean serialization examples

Because of the lack of availability of a Java Developer's Kit 1.1 version of any major Java development tool, the files are placed as-is, with Solaris Makefiles. As you begin to develop your applications, or wish to compile the samples, you will need to make a tool selection and create project files for the tool.

Developer's Kits

The `Solaris` directory contains the Java Developer's Kit 1.1 (JDK) and the Beans Developer's Kit April 1997 (BDK) for the Solaris platform. The `Windows` directory contains the JDK and BDK for the Windows 95/Windows NT platform.

Windows 3.1 and Macintosh versions of the JDK and BDK are not available on the CD-ROM. Of course, the same sample code should work on every platform. For simple applications at least, write once, run everywhere is a reality.

Software

Penumbra Software in Atlanta, Georgia graciously allowed Prentice Hall and I to include their Java development environment Super Mojo on this CD. Super Mojo is a 100 percent Java application that is capable of being both a GUI Builder for JavaBeans as well as a full-fledged development environment for Java. Super Mojo is located in the `SuperMojo` directory. Currently, Penumbra was only able to make available a version of their tool with Windows 95 support files. For more information on cross-platform development, consult their Web site (www.PenumbraSoftware.com).

As always, the lawyers wanted their say. Consult the license agreements for each product, and have fun. As far as the sample code is concerned, you may freely re-use, modify, drink, eat, and otherwise enjoy every last byte contained on the CD or in the book.

Index

Java™ Development Kit
Version 1.1.1
and
BDK Version 1.0 Combined
Binary Code License

This binary code license ("License") contains rights and restrictions associated with use of the accompanying software and documentation ("Software"). Read the License carefully before installing the Software. By installing the Software you agree to the terms and conditions of this License.

1. Limited License Grant. Sun grants to you ("Licensee") a non-exclusive, non-transferable limited license to use the Software without fee for evaluation of the Software and for development of Java™ compatible applets and applications. Licensee may make one archival copy of the Software. Except for the foregoing, Licensee may not re-distribute the Software in whole or in part, either separately or included with a product. Refer to the Java Runtime Environment Version 1.1 binary code license (http://www.java-soft.com/products/JDK/1.1/index.html) for the availability of runtime code which may be distributed with Java compatible applets and applications.

2. Redistribution of Demonstration Files. Sun grants Licensee the right to use, modify and redistribute the Beans example and demonstration code, including the BeanBox ("Demos"), in both source and binary code form provided that (i) Licensee does not utilize the Demos ina manner which is disparaging to Sun; and (ii) Licensee indemnifies and holds Sun harmless from all claims relating to any such use or distribution of the Demos. Such distribution is limited to the source and binary code of the Demos and specifically excludes any rights to modify or distribute any graphical images contained in the Demos.

3. Java Platform Interface. Licensee may not modify the Java Platform Interface ("JPI", identified as classes contained within the "java" package or any subpackages of the "java" package), by creating additional classes within the JPI or otherwise causing the addition to or modification of the classes in the JPI. In the event that Licensee creates any Java-related API and distributes such API to others for applet or application development, Licensee must promptly publish an accurate specification for such API for free use by all developers of Java-based software.

4. Restrictions. Software is confidential copyrighted information of Sun and title to all copies is retained by Sun and/or its licensors. Licensee shall not modify, decompile, disassemble, decrypt, extract, or otherwise reverse engineer Software. Software may not be leased, assigned, or sublicensed in whole or in part. **Software is not designed or intended for use in on-line control of aircraft, air traffic, aircraft navigation or aircraft communications; or in the design, construction, operation or maintenance of any nuclear facility. Licensee warrants that it will not use or redistribute the Software for such purposes.**

5. Trademarks and Logos. This License does not authorize Licensee to use any Sun name, trademark or logo. Licensee acknowledges that Sun owns the Java trademark and all Java-related trademarks, logos and icons including the Coffee Cup and Duke ("Java Marks") and agrees to: (i) to comply with the Java Trademark Guidelines at http://java.com/trademarks.html; (ii) not do anything harmful to or inconsistent with Sun's rights in the Java Marks; and (iii) assist Sun in protecting those rights, including assigning to Sun any rights acquired by Licensee in any Java Mark.

6. Disclaimer of Warranty. Software is provided "AS IS," without a warranty of any kind. ALL EXPRESS OR IMPLIED REPRESENTATIONS AND WARRANTIES, INCLUDING ANY IMPLIED WARRANTY OF MERCHANTABILITY, FITNESS FOR A PARTICULAR PURPOSE OR NON-INFRINGEMENT, ARE HEREBY EXCLUDED.

7. Limitation of Liability. SUN AND ITS LICENSORS SHALL NOT BE LIABLE FOR ANY DAMAGES SUFFERED BY LICENSEE OR ANY THIRD PARTY AS A RESULT OF USING OR DISTRIBUTING SOFTWARE. IN NO EVENT WILL SUN OR ITS LICENSORS BE LIABLE FOR ANY LOST REVENUE, PROFIT OR DATA, OR FOR DIRECT, INDIRECT, SPECIAL, CONSEQUENTIAL, INCIDENTAL OR PUNITIVE DAMAGES, HOWEVER CAUSED AND REGARDLESS OF THE THEORY OF LIABILITY, ARISING OUT OF THE USE OF OR INABILITY TO USE SOFTWARE, EVEN IF SUN HAS BEEN ADVISED OF THE POSSIBILITY OF SUCH DAMAGES.

8. Termination. Licensee may terminate this License at any time by destroying all copies of Software. This License will terminate immediately without notice from Sun if Licensee fails to comply with any provision of this License. Upon such termination, Licensee must destroy all copies of the Software.

9. Export Regulations. Software, including technical data, is subject to U.S. export control laws, including the U.S. Export Administration Act and its associated regulations, and may be subject to export or import regulations in other countries. Licensee agrees to comply strictly with all such regulations and acknowledges that it has the responsibility to obtain licenses to export, re-export, or import Software. Software may not be downloaded, or otherwise exported or re-exported (i) into, or to a national or resident of, Cuba, Iraq, Iran, North Korea, Libya, Sudan, Syria or any country to which the U.S. has embargoed goods; or (ii) to anyone on the U.S. Treasury Department's list of Specially Designated Nations or the U.S. Commerce Department's Table of Denial Orders.

10. Restricted Rights. Use, duplication or disclosure by the United States government is subject to the restrictions as set forth in the Rights in Technical Data and Computer Software Clauses in DFARS 252.227-7013(c)(1)(ii) and FAR 52.227-19(c) (2) as applicable.

11. Governing Law. Any action related to this License will be governed by California law and controlling U.S. federal law. No choice of law rules of any jurisdiction will apply.

12. Severability. If any of the above provisions are held to be in violation of applicable law, void, or unenforceable in any jurisdiction, then such provisions are herewith waived to the extent necessary for the License to be otherwise enforceable in such jurisdiction. However, if in Sun's opinion deletion of any provisions of the License by operation of this paragraph unreasonably compromises the rights or increases the liabilities of Sun or its licensors, Sun reserves the right
to terminate the License and refund the fee paid by Licensee, if any, as Licensee's sole and exclusive remedy.

JDK1.1 BCL 2-9-97#

More Tools for Developers

JavaBeans Developer's Resource
Prashant Sridharan
1998, 384pp, paper, 0-13-887308-9

A Book/CD-ROM Package

The JavaBeans API will be pivotal in helping companies transition from monolithic applications to secure collections of distributed, networked mini-applications. This is a complete guide to using JavaBeans — by one of the Sun engineers who created the API. This book shows developers how to use the JavaBeans API to build reusable Java object components that can be customized and packaged at will. This author introduces Java's component model, discusses JavaBean properties, events, introspection and persistence; and covers JavaBean networking. All code appears on the accompanying CD-ROM, plus a beta version of Super Mojo, a Beans GUI builder.

CGI Developer's Resource:
Web Programming in Tcl and Perl
J.M. Ivler
1997, 624pp, paper, 0-13-727751-2

A Book/CD-ROM Package

This book introduces intermediate to advanced-level developers to Web CGI programming, and presents the first end-to-end methodology for Web CGI implementation. CGI scripts are presented — including practical e-mail and database front ends, and calendar applications. The author also covers advanced topics such as environment variables. The book includes detailed coverage of intranets, CGI system management and security issues; log files; and the quirks of Netscape, Microsoft and other servers. Finally, it considers the future of CGI, plug-ins, the Java Virtual Machine, Tcl and Perl.

JDBC Developer's Resource
Art Taylor
1997, 752pp, paper, 0-13-842352-0

A Book/CD-ROM Package

This book is a comprehensive tutorial and reference for learning and using JDBC. It begins by introducing the JDBC standard and its relationship to ODBC; then shows how JDBC can be used to enable a wide variety of applications. It shows how JDBC provides for enhanced security, through techniques such as trusted applets. An extensive tutorial section walks developers through every step of developing three sample applications, demonstrating most of the techniques developers will need, including how to implement multithreading support, register drivers, and execute SQL statements. All code appears on the accompanying CD-ROM — along with the exciting new Mojo rapid application development environment for Java, and JDBC/ODBC drivers from Visigenic.

ActiveX Developer's Resource
Kamran Husain
1997, 464pp, paper, 0-13-270786-1

A Book/CD-ROM Package

This book brings together all the critical information experienced developers need to successfully create ActiveX controls.
ActiveX Developer's Resource first lays the groundwork for ActiveX development by walking through the basics of OLE technology. Developers learn how to install the ActiveX Developer's Kit — and what pitfalls to avoid. With the basics in hand, developers will learn to create controls with Internet data download features, and then move on to Microsoft's cutting edge technologies, including Authenticode security features, Internet conferencing, and both client-side and server-side database interface issues.